THE MARTHA'S VINEYARD 🐚 COOKBOOK

A Diverse Sampler from a Bountiful Island

This is a culinary tribute to one of the most beautiful and unspoiled spots on the Atlantic coast, an island with a character all its own.
— **Honolulu (Hawaii) Star-Bulletin**

Practically all of the recipes can be prepared as easily in the Pacific Northwest as (on) the Cape.
— **Oregon Journal**

Universal in gustatory appeal.
— **King Features Syndicate**

An unusually large collection of appealing recipes.
— **Journal papers, Washington, D.C.**

A great opportunity to prepare totally different dishes from the same basic foods.
— **Chattanooga (Tennessee) Free Press**

A rare delight — an attractive book that is a treat to read, and no doubt an equal treat from which to eat.
— **Independent Journal, San Rafael, California**

A delicious cookbook in more than one sense; it can be enjoyed by cooks and browsers alike.
— **Kliatt Paperback Book Guide**

A beautiful and fascinating book. — **St. Louis (Missouri) Globe Democrat**

Will enchant food lovers everywhere.
— **Leisure-Dining Magazine, Connecticut**

A delightful collection of diverse recipes reflecting its varied heritage.
— **The Trenton (New Jersey) Times**

Some cookbooks bring on a yawn; others glaze the eye. But The Martha's Vineyard Cookbook lures one on with a Mona Lisa smile . . . Interwoven with charming historical tidbits are 250 bright-as-buttercup recipes culled from both the old and new Martha's Vineyard dweller.
— **Book Nook by Bea, The Quoddy Times, Franklin, Maine**

If, after reading this book, you haven't developed a strong yen to visit Martha's Vineyard, you are a hopeless landlubber and should stay home.
— **The Milwaukee (Wisconsin) Journal**

Any cookbook which has its inspiration and its roots in Martha's Vineyard can't be bad . . . The recipes read well using a clear, no-nonsense format.
— **WEEI Radio, Boston, Massachusetts**

My copy of The Martha's Vineyard Cookbook is already looking used . . . a sign of a cookbook that has already made a place for itself in my kitchen.
— **The Berkshire Courier, Great Barrington, Massachusetts**

More than 250 delectable recipes will delight adventuresome cooks, and local lore will entertain curious readers.
— **The Warner Robins (Georgia) Independent**

. . . combines food lore and recipes.
— **The Muncie (Indiana) Evening Press**

The authors have also succeeded in creating a marvelous history of Martha's Vineyard . . . It reads almost eloquently in spots — stirring nostalgia and creating mental images.
— **The Day, New London, Connecticut**

One of the best things about the cookbook are the explanations of matters locals take for granted but which give a newcomer pause.
— **The Keene (New Hampshire) Sentinel**

This book recaptures the spirit and character of people who remained rugged individualists. It will make you plan to visit Martha's Vineyard.
— **The Evening Outlook, Santa Monica, California**

That islanders of Martha's Vineyard have a bounty of native viands as well as a cornucopia of mouth-watering recipes for their preparation is the revelation of The Martha's Vineyard Cookbook.
— **Cape Cod Life Magazine**

Yankee cooking at its best.
— **The Newtown (Connecticut) Bee**

. . . a grand addition to any culinary library . . . This flavorful collection of Vineyard recipes is ideal for the summer visitor who, during the winter months elsewhere, craves the tastes . . . It should not be missing from the Island kitchen . . . and when a relative or friend comes for a visit, what a perfect gift to help them understand a bit of Vineyard history and personalities while giving them a collection of the Island's most delectable fare.
— **Vineyard Gazette**

Chowder and muffins, sure, but the book is nicely flavored with island folklore, enough, in fact, to make you want to start making vacation plans.
— **The Sunday Republican, Springfield, Massachusetts**

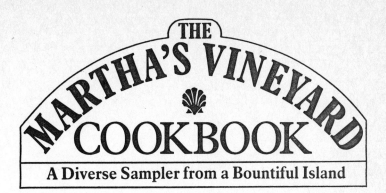

THE MARTHA'S VINEYARD COOKBOOK

A Diverse Sampler from a Bountiful Island

By

LOUISE TATE KING

AND

JEAN STEWART WEXLER

Illustrations by Grambs Miller

The Globe Pequot Press

Chester, CT 06412

Second Printing, May 1983
Third Printing, September 1983
Fourth Printing, May 1984
Fifth Printing, February 1987

ISBN: 0-87106-915-6

Library of Congress Catalog Card Number: 70-144180

Designed by Lydia Link
Cover design by Barbara Marks

FOR OUR MOTHERS,

Pearl and Bona

Contents

Introduction

Add ten years to a volume of recipes already as well aged in wisdom and practicality as these, and the extra decade is nothing much — except as it may represent absence from kitchens where it ought to be but isn't because the first edition was sold out. It is ten years since the hard cover Martha's Vineyard Cookbook came out, and here is the subtler and a bit more pliable edition in paper covers, certain of the welcome it will have.

Along with most of maritime New England, Martha's Vineyard has been a victim of the misguided impression that its cooks were chiefly inclined to the overcooking of vegetables, monotonous preparation of the stoutest foods, and a Puritanical avoidance of delicacy and imagination. In spite of evidence to the contrary, these assumptions have persisted. They have persisted to such an extent that the present cookbook brought not only revelation but some of revelation's best delights — in this case the mouth-watering delights that lie beyond expectation.

It is true that Vineyard housewives could make sea voyage gingerbread that would last well around Cape Horn and into the Pacific or even into the Arctic; and it is true that a biting northeaster and a hard day's work on the water would assist the ingestion of a hearty eel stifle. But times have changed, old exigences have been completely relaxed, and today's eel stifle may be put down as a gourmet dish. Yes — read what it says here. Or, for variety, here is an invitation to eels with herbs, including sage, rosemary, thyme, and so on. Who, ten years ago, would have expected so much?

Half a century ago swordfish was hardly known in the important markets with the exception of Boston. Vineyard recipes helped in the missionary spread of swordfish fame, now far flung; and there are imaginative ways of cooking swordfish. Nobody wants to be in a rut when there are inviting possibilities to explore. Ever try swordfish with fennel?

If, besides the resourcefulness exhibited in these pages, resulting in so wide a range of choice, there is a characteristic emphasis, it lies not in any stuffiness of tradition, but in basic excellence with chowders, shellfish and seafood generally, and in the rewarding use of the Island's bounty — windfall apples, elderberries and elder flowers, cranberries, wild grapes, beach plums, blackberries, beach peas, Irish moss, and so on. Not to be overlooked is the contribution in such diverse forms as Easter bread and linguica which came by sea in the whaling era of the past century. So it is that a hint runs from first to last of the savor provided by blown spray, insular kinship and the lean paradox of the Vineyard's own soil.

HENRY BEETLE HOUGH

Foreword

A cook book about Martha's Vineyard, the picturesque island lying five miles south of the heel of Cape Cod, could well be a New England cook book. Or it could be a seafood cook book, describing ways to prepare the fish and shellfish that live in the Island's ponds and in the salt waters that encircle it. Vineyarders do use these foods from the sea—and have for the three-hundred-odd years since the Island acquired its present name: "Martha's" after the daughter of one of the first settlers, Bartholomew Gosnold; "Vineyard" because of the profusion of wild grapevines that still blanket large sections of the Island's interior.

But today's Vineyarders draw on an expanded heritage in preparing their meals. Some of their recipes, like a simple but satisfying cornmeal mush (called Hasty Pudding) were used by the Wampanoag Indians who hunted and trapped amongst the riches of the Island long before the white men moved in. Some were brought in by the Portuguese fishermen who signed on with the Edgartown whalers when they stopped off at the Azores and the Cape Verde Islands and who returned with the ships to settle and prosper in the quiet Island towns. Other dishes have English or Scottish origins and were prepared by the wives of the whaling captains and other early settlers, whose descendants still live in the proud white houses with their widow's walks. And much of their food came, as it still does,

from the Island's own riches — the meadows and woodlands, the Great
Ponds and the smaller fresh-water ponds.

New England ways of cooking are traditional on the Vineyard, but individual adaptations have crept into the lore, and an Island chowder — or
stifle, or blueberry pudding — will taste a little different from one made in
Boston, or even one made on Cape Cod. Of course we may be prejudiced.
Swordfish straight off the boats at Menemsha, the farmers' first sweet
corn, summer's first blueberry pie, a delectable chowder made from the
unappetizing creatures your children dug out of the primeval black muck
of a Great Pond — this is Vineyard fare that somehow would never taste
the same "off-Island."

Ecology — the relation of organisms to their environment — has become a primary concern in populated areas throughout the world. Preserving a delicate balance between man and nature is vital on the
Vineyard, whose boundaries are defined forever by the sea. The Great
Ponds must remain saline and unpolluted to maintain the fish and shellfish that inhabit them, valuable sources of food and income. There must
be farmers to plant and land for them to plant on, space for cows and
sheep to graze and poultry to range, if the Island is to survive in the way its
residents want it to survive. Vulnerable to two vastly different but almost
equally threatening forces — the sea that ravages its coastline and devel-
opers who have begun to ravage its beauty — Martha's Vineyard is constantly struggling to sustain its environmental heritage.

First published in 1971, the hardcover edition of this cookbook went
out of print ten years later, to the dismay of many people who discovered
it too late. We are delighted to have it reappear in paperback form, and
hope that in it new readers will find not only interesting suggestions for
preparing food, but a reflection of the essence that defines this very special island.

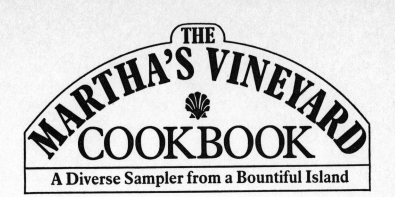

THE MARTHA'S VINEYARD COOKBOOK

A Diverse Sampler from a Bountiful Island

Chowders

Chapter 1

. . . chowder, if built with due respect for both clock and calendar, improves with age. In many chowder recipes one encounters the phrase "remove to back of stove," and there is a good deal of eloquence there. On the back of the stove is where much of the perfection comes in.

—*Vineyard Gazette,*
APRIL 1, 1960

The word "chowder" probably derives from the French word *chaudière,* meaning an iron pot. On their native islands of Guernsey and Jersey, the Channel Islanders who settled along the north shore of Massachusetts over three hundred years ago had long combined food from the sea with the rich milk from their cows in the iron pots they used for cooking. Other settlers in the new land, after sampling this delightful combination, soon were concocting chowders from whatever base they had at hand, applying the resourcefulness and ingenuity long identified with the New England housewife. Besides fish, clams, lobsters, scallops, shrimp, oysters, eels, chickens, beefsteak, corn, potatoes, parsnips—even eggs—went into the pot with the bread, onions, and milk. Tomatoes, however, used instead of milk in the chowders made further south, have always remained anathema in the chowders of New England.

In early days corn was the staple of the Vineyard diet through the winterbound months, and early chowders were a thin corn gruel to which was added fish, eels, shellfish, or some sort of meat. Potatoes in place of bread, now traditional in the chowders of Martha's Vineyard, are said to have been introduced by one John Pease, who came from Salem, Massachusetts, to settle in Edgartown around 1656. He had eaten potatoes in the Virginia colony; and one lean fall, when Vineyard grain crops had been devastated by flocks of wild fowl (probably wild pigeons), he begged a few potatoes from the trading vessels that moved along the eastern coast and tried them in his chowder, with historic results. Later, salt pork was added to fill out and enrich the chowders when clams were poor in flavor; it too became traditional. On the Vineyard, the browned bits of salt pork are often left in the finished chowder as they were three hundred years ago, not removed as they usually are in mainland chowders.

Chowders, like stews and other dishes developed when cooking was a pleasurable and time-consuming art, do need to be "built" with care and allowed time to mellow. Vineyard housekeepers, working in the same houses or home sites as their whaling-wife or Wampanoag (the Indian tribe native to the Vineyard, a branch of the Algonquians) ancestors, today use blenders, electric stoves, and freezers to prepare and preserve their chowders. But, to quote a letter written by the grandmother of a present-day West Tisbury cook, chowder is still "better the second day than the first, and the third day than the second, if it lasts that long."

There are many chowders, all structured the same way. We have included only the ones that we consider most indigenous to the Island. Following the basic procedures detailed in the Basic Recipe, you can concoct your own. Or see what you can produce from this list for a salt-pork chowder, taken from the recipe book of a "Boston Housekeeper" of 1854: salt pork, onions, sweet herbs, fresh sliced cod, biscuits, Madeira wine, Jamaican pepper, stewed mushrooms, oysters, and truffles. With this, we leave you on your own!

VINEYARD CLAM CHOWDER

The clams in this heartwarming, satisfying brew are known off-island as steamers; quaintly enough, they are also named Nanny-Noses. This is *the* clam of New England; it is a soft clam, thin-shelled, with a projecting neck. Unlike its sturdier-flavored relative, the hard-shelled clam (known on the Vineyard as the "quahog,"* its name resulting from the longer, less-pronounceable Algonquian Indian *p'quaughaug*), the steamer imparts a delicate, subtle sea flavor to chowder; the quahog produces a robustly aromatic dish. Vineyarders, like all New Englanders, without question imply the use of the soft clam when they set out to build a clam chowder.

The quahog finds its way into chowders, too. But the dish is

---

* Pronounced "ko'-hog" and also spelled "quahaug."

then specifically labeled "quahog chowder." Here on the Island a clam and a quahog are thought of as two very different bivalves. And so they are. The quahog in its youthful stages is recognized off-Island as the familiar little-neck or cherrystone clam. Then it is at its tender best, eaten raw on the half shell. Or the clams are broiled, with appropriate seasonings, as Clams Casino or Quahogs Rockefeller—for example (see pages 57 and 55). Grown up and measuring three inches or more in diameter, the quahog is chopped or ground and forms the basic ingredient of quahog chowder.

BASIC RECIPE

8 to 10 portions

1 quart shucked steamer
   clams, including their
   liquor
¼ pound salt pork, cut into
   ½-inch dice
2 medium onions, chopped
   medium fine
4 medium potatoes peeled,
   cut in ½- to ¾-inch dice
   (about 3 cups)

4 cups rich milk (or half milk,
   half evaporated milk)
2 tablespoons butter
Salt to taste
¼ teaspoon freshly ground
   black pepper

Lift clams out of their liquor; this helps somewhat to drain off the sand. (Some cooks rinse the clams briefly in running water.) Strain the clam liquor through a strainer lined with cheesecloth or a clean dish towel; set aside. Separate the firm parts of the clams from the bellies, or soft parts. Cut away the black portion of the necks, if desired. Coarsely chop only the firm part, or put through the coarse blade of a food chopper. Set aside the clams, keeping separate the firm and soft parts.

In a heavy kettle or Dutch oven cook diced salt pork over moderate heat until crisp and golden. Remove the dice, drain on a paper towel, and set aside. To the fat in the kettle add the chopped onions; cook slowly until tender and transparent. Add

(continued)

the diced potatoes, the strained clam liquor, and sufficient water to rise about 1 inch above the potatoes. Simmer, covered, until potatoes are tender, but don't overcook them. Add the chopped firm parts of the clams; simmer a little longer—about 5 minutes. Add the soft parts of the clams and the reserved salt-pork bits; cook 5 minutes longer.

In a saucepan heat the milk with the butter over moderate heat; it must not boil. Add to the chowder kettle. Add salt to taste and the black pepper. (Salt may not be needed; if the clams are very fresh they contribute considerable saltiness; so, too, the salt pork.) Remove kettle from heat immediately and allow chowder to "ripen" at least an hour or two.

Reheat, uncovered, on low heat until the mixture begins to steam. It must not boil or it will curdle. Remove from heat and serve immediately. The use of a double boiler is recommended; set the top of the double boiler over, not in, boiling water. Serve the chowder in heated bowls.

Optional: Vineyard cooks rarely thicken their chowders, thinking, with culinary justification, that the potatoes will bind the mixture sufficiently. If, however, you wish a thickened chowder, blend 3 tablespoons softened butter with 3 tablespoons flour; stir this mixture gradually into the chowder kettle several minutes before the heated milk is added. Stir over very slow heat until chowder thickens slightly. Do not allow it to boil or the mixture will curdle. If this happens, drain off the liquids and blend them in an electric blender 5 to 10 seconds. The result: a fully reconstituted mixture.

Note: Common crackers are traditionally served with chowders, usually split and soaked in milk, then added to each bowl of chowder. Toasted (see notes about them under Fish Chowder, page 10), they make a good accompaniment, too. Legend has it that these crackers were first made in Massachusetts one hundred or more years ago by Artemus Kennedy, who baked them on the floor of a brick oven, then peddled them on horseback, using his saddlebags as containers. Today's efficient methods of preparation and transportation make them available in any good grocery store.

QUAHOG CHOWDER

8 to 10 portions

In New England we simply ask the fish-market man for qua-hogs for chowder and all is well. Elsewhere, however, it is pru-dent to request *clams* for this chowder, whereupon one receives the familiar hard-shelled bivalve, a grade or two larger than the cherrystone clam. This, the quahog, differs considerably in struc-ture from the steamer clam. It ingests less sand than the steamer; there is less likelihood, therefore, of encountering these annoying particles.

Buy 1 quart of these clams, shucked. Lift them out of their liquor, chop them coarsely by hand or, using the coarse blade, put them through a food chopper. Put the liquid through a fine strainer lined with cheesecloth or a clean dish towel.

Proceed with the Basic Recipe (see page 5).

FISH CHOWDER

Among the chowders, fish chowder in particular invites ex-periment. If you already know the dish as made with the tradi-tional cod or haddock, try making it with some other fish. John Pachico, long-time fish vendor on the Vineyard, recommends an elegant blending of swordfish and striped bass. Blackfish or black bass (known on the Vineyard as "tautog" and catchable from nearly any rocky shore) and filleted flounder, which Vine-yarders call "sole," are both good in any combination. This meld-ing of various fish textures and tastes adds character to an al-ready delicious dish. If a family fishing expedition leaves you with an assortment of fish you don't quite know what to do with, have the fishermen clean and bone them, and toss them all in the chowder pot.

Off-Island, or if no one in your household wants to bother with catching or cleaning fish during your stay on the Vineyard,

(continued)

have your fish dealer fillet whatever fish you choose. Be sure to have him give you the bones, skin, heads, and tails for making your fish stock, the most important ingredient in this chowder. One Island fishmonger stews these trimmings in sea water, a masterful touch. If sea water for you means a trip to the East River or to some polluted bay, use bottled clam juice to make your stock, or settle for the water from your kitchen faucet.

8 to 10 portions

FISH STOCK

Trimmings from a 4-pound cod or haddock, or from 4 pounds of fish of choice (heads, bones, skin, tails)
3 or 4 stems from fresh parsley
1 small onion, peeled, thinly sliced
6–8 whole black peppercorns
Cold water to cover fish (or half bottled clam juice, half water)

½ carrot, cut into ¼-inch-thick circles (don't bother to peel it)
1 small stalk celery
1 tablespoon lemon juice
1 bay leaf
Salt to taste (less if using clam juice; as the clam juice cooks down it gets saltier)

Place these ingredients in a 4- to 6-quart kettle, preferably enamel or stainless steel, using enough cold water (or half clam juice, half water) to rise an inch or two above the surface of the fish trimmings. Bring to a boil, then, reducing heat to low, cook at a gentle simmer for ½ hour. Strain the stock through a fine strainer; reserve it.

P'quaughaug

THE CHOWDER

¼ pound salt pork, cut in ½-inch dice

2 medium onions, chopped medium fine

4 medium potatoes, pared and cut into ½-inch dice (about 3 cups)

2 cups reserved fish stock

The raw fish, trimmed, boned, skinned, and cut in 2-inch chunks (at least 2½-3 pounds)

4 cups rich milk (or half milk, half evaporated milk)

2 tablespoons butter

Salt to taste

¼ teaspoon freshly ground black pepper

Chopped parsley (optional)

Over moderate heat cook the salt-pork dice in a heavy 4- to 6-quart kettle or Dutch oven until crisp and golden. Remove the "cracklings," drain on a paper towel, and reserve. Add the onions to the fat in the kettle; cook slowly until transparent. Add the diced potatoes and the reserved fish stock. There should be enough of this liquid to cover the potatoes by an inch or two. Add water, if necessary. Simmer the potatoes over low heat until tender. Do not overcook them. Add the cut-up fish and the reserved salt-pork cracklings and cook very slowly 8 to 10 minutes. It is important not to overcook the fish; it is done when it flakes easily when pierced with a fork.

In a saucepan heat the milk with the butter; be careful not to let it boil. Add it to the chowder with salt to taste and the black pepper, and remove immediately from heat. Allow the chowder to "ripen" for at least an hour or two.

At serving time heat slowly and carefully so that it does not boil, and serve immediately. The use of a double boiler is recommended; set the chowder over, not in, boiling water.

A garniture of chopped parsley may be sprinkled over the chowder in each serving bowl.

Note: The chowder may be thickened slightly with a paste

(continued)

of 3 tablespoons softened butter and 3 tablespoons flour, added to the chowder gradually a few minutes before the heated milk goes into the chowder kettle.

Traditional Island accompaniments: A dish of sour pickles and some common crackers or pilot crackers. Or try the common crackers split, soaked in hot water until soft, drained, spread with softened butter, and toasted under the broiler.

LOBSTER CHOWDER

6 generous portions

To prepare this aristocrat of chowders, place 2 live lobsters each weighing 1½ pounds in a kettle of suitable size. Pour on enough salted boiling water to rise about 2 inches above the lobsters. (Fresh clean sea water is ideal.) Over high heat cook until water returns to a boil; reduce heat and simmer about 10 minutes. Remove lobsters from kettle and cool them. Boil the liquid in the pot over high heat, uncovered, until it is reduced to 2 cupfuls. Strain the liquid and reserve it.

When the lobsters are sufficiently cool to handle, split them lengthwise along the back with a sharp knife. Remove the meat, including the roe (if any) and the liver (tomalley). Crack the claws; remove the meat. Cut the lobster meat into 1-inch slices.

Proceed with the Basic Recipe (see page 5), substituting the reserved liquor for the clam liquor. Add the lobster meat, the roe, and the liver approximately 5 minutes before the heated milk goes into the chowder kettle.

If live lobster is not available, frozen lobster meat is a fair substitute, provided that bottled or canned clam juice—2 cupfuls of it—is used to replace the stock one obtains from boiling live lobsters.

Note: Be cautious about adding additional salt to the chowder. The reduced lobster liquor (if you are boiling live lobsters) or the clam juice (if you are using frozen lobster meat) may be salty enough.

BAY SCALLOP CHOWDER

6 to 8 portions

Small and sweet, incomparable in flavor, bay scallops are found in salt-water ponds and bays, ranging south from northern New England to Hatteras and even farther. Improved marketing techniques bring this remarkable shellfish, fresh and delicious, within reach of adoptive Vineyarders and others living in the cities along the northeastern seaboard. Frozen properly, these little scallops now travel even farther afield, attracting new members into a dedicated gourmet fellowship.

Substitute 1½ pints bay scallops (and only bay scallops will do in this particular recipe) plus their liquor, for the clams in the Basic Recipe (see page 5). There will be little liquor accompanying the scallops. However, strain it carefully to remove shell particles (and even bits of seaweed); add it to the water required to cook the diced potatoes. Or better still, combine it with part bottled clam juice and part water for additional flavor.

Reduce the quantity of diced potatoes given in the Basic Recipe; 2 cups is the proper amount for this particular chowder; then proceed with the Basic Recipe, adding the scallops 5 minutes before the heated milk goes into the chowder kettle. Be careful not to overcook these delicate beauties. Overcooking toughens and shrinks *all* shellfish, destroying the perfection of the finished dish.

Optional: This chowder may be prepared without salt pork, if a little less robust flavor is desired. Substitute 3 or 4 tablespoons good table butter for sautéeing the chopped onions. A restrained sprinkle of cayenne pepper may be sprinkled over each bowl of chowder.

OYSTER CHOWDER

8 to 10 portions

Substitute 1 quart shucked fresh oysters for the clams in the Basic Recipe (see page 5). Pick over the oysters to remove bits of shell. Strain the liquor and add it to the water required to cook the potatoes. Or, for superior flavor, combine bottled or canned clam juice with the water in equal amounts. Proceed with the Basic Recipe.

You may cut the oysters in half if they are large and plump. Do not overcook them; 5 minutes of slow simmering in the chowder base is sufficient. Add the hot milk immediately and remove chowder kettle from heat.

BEEFSTEAK CHOWDER

6 generous portions

¼ pound lean salt pork, cut in
  ½-inch dice
2 cups onions, coarsely
  chopped
Flour
2 pounds bottom round or
  chuck beef, cut in 1-inch
  squares
About 1 teaspoon salt
Freshly ground black pepper
2–3 cups beef stock (or 2–3
  cups boiling water com-
  bined with 2 beef bouillon
  cubes)
3 cups potatoes, cut in ½-inch
  dice
3 cups rich milk (or half milk,
  half evaporated milk)

Cook salt-pork dice in a Dutch oven or heavy casserole over moderate heat until crisp and golden. Remove pork bits with a slotted spoon, transferring them to a paper towel to drain. Reserve them. Add the onions to the fat in the pan and cook until golden and transparent; remove from pan with slotted spoon and set aside.

Sprinkle about 2 tablespoons flour over the beef, then add salt and fairly generous grindings of pepper. (Remember there is salt in the pork fat.) Over high heat, sauté the beef pieces until they brown, then turn and brown the other side. Be careful not to let them brown too deeply. Add the onions and sufficient beef stock barely to cover the ingredients. Bring to a simmer, cover, and maintain a slow simmer until beef is tender—about 2 to 3 hours. Add additional beef stock occasionally to keep meat covered. Add the diced potatoes and enough additional beef stock, if necessary, just to cover the ingredients again. Continue to simmer until the potatoes are tender. Heat the milk separately and just before it comes to a boil add it and the reserved salt-pork dice to the rest of the chowder. Taste carefully, and season with additional salt and pepper if necessary.

CHICKEN CHOWDER

A culinary delight, this chowder merits wider familiarity off-Island. In whaling times it was undoubtedly served up in many distant and exotic ports and places, when an ingenious Vineyard housewife, traveling with her husband on a 3- or 4-year sea voyage (as many did), concocted a delicious version from a Peruvian or Hawaiian fowl, if she was fortunate enough to get her hands on a suitably-fleshed victim. It does involve two days of preparation, but the result is well worth waiting for.

12 portions

FIRST DAY

Fowl weighing 5–6 pounds, cut up for stewing	8–10 whole peppercorns
2 carrots, unpeeled	2 stalks celery
1 large onion, unpeeled, quartered	3 or 4 pieces of parsley, stems only
	2 teaspoons salt

In a large kettle place all ingredients, pouring on sufficient cold water to cover them by 2 inches. Cover the kettle tightly, place over moderate heat and bring to a good boil. Reduce heat to low and simmer, covered, until chicken is tender, approximately 2 to 3 hours. Skim as needed. Remove chicken carefully

(continued)

from kettle and allow it to cool. Strain chicken stock, discard
vegetables, and return stock to kettle; reduce it to 4 to 4½ cups
by boiling it uncovered. Skin the cooled chicken, remove bones,
and cut meat into 1-inch chunks. Return this meat to the chicken
stock; cool and refrigerate.

SECOND DAY

2 medium onions, chopped
fine

4 tablespoons chicken fat,
removed from refrigerated
chicken mixture (or
½ pound salt pork, cut in
½-inch dice)

4 medium potatoes, pared and
cut in ½-inch dice

4 cups chicken stock
Cut-up chicken
4 cups rich milk (or half milk,
half evaporated milk)
White pepper
Salt

In a heavy kettle slowly sauté the onions in the chicken fat or
salt-pork fat until pale golden and translucent. (If salt pork is
used, try out diced bits before adding onions. Drain and reserve
them.) Remove chicken pieces from cooled chicken stock. Add
the diced potatoes and enough chicken stock barely to cover
them. Cook over low heat until potatoes are tender. Add the
cup-up chunks of chicken; simmer 10 minutes. Add reserved salt-
pork dice, if used. Heat the remaining chicken stock with the
milk and add to chowder. Season with pepper and salt if necessary. Simmer another 10 minutes.

Optional: Some Vineyard cooks thicken the chowder with a
paste of 3 tablespoons softened butter and 3 tablespoons flour.
Blend softened butter with flour, and gradually add this paste to
the chowder, stirring carefully after each addition.

This chowder, especially, is "better the second day than the
first."

HENRY BEETLE HOUGH'S CHICKEN CHOWDER

When asked for his favorite recipe, Henry Beetle Hough, editor of the *Vineyard Gazette,* replied that he thought it was his mother's recipe for chicken chowder. Quoted intact from a clipping he sent us from the *Gazette* files for the year 1923, here is the recipe:

> Following recent editorial discussion of chowder, several readers have requested a recipe for chicken chowder. The formula, an invaluable one, seems to deserve a place in this department. Accordingly, the recipe of a Vineyard housewife and cook of considerable reputation is given as follows:
>
> Put three slices of salt pork into an iron kettle. One tablespoon of butter can be used instead. Remove the pork after it has cooked out. Slice in four or five onions and cook, but not long enough for them to brown. When onions are cooked, put in three pints of boiling water. Add one chicken, cut in pieces. Cook about two and a half hours, then slice in three or four potatoes. Cook about a half hour. Heat a quart of milk. Mix two tablespoons of flour together with enough cold water to make a thin paste. Stir together well, then add salt and pepper to taste, smooth out and add to milk. Bring milk to boil and add to ingredients in the kettle. Bring whole to a boil and then set on back of stove.
>
> . . . and the concoction is as good or better the second day as it is the first.

The use of a good plump fowl is suggested.

EGG CHOWDER

6 generous portions

Five or 6 sliced hard-boiled eggs replace the clams in the Basic Recipe (see page 5). Cook the raw diced potatoes in chicken stock instead of water and clam juice. Add the sliced eggs at the same time as the heated milk and garnish each serving with a sprinkle of cayenne pepper.

CORN CHOWDER

6 to 8 portions

This is an estimable luncheon dish. In place of the clams in the Basic Recipe (see page 5), use 3 cups canned cream-style corn, or half cream-style and half whole-kernel corn. Add with 2 cups water or chicken stock to the diced raw potatoes. (Use only 2 cups potatoes and 3 cups milk.)

Optional but definitely superior: Corn on the cob, in season, may replace the canned corn. At least a half-dozen ears, depending on their size, will be required to produce 3 cups corn. To strip the cobs, cut each row of corn lengthwise through the kernels with a sharp knife. Using the back of a knife, scrape each ear also, being careful not to scrape too close to the cob.

Some Vineyard cooks choose to boil the stripped cobs in enough water to cover and use the resulting liquid to replace the liquid required in the Basic Recipe.

POTATO CHOWDER

4 to 6 portions

After their introduction to the New World colonies, potatoes became a staple crop, and although they are a basic ingredient of all chowders, New Englanders appreciated this sturdy vegetable sufficiently to prepare a chowder minus clams, fish, beef, or what have you, allowing the potato the stellar role.

For Potato Chowder, follow the Basic Recipe (see page 5), but eliminate the clams and clam liquor. If the raw diced potatoes are cooked in chicken stock instead of water, the finished chowder is even better. Garnish each serving with chopped fresh chives or parsley.

PARSNIP CHOWDER

8 portions

Vineyarders consider the parsnip a "respectable" vegetable. For generations the winter's supply of potatoes, carrots, and other root vegetables was stored in root cellars, but the parsnip wintered in the ground until late February, when it was time to dig the first mess of this useful vegetable. The parsnip's sweetness contributes considerable flavor to this chowder.

Peel and cut into ½-inch cubes sufficient parsnips to make 3 cups. Substituting the parsnips for the clams, and using only 2 cups of potatoes, proceed with the Basic Recipe (see page 5), cooking the parsnips with the raw potatoes. Again, it is suggested that chicken stock replace water and clam liquor for cooking these vegetables. Garnish each serving with a sprinkle of chopped fresh parsley.

Optional: Some of the old recipes call for the addition of ½ cup of finely rolled cracker crumbs; others, as suggested optionally in the Basic Recipe, for thickening with butter and flour.

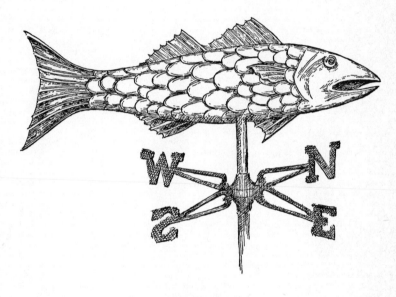

Fish

Chapter 2

Whales, Tortoises, both on land and sea, Seales, Cods, Mackerel, Breames, Herrings, Thornbacke, Hakes, Rockefish, Dogfish, Lobsters, Crabbes, Muscles, Wilks, Cockles, Scallops, Oisters.

—BRERETON (1602), IN BANKS,
History of Martha's Vineyard

Alewife, Bass, Bluefish, Butterfish, Cod, Dogfish, Eel, Flounder, Goosefish, Haddock, Hake, Halibut, Mackerel, Marlin, Perch, Pollock, Puffer, Sculpin, Sea Robin, Scup, Shark, Shockfish, Skate, Skipjack, Smelt, Squeteague, Sting Ray, Sturgeon, Swordfish, Tautog, Tomcod, Toadfish, Trout, Tuna, Whiting.

—COMPILED FROM ELVIN, *The
Fishes of Martha's Vineyard*
(1966)

Martha's Vineyard has a long and honorable history of fishing and fishermen. The journal of the Gosnold expedition to the Island in March, 1602, reports that the crew "had pestered our ship so with Cod fish that we threw numbers of them over-bord again." The abundance of these fish gave the area its name—Cape Cod. Early records are full of references to fish and fishing. The Island Indians, hospitable from the beginning to the English adventurers, taught the new settlers ingenious methods for capturing this elusive but essential food; and many of the Island's waters bear names deriving from the Indians' use of them—Katamuck (Katama), a crab-fishing place, for instance, or Quanaimes (Quenames), the long-fish place.

Despite pollution, overcommercialization, and all the other hazards of our technological age, the magic and mystery of the primitive rituals involved in taking food from the sea still persist on the Island. Traps and nets are still spread out to dry behind the weatherworn houses of the fishermen; and be it fair weather or foul, the *Kennebec* and the *Elizabeth L* chug through Menemsha Bight into the uncertain waters of the Sound and return with their holds heavy with glistening cod or monstrous green lobsters. Little boys dangle their lines from every bridge and dock on the Island, and in the fall the

fires of the bass fishermen glimmer here and there on the misty
beaches as the men cast their lines out into the dark water all through
the night.

Proportionately, salt-water fish are of course more important and
more abundant on and around the Vineyard than are fresh-water
fish. Many of the pretty land-locked ponds can yield up a good mess
of shiny sunfish in a short time, however; and trout fishermen often
net beautiful specimens of these sleek, spotted fighters in certain
ponds or along the fresh, sparkling streams that traverse some parts
of the Island.

SWORDFISH

A summer on the Vineyard without swordfish is almost as unthink-
able to some people as a summer on the Vineyard without sun is to
others. Those picturesque fishing trawlers with the elongated metal
structures, or pulpits, on their bows are not just tied up at the docks
for tourists to snap their pictures. They are working boats coming
in sometimes with as many as 400 swords (weighing an average of
100 to 150 pounds apiece) after a 2-week trip. The big fish are still
spotted from the pulpit and harpooned, as they have been for generations; but a modern concession is the employment of pilots flying
Piper Cub planes that take off from the Vineyard, find where the
swordfish are, and report their location to the fishermen by citizens'
band radio. The pilots are paid by the hour and also get a percentage
from the catch.

Years ago, local boats used to rig for swordfish and go down as far
as Cape May to meet the fish as they made their annual migration
northward, sometimes following the schools as far north as Nova

Scotia, but since spotting by plane was introduced, the local hauls have increased so that the boats don't need to venture so far away from home to fill their holds.

The long-line method is also used for catching swordfish—an apt name, as up to ten miles of mackerel-baited line are let out behind the boats. For understandable reasons, the harpoon method is preferred, as the captain of the *Kennebec* would undoubtedly have made clear to anyone after he and five other men once spent forty-eight hours straight, working in shifts, untangling their long line, baited every twenty feet and not only snarled but loaded with sharks, tuna and—the only conceivable prize after such an ordeal—about 300 swordfish. To avoid getting entangled with other craft as well, the draggers go out at dusk to lay out the long lines, then haul back about eight-thirty in the morning while most pleasure-craft owners are still dawdling over coffee.

Thanks to these fishermen, Vineyarders are able to buy and relish swordfish from mid-June until the end of September, in a good season—and if you happen to be around Menemsha the day the first swords are brought in you'll probably hear about it, as word spreads through the community the way word of the arrival of spring warblers is passed from one birdwatcher to another. And, once you've become addicted to freshly caught swordfish, you're not likely to settle for any other kind. Choose some other item on the menu if you go out for a seafood dinner at a restaurant during the winter.

CHARCOAL-BROILED SWORDFISH

Two factors are important here. First, the swordfish steaks should be marinated in an aromatic mixture of herbs, oil, lemon juice, and seasonings after being cut into serving-size portions. But, more important: never, never purchase anything but the freshest swordfish. During the summer, this is not difficult if one lives in the North Atlantic states (though we, of course, feel Vineyard-bought swordfish is matchless). At the risk of antagonizing the frozen-food processors, we do not recommend frozen swordfish at any time.

(continued)

Swordfish, ½-¾ pound per serving, cut *at least* 1½ inches thick	Marinade (see below) Lemon wedges Melted butter

Marinate fish pieces at least 4 hours, turning several times. Drain pieces well; broil over charcoal (or about 4 inches from broiler heat in your kitchen range) about 6 to 7 minutes on each side for 1½-inch slices, or until fish begins to flake when tested with a fork. Serve with lemon wedges and pour a little melted butter over the top.

Note: The fish may be broiled on one side only—approximately 12 to 14 minutes.

SWORDFISH MARINADE

Makes about 1½ cups

1 cup vegetable oil	½ teaspoon dried basil (or 1 teaspoon chopped fresh basil)
Juice of 2 lemons	
2 tablespoons white-wine vinegar (optional)	
1 teaspoon salt	Very small pinch cayenne pepper
⅛ teaspoon freshly ground black pepper	1 medium clove garlic, minced (optional)

Stir together all ingredients.

YVONNE'S SWORDFISH WITH FENNEL

Many summer Vineyarders feel swordfish is what you have for your annual first dinner on the Island (if it is in season), and what you serve your guests for *their* first dinner on the Island. A French friend, visiting one of the authors, was enchanted both by the pearl-pink beauty of the slab of fresh swordfish and by the flourishing bed of fennel in the vegetable garden. Good cook and fellow gardener, she asked if she might prepare the fish a European way by broiling it in a nest of fennel.

If you can find fennel (or grow a little in your Island flower bed—it is quick-growing and very decorative), this recipe can win over even the purists who feel good fish should be left strictly unadorned. The method is equally good for bluefish, sea bass, or any broiling fish.

4 portions

2–3 pounds swordfish, preferably in slab at least 1½ inches thick
4 tablespoons melted butter
Salt and pepper
Enough sprigs of fennel to cover top and bottom of fish

Pat fish dry with paper towels. Rub with melted butter (fish should not be too cold or butter will congeal on hand or utensil instead of fish). Salt and pepper to taste. Lay half the fennel sprigs on a broiling pan or foil, place fish on these, and cover with remaining sprays. Use plenty of fennel. Place about 4 inches below broiler heat and cook until fish flakes in center when tested with a fork. This is usually in 10 to 20 minutes, depending on thickness of fish. Do not overcook—flavor is diminished and texture not as firm. Serve with the cooked fennel, or remove if desired.

Note: It is not necessary to turn the fish while it is broiling; simply cook it a bit longer.

SKEWERED SWORDFISH

8 portions

Swordfish Marinade (see page 24)
1 tablespoon soy sauce
1½-2 pounds fresh swordfish, sliced 1 inch thick, cut into 24 cubes
24 medium-sized mushrooms
16 small white onions, peeled and parboiled 5 minutes
2 large green peppers, cut into twenty-four 1½-inch squares
16 cherry tomatoes
About ½ cup melted butter
Salt
Freshly ground black pepper
Fennel sprays (optional)

(continued)

Prepare marinade, adding the soy sauce to the other ingredients. Marinate swordfish cubes at least 2 to 3 hours. Remove from marinade and drain well, then dry with paper towels. Preheat broiler to maximum. (A charcoal grill is preferable, but if used should be started about 20 minutes before swordfish is removed from marinade.)

Thread 8 ten- to twelve-inch skewers with fish and vegetables. Brush with melted butter and sprinkle with salt and pepper to taste. If you like, tie 1 or 2 fennel sprays lengthwise on each skewer.

Broil 5 to 6 minutes, turn skewers, broil another 5 to 6 minutes. Skewers may be brushed again with melted butter while cooking.

STRIPED BASS

Two types of bass are found in Vineyard waters—the black bass (also called blackfish), which according to one Island fisherman-writer is "by all odds the finest chowder fish," and the more familiar "striper," or striped bass, whose popularity has undoubtedly increased since the establishment of the annual Martha's Vineyard Striped Bass Derby, which runs from September 15 to October 15 and lures thousands of fishermen across on the ferry. Awards are given for varied enough reasons to entice almost everyone. The one for the biggest fish of the derby is of course everyone's goal; but there is also competition for the biggest fish each day, the biggest one caught by a man, a woman, a child, from a boat, from the shore, by an Islander, by an off-Islander. The weighing-in station on Oak Bluff's main street becomes a night-long social center, where pipes and cigars are chewed on as tales are swapped involving jigs, tides, spots most plagued by mosquitoes, big ones that got away, and all the traditional lore of dedicated fishermen. And when a 75-year-old Chilmark woman hauls in a 54-pound beauty, another item is added to the annals for the years to come.

Most of us have to content ourselves with buying our bass, all cleaned, cut up, and ready to be stuffed and baked or broiled in the backyard. The more fortunate fishermen can not only consume their prizes, or give them to their friends, but pile great stores of this meaty, firm-fleshed fish in their freezers to feast on through the winter.

BAKED STRIPED BASS
WITH HERB STUFFING

4 generous portions

4–5-pound striped bass, cleaned (leave head on)

Salt and freshly ground black pepper

3 or more tablespoons butter

½ cup chopped shallots or green onions (use some of green stems)

1 clove garlic, minced fine

½ cup finely chopped celery

½ cup coarsely chopped fresh mushrooms

1 tablespoon chopped fresh chervil (or 1 teaspoon dried)

½ teaspoon chopped fresh sage leaves (or ¼ teaspoon dried)

½ teaspoon minced fresh summer savory (or ¼ teaspoon dried)

½ teaspoon minced fresh basil (or ¼ teaspoon dried)

¼ cup chopped fresh parsley (the Italian type is best)

1 cup dry white wine

6 slices whole-wheat bread, toasted and coarsely crumbled

¼ cup grated Parmesan cheese

¼ cup olive oil

4 slices salt pork, thinly sliced (optional)

1 teaspoon lemon juice

Lemon wedges

Parsley sprigs

(continued)

Preheat oven to 400° F.

Rinse fish well under cold water, dry with paper towels, rub with salt and pepper inside and out.

Over moderate heat melt butter in a heavy skillet; when butter foam subsides, add shallots or onions, garlic, and celery. Reduce heat and sauté about 5 minutes, or until vegetables are wilted. Stir occasionally. Add a little more butter if indicated. Turn heat to high, add mushrooms and cook 3 or 4 minutes more. Add chervil, sage, savory, basil, parsley, and only ½ cup of the wine; stir well, reduce heat, and let simmer for several minutes.

Remove skillet from heat, stir in bread crumbs and grated cheese, lifting lightly with a 4-tined fork to combine all ingredients. Additional salt and pepper may be added, if required. Allow mixture to cool slightly.

Stuff fish with the herb-crumb mixture. Fill lightly to allow for expansion of the stuffing. Close cavity with toothpicks or small skewers. Rub fish with 2 tablespoons of the olive oil. Dust lightly with extra salt and pepper if desired. Place fish in a shallow baking pan lined with greased foil. The optional salt pork slices may be placed on top of the fish at this point.

In a small saucepan heat remaining wine and olive oil and the lemon juice. Pour it over fish and bake, uncovered, about 30 to 45 minutes, or until fish flakes easily when pierced with a fork. While the fish is baking, baste it three or four times with the liquids in the baking pan. Remove toothpicks or skewers, transfer fish to a heated platter.

Serve the fish very hot, garnished with lemon wedges and sprigs of parsley.

STRIPED BASS BAKED WITH MILK

4 generous portions

4–5-pound striped bass,
cleaned, head removed

¼ teaspoon freshly ground
black pepper

¾ teaspoon salt

1–2 tablespoons softened
butter

1½ cups rich milk (or half
milk, half cream)

1 tablespoon butter

Paprika

Parsley sprigs

Preheat oven to 350° F.

Rinse fish well under cold water, dry with paper towels, rub inside and out with the pepper and half of the salt. Spread 1 or 2 tablespoons of the softened butter on both sides of the fish.

In a small saucepan, heat the milk and 1 tablespoon butter until milk barely simmers, remove from heat. Place the fish in a shallow baking dish, preferably an enamel or glass dish, sprinkle with the remainder of the salt and dust lightly with paprika. Pour the heated milk mixture around the fish and bake about 40 to 45 minutes, or until fish flakes easily when pierced with a fork. Baste frequently with the milk mixture.

Transfer to a heated platter, pour some of the pan juices over the fish and garnish with parsley sprigs.

Gay Head Light

BLUEFISH

Fishing for "blues," according to Island chronicler Joseph Chase Allen, was probably the first Vineyard sport. Years and years ago, when the bluefish schooled along the shores, young and old lined the beaches and fished for the fun of fishing, throwing most of their catch down to flop their lives away on the sand. To get in form for these outings, the fishermen held casting practice sessions with their heavily leaded lines in Island meadows, and Joe Allen comments that "distances to which these Vineyarders could cast a bluefish jig were unbelievable, fifty fathoms being considered only moderately fair."

No one parts with a just-caught bluefish these days without good cause, such as being able to present a cleaned 10-pounder to the lady the fisherman is courting. Many consider them the finest-flavored fish of all, rating them even higher than the striped bass or swordfish. This is a moot point which we will not debate here; but from the tiny "snappers" that weigh only a few ounces to the huge "choppers" often caught off shore on trolling jigs thrown out from boats, blue-fish, when carefully prepared, are a sea delicacy worthy of the highest praise.

BAKED BLUEFISH
[A Gay Head recipe]

4 to 6 portions

½ loaf day-old home-style bread, crusts removed
1½ teaspoons poultry seasoning
½ cup ground salt pork
¼ teaspoon freshly ground black pepper
1 tablespoon melted butter

½ cup boiling water
4 bluefish fillets, weighing a total of approximately 3 pounds
8 lemon slices
8 thin slices salt pork
Additional lemon slices (optional)

Parsley sprigs

Preheat oven to 375° F.

Prepare the bread stuffing as follows: Cut the bread into ½-inch cubes. In a mixing bowl combine the bread, poultry seasoning, ground salt pork, pepper, and melted butter. Using a fork for mixing, gradually add the boiling water, lifting and combining all ingredients, until properly moistened. Spread the stuffing equally on two of the bluefish fillets; cover with the remaining fillets. Place 8 lemon slices on the fish, then the thin salt pork slices.

Bake the fish in a shallow casserole or baking dish (try lining with aluminum foil for easy cleanup) about 25 minutes. The fish is ready for the table when it flakes easily when pierced with a fork. Serve with additional lemon slices, if desired, and garnish with parsley sprigs.

Note: As an alternative dressing, the Parsley Stuffing (page 247) or the Herb Stuffing for the Baked Striped Bass (page 27) is suggested.

BLUEFISH PROVENÇALE

[*Baked with Aromatic Herbs and Seasonings*]

An entrée from Louise Tate King's restaurant, this is a considerably simplified version of a traditional French dish from Provence where tomatoes, garlic, and olive oil are part of the culinary heritage. There tuna is likely to be used in preparing this dish. An asset is that you may prepare it ahead by browning the bluefish slices quickly, preparing the sauce ahead, and combining all a half hour or so before serving time.

4 portions
    4–5-pound bluefish, cleaned
        and cut into 2-inch thick
        slices (bone in)

MARINADE

1 cup olive or vegetable oil
½ cup red-wine vinegar
1 tablespoon lemon juice
1 teaspoon salt

¼ teaspoon freshly ground
    black pepper
2 cloves garlic, minced fine

(continued)

Place the bluefish slices in a shallow container; combine the 1 cup oil, vinegar, lemon juice, 1 teaspoon salt, pepper, and 2 of the cloves minced garlic and pour over the fish. Marinate the fish in this mixture two to three hours, turning occasionally. Refrigeration is not required.

Preheat oven to 450° F.

Remove fish from marinade; dry it thoroughly with paper towels. Discard marinade.

2 tablespoons butter	1 teaspoon salt
2 tablespoons olive or vege- table oil	¼ teaspoon freshly ground black pepper
1 cup onions, thinly sliced	1 cup dry white wine
3 cups fresh tomatoes, cut in chunks (**canned** may be substituted)	4 tablespoons tomato paste
	2 beef bouillon cubes
	½ cup chopped parsley
2 cloves garlic, minced fine	½ teaspoon dried thyme

Scant teaspoon dried orégano

Over high heat melt the butter with the oil in a heavy skillet until the butter foam subsides. Quickly brown the fish on both sides, allowing 2 to 3 minutes per side. Remove from skillet and arrange in a shallow, flameproof baking dish.

In the same skillet, over moderate heat, cook the onions until transparent. Add a little more butter or oil if the onions demand it. Add the tomatoes, the remaining 2 cloves minced garlic, the remaining teaspoon salt, pepper, wine, tomato paste, bouillon cubes, ¼ cup of the chopped parsley, thyme, and orégano. Cook over high heat, stirring frequently, about 10 minutes, allowing the liquids to evaporate sufficiently so that sauce is thickened slightly.

Pour the sauce over the bluefish slices, sprinkle with the remaining ¼ cup chopped parsley, cover the dish tightly with foil and bake 15 to 20 minutes, or until the fish flakes easily when pierced with a fork.

Transfer the fish to a heated platter; keep warm. Place the baking dish with its remaining sauce over high heat and boil rapidly, stirring constantly, until about 2 cups of sauce remain. Pour sauce over fish slices and serve immediately.

Note: The sauce may be thickened slightly with a paste of 1 tablespoon flour mixed with 1 tablespoon softened butter.

CODFISH SOUFFLÉ

This sturdy-sounding dish was offered in the *Vineyard Gazette* in March, 1910. We reprint it here verbatim, but must point out that either cook or typesetter forgot to include the mortared and pressed fish in the final dish! We suggest you pour the prepared sauce over the neglected fish, which presumably you have left resting in its basin, before you place the soufflé in its well-buttered tin. It might be easier to press the fish through a colander or food mill and forget the mortar and sieve altogether. We suggest also that the eggs be separated so that the yolks may be added to the sauce and the stiffly beaten whites folded into the sauce just before turning the mixture into its baking dish.

Preheat your oven to 375° F.

4 portions

12 ounces cooked codfish	1 gill cream
2 tablespoons butter	½ teaspoon salt
2 tablespoons flour	Black pepper
1 gill fish stock*	Nutmeg
3 eggs	Paprika

Pound the fish in a mortar, then rub it through a sieve into a basin. Melt the butter in a saucepan, stir in the flour, cook over a slow fire several minutes without letting the flour get brown. Moisten with the fish stock and continue to stir until mixture becomes a smooth paste. Beat in the eggs one by one, add the cream and season with salt, pepper, nutmeg and paprika. Put into a well-buttered soufflé tin, cover with greased paper and steam or bake 40 minutes. Serve with tomato or anchovy sauce.

* A gill equals ¼ pint of liquid, ½ cup in today's terms.

HERRING

Next to the whale—which, however colorful, does not figure in a Vineyard cook book—the lowly herring seems to have the most interesting Island history. During the 1920's and 1930's, hundreds of thousands of barrels (some fishermen brought in a thousand a night during the 6-week spawning season) of these silvery fish were trapped in the herring creek off Edgartown Great Pond and used to make, of all things, artificial pearls. Ac-

cording to a fascinating account in the *Vineyard Gazette* of May 24, 1923, two Cape Cod men evolved a process for converting the scales from the herrings' bellies (no other part of the fish was used) into a liquid into which glass beads were dipped to produce so-called Priscilla pearls. Since the days of salting and pickling these fish had already passed, the remains were not eaten but were "plowed into the ground for fertilizer." The *Gazette* doesn't say where, but perhaps this accounts for the lushness of some of our Vineyard gardens.

Salted and smoked, the herring used to be known on the Vineyard as Oldtown Turkey. "Alewives" is a more familiar name for these fish. Webster's gives two possible derivations for this euphonious term; we prefer the second: "possibly . . . American Indian (a form *aloofe* is recorded in 1678) ."

Little used today by American housewives, herring have long been an important food fish and are still an important part of European cuisine, particularly Scandinavian. Today's Vineyarders still trap the herring when they come wriggling up the creeks off the Great Ponds every spring as they have for untold centuries, but nowadays this is mainly to extract the females' roe. As herring is both plentiful (though seasonal) and good, it deserves to be eaten more often, particularly in one of its many pickled forms.

PICKLED HERRING

4 portions

1 large dried, salted herring
1 medium-sized red onion,
  sliced
10 whole allspice
¾ cup white vinegar
¼ cup water

¼ cup sugar
6 whole peppercorns
1 large bay leaf
2 tablespoons chopped fresh
  dill

Soak fish overnight in cold water to cover. Drain and rinse. Clean, remove head if necessary, then cut into fillets by carefully slicing the strips from the bones. Arrange fillets in a flat glass or ceramic serving dish and lay onion slices on top of them. Crush 6 of the whole allspice and sprinkle over onions. Combine vinegar, water, sugar, 4 allspice, peppercorns, and bay leaf in a small saucepan and bring to a boil. Let mixture cool, then strain and chill before pouring over fish fillets. Allow fillets to marinate at least overnight in refrigerator (covered with waxed paper or foil) before serving. Garnish with fresh dill.

SAUTÉED FRESH HERRING ROE

4 portions

16–20 fresh herring roes,
  whole
1 teaspoon salt
¼ teaspoon freshly ground
  pepper
Flour or cracker meal

1 beaten egg (optional)
About 2 tablespoons butter
About 2 tablespoons vegetable
  oil
Cooked bacon
Few sprigs parsley

Place a heavy 10- to 12-inch skillet (preferably black iron) over low heat. Season roes with salt and pepper and coat them with flour or cracker meal. Handle them gently; they are fragile. Roes may be dipped into beaten egg before coating with flour or meal. Add half butter, half oil to skillet in sufficient quantity

(continued)

to cover the bottom well. Increase heat to moderate. When butter foam subsides, add the roes and sauté each side until golden brown. Do not overcrowd skillet. If necessary, sauté one batch and remove to a heated platter, then repeat the process. Serve with crisp, golden bacon, and garnish with a few sprigs of parsley.

JOHN PACHICO'S HERRING ROE BAKE

Mr. Pachico, skilled fisherman and former proprietor of a Vineyard Haven fish market, suggests this simple method of preparation. The finished dish is unexpectedly good, and it is not only quickly prepared but, unlike sautéed roe, requires no attention while it is cooking.

4 portions

12 slices raw bacon	Salt and freshly ground
16–20 whole fresh herring roes	pepper
Flour or cracker meal	2 eggs, lightly beaten (optional)

Preheat oven to 475° F.

Place half the bacon slices on the bottom of a shallow casserole or baking dish. Dip the roes into flour or cracker meal. Handle them gently; they are fragile. Season well with salt and pepper. If desired, dip first into beaten eggs and then into flour or cracker meal. Carefully distribute the roes over the bacon. Cover with remaining bacon slices. Bake approximately 25 minutes. If bacon topping is not crisp enough, place dish under the broiler for a few moments.

The Red Nun

FILLET OF SOLE LOUISE

6 portions

6 small fillets of very fresh sole
(or flounder or halibut)
Dry white wine
Bottled clam juice
2 tablespoons chopped shallots (or white part of
scallions)
¼ teaspoon salt

¼ teaspoon white pepper
1 tablespoon fresh lemon juice
5 tablespoons butter
2 tablespoons flour
1 cup cream or rich milk
18 large fresh shrimp, shelled
and deveined

Preheat oven to 400° F.

Carefully place fish in an enamel or glass baking dish, about 9
by 14 inches, so that all are equally spaced. If the tails seem especially thin, turn them under an inch or so. Pour enough wine and
clam juice (in equal quantities) over fillets barely to cover them.
Spread chopped shallots or scallions over top, season with salt
and pepper, sprinkle with the lemon juice, and dot with 2 tablespoons of the butter. Cover baking dish tightly with a piece of
aluminum foil. Bake approximately 10 to 12 minutes, then lift a
corner of the foil and check fish. It should appear opaque and
should be just starting to flake.

Remove baking dish from oven and allow fish to cool for an
hour. If the fish is very fresh, this will make it easier to remove
from the pan. With a spatula or pancake turner (or both), carefully transfer fish to a heatproof platter. Strain the fish stock. Reduce it to 1 cup by boiling rapidly in an uncovered pan. Make a
roux by melting the remaining 3 tablespoons butter in a saucepan over moderate heat, then adding the flour and blending it in
thoroughly. Allow roux to simmer several minutes, then add the
fish stock and cream or milk. Bring the mixture to a simmer,
stirring constantly. Taste for seasoning. Pour any accumulated
liquids from fish platter into sauce. Stir well, then pour sauce
over fish.

(*continued*)

Simmer shrimp slowly in boiling salted water for 3 to 5 minutes. Cut in half lengthwise and garnish each fillet with 6 pieces. Heat in 450° F. oven only long enough to bring fish to serving temperature.

Note: Prepare this dish in the morning if you like, saucing and garnishing the fish just before reheating.

POACHED HADDOCK OR CODFISH WITH EGG SAUCE

Off-Island, this is sometimes referred to as "Cape Cod Turkey." Incidentally, Vineyarders who schedule a trip to the mainland often say that they are going to the United States of America. A small smile invariably accompanies this statement, and in it can be read a quiet contentment, a strong feeling of "place"—engendered, perhaps, by the Island's physical and psychological insularity. Also revealed is the inimitable flash of Yankee humor, never far below the surface.

3 to 4 portions

4-pound haddock or codfish (pollock, which runs in the fall, is also good), cleaned and left whole	Salt Egg Sauce (see below)

If time permits, sprinkle fish with ½ cup salt inside and out and let it stand overnight. Then rinse thoroughly. Otherwise, salt fish and let stand at least half an hour, then rinse. Fill 6- to 8-quart pot or fish steamer with enough water to cover fish; add about 2 tablespoons salt. Bring water to simmering point. Carefully tie the fish in cheesecloth and place it in the pot of simmering water. Allow it to simmer for about 30 minutes. Fish will be done when it just barely begins to flake when tested with a fork. Transfer fish to a heated platter, remove cheesecloth and serve with Egg Sauce.

Note: Canadian salt cod (use 1½ pounds fillets) may also be used in this recipe, but the fish must be "freshened" to remove its salt. To do so, soak it in water to cover for at least 12 hours, draining water and replacing it with fresh water at least twice during this period. Or the salt cod can be covered with cold water, brought to a simmer, and drained at once; repeat this process three times, until the fish loses enough salt to be edible when tasted. The fish must *not* be boiled during this desalting process.

EGG SAUCE

4 portions

2 tablespoons butter	1½ cups milk (or half milk,
2 tablespoons flour	half chicken stock or
¼ teaspoon dry mustard	canned chicken broth)
¼ teaspoon salt	2 hard-boiled eggs, sliced

Melt butter in small saucepan over moderate heat, add flour, mustard, and salt and stir thoroughly until well blended. Reduce heat. Cook a minute or so longer. Slowly stir in the milk or milk and stock. A wire whisk is good for this purpose. Still stirring, cook slowly until mixture comes to a simmer. Add the hard-boiled eggs and serve immediately.

SCUP (PORGIE) AU GRATIN

Scup is suggested in this recipe from the files of the *Vineyard Gazette*. Filleted flounder makes an admirable substitute, as do other filleted fish—young mackerel, haddock, or pollock. Nor is it essential to adhere conscientiously to the amounts of other suggested ingredients. For instance, a little more zucchini or tomato, particularly if both are freshly plucked from one's garden, heightens enjoyment of the finished dish.

(continued)

4 portions

4 servings filleted scup (or
  other filleted fish)
1½ teaspoons salt
¼ teaspoon freshly ground
  black pepper
2 small zucchinis, sliced
  ½ inch thick
2 medium tomatoes, coarsely
  chopped (or 1 cup drained
  canned tomatoes)
2–3 tablespoons finely
  chopped shallots or
  green onions

½ cup fresh bread crumbs,
  preferably from day-old
  home-style bread
½ cup melted butter (or half
  butter, half oil)
2 tablespoons lemon juice
¼ cup grated Parmesan
  cheese (freshly grated is
  preferable)

Preheat oven to 425° F.

Place fish fillets in shallow baking dish, season lightly with
about half the salt, dust with pepper. Cover with zucchini slices,
tomatoes, and shallots or green onions. Sprinkle remaining salt
over vegetables, dust with pepper. Combine bread crumbs, butter and lemon juice in a small bowl, mix, then spread over vegetables. Top with grated cheese. Bake until fish flakes easily when
tested with a fork, about 20 to 30 minutes.

BAKED FISH FILLETS WITH
FRESH PARSLEY STUFFING

4 portions

4 medium-sized fish fillets
  (flounder, sole or
  haddock)
½ teaspoon salt
¼ teaspoon freshly ground
  black pepper
Parsley Stuffing (page 247)

3 tablespoons melted butter
  (or half butter, half
  vegetable oil)
Paprika (optional)
Lemon wedges
Parsley sprigs

Preheat oven to 375° F.

Rinse the fillets well under cold water; wipe dry with paper towel. Halve them lengthwise. Sprinkle them with salt and pepper. Divide the stuffing into 8 equal portions and spread it on the fish fillets. Roll them and secure with toothpicks. Place in a shallow baking dish, cut side down.

Pour the melted butter over the fish, and dust lightly with paprika, if desired. Bake, uncovered, about 20 to 25 minutes. Do not overcook; the fish is done when it flakes easily when prodded with a fork.

Remove toothpicks, transfer fish to a heated serving platter; pour or spoon the pan juices over the fish and garnish with lemon wedges and sprigs of parsley.

SAUTÉED FISH

A popular Vineyard version of fried fish, good for small freshwater fish as well as for the little mackerel, snapper blues, scup, flounder, and other salt-water dwellers that are too small for broiling or baking.

4 portions

5 tablespoons butter (or half butter, half vegetable oil)	2 eggs, beaten
	Salt
8–12 small fish, cleaned (or 2–3 pounds filleted fish)	Freshly ground black pepper

In a heavy skillet (preferably black iron), heat the butter until foam subsides. Dry each fish or fillet slightly with a paper towel, dip in beaten eggs, place in skillet, and brown over moderate heat. (The egg will run a little; scrape it back toward the fish pieces.) When one side of fish is browned, dribble a little additional beaten egg on top of each piece, salt and pepper lightly, and turn over to brown on other side. Salt and pepper to taste; serve very hot.

CAPTAIN POOLE'S FISH

Two Menemsha stalwarts are said to be uncompromising about how fish is to be eaten, and if anyone should know about such matters, they should: it must be rolled in cornmeal and fried in salt-pork fat. Captain Donald Poole insists there is "no other way to cook fish." This is the way he ate it as a boy and this is how his wife prepares it for him now. Even his son Everett's magnificent swordfish receives this treatment. Everett himself, according to his mother, is not quite such a diehard and will sometimes settle for fish that has been broiled or baked.

If you've always used some other kind of fat for frying fish, try using salt pork, and you may be as reluctant as the Pooles are to give it up.

4 portions

4 frying-size fish (mackerel or ocean perch should be good) or 4 good-sized fish steaks or fillets

2 teaspoons salt (slightly less if preferred)

½ teaspoon black pepper

½ cup yellow cornmeal

Piece of salt pork (about ¼ pound), cut in ½-inch dice

Lemon wedges or tartar sauce

Clean fish and remove heads, if using whole fish. Rinse in cold water, pat dry with paper towels. Rub all surfaces (including inside cavities if using whole fish) with combined salt and pepper, then roll in cornmeal. Cook salt-pork dice over moderate heat until skillet has a good coating of fat—at least ¼ inch deep. Remove dice; fry fish in hot fat over moderate heat until crisp and brown on both sides. This should take 6 to 8 minutes. Fish should flake easily when tested with fork. Do not overcook. Drain slightly on paper toweling and serve very hot. Browned salt-pork dice may be served with fish for those who like it, as may the traditional lemon wedges or tartar sauce.

MIXED SEAFOOD IN CLAM SHELLS

Sometimes, instead of arriving home with a catch of handsome bluefish or a mess of steamers, children, husband, or house guests show up in the kitchen and proudly present the cook with a conglomeration of sea treasures that, if used separately, wouldn't even make enough appetizers to go around. The next time this happens, try this recipe, adapted to utilize whatever you find dumped in the kitchen sink. Mussels instead of clams could be used, or several of each; more fish and less crab could be used, or vice versa. Almost any way, it's good.

4 portions

6–8 medium quahogs

2 or 3 small fish: flounder, scup (porgy), tautog, or perch; cleaned but left whole

Canned clam juice

Meat from 8 rock crabs (or 2 or 3 blue crabs or ¾ cup cooked crabmeat)

1 cup fresh bread crumbs (use day-old French or Italian-type if possible)

⅓ cup each chopped onion, green pepper, and celery

2 tablespoons melted butter

1 teaspoon chopped fresh parsley

2 slices bacon, cooked crisp

Salt and pepper

Paprika

Preheat oven to 400° F.

Open the quahogs, reserving liquid and at least 12 shells. Wash the shells.

Place the fish in a saucepan of sufficient size, add the reserved quahog liquor and sufficient canned clam juice barely to cover the fish. Cover tightly and cook over gentle heat about 5 to 10 minutes, or until fish flakes easily when prodded with a fork.

While fish is poaching, chop clams fine; place in mixing bowl with crabmeat, bread crumbs, onion, green pepper, and celery.

Remove fish from its poaching liquid, reserving several table-spoons liquid; place on cutting board and discard skin, remove flesh from bones, using two forks. Add fish, melted butter, and chopped parsley to bowl. Crumble the bacon over the mixture. Mix lightly with a fork, adding several tablespoons of the re-served fish liquor. Salt and some freshly ground pepper may be added to taste.

Place the seafood mixture in the quahog shells, dividing it evenly. Bake the filled shells in a shallow pan, covered tightly with foil, about 20 minutes. Remove foil, sprinkle the shells lightly with paprika, and place under a moderately-heated broiler long enough to brown.

You may cook these also over a charcoal grill by wrapping each filled shell in heavy foil and placing them on the grill about 25 minutes.

Serve in the shells.

EEL

Dreaded by timid bathers, despised by most fishermen, and scorned by contemporary cooks, at least in America, these snakelike water creatures with a unique and fascinating life history can be transformed into epicurean delicacies. In pioneer days eels were used in coastal settlements as an important food and were trapped largely in eel pots. Nowadays, eels are usually caught—off the Menemsha docks, for instance—by someone who is fishing for something else, and discarded as quickly as they can be freed from the fishhook.

If you land an eel, and can survive the dehooking, skinning, and hacking-to-pieces processes, try cooking the eel meat. It has a rich, slightly oily flavor and tastes more like chicken than fish, according to devotees. There are several ways to disgorge the hook from the eel's mouth, but they are too involved to be described here. If there is an Islander nearby, ask him. To skin an eel, cut through the skin all the way around just below the head. Hold the eel's head in one hand, and yank the skin off with a pair of pliers (don't forget to kill your prey first by striking him hard on the head with some heavy object). Pull hard, and remember the eel is proverbially slippery. Slit the belly and remove the innards. Hack off the head; then cut the meat into chunks of 2 or 3 inches. Wrap these in foil and refrigerate until used. Like any fish, eel should be eaten (or pickled) soon after it is caught.

EELS WITH HERBS

4 to 6 portions

1½ pounds cleaned, skinned
  fresh eels
4 tablespoons butter
½ cup chopped spinach or
  sorrel
½ cup chopped fresh parsley
2 tablespoons fresh chervil
  (or 1 tablespoon dried)
1 teaspoon chopped fresh
  tarragon (or ½ teaspoon
  dried)

Pinch each of dried sage,
  thyme, and rosemary
½ teaspoon salt
¼ teaspoon freshly ground
  black pepper
1 cup white wine
1 cup or more chicken stock
  (or canned chicken broth)
2 egg yolks, lightly beaten
1 tablespoon lemon juice

Rinse eels in cold water; dry thoroughly with paper towels or they will not brown when sautéed. Cut them into 2- to 3-inch pieces.

Heat butter in a heavy skillet over moderate heat until foam subsides; add eels and brown evenly on all sides. Add the spinach or sorrel and the herbs; add the salt and pepper. Pour the wine and chicken stock over the eels and herbs, using enough broth barely to cover fish. Cover pan tightly and reduce heat; simmer the eels about 20 minutes, or until a fork pierces the flesh easily.

Remove eel pieces; place in shallow casserole or bowl.

Pour pan liquids into top of a double boiler; place over, not in, boiling water in bottom of double boiler. Stir egg yolks into liquids and cook, stirring constantly, until sauce thickens slightly. Stir in lemon juice; pour sauce over eels. Sauce will thicken as it cools. Chill well in refrigerator before serving.

MARTHA'S VINEYARD EEL STIFLE

6 to 8 portions

¼ pound salt pork, cut in
½-inch dice

4 medium onions, cut ½ inch
thick

4 cups sliced potatoes, ½ inch
thick

2 pounds eels, skinned and cut
in 1-inch slices

¾ teaspoon salt

¼ teaspoon freshly ground
black pepper

Flour

Prepare eels according to directions on page 45. In a heavy iron or cast-aluminum kettle, cook the salt-pork dice over moderate heat until crisp and golden. Drain on paper towels and reserve. Place a layer each of onions, potatoes, and eels in the kettle. Sprinkle with some of the salt and pepper and about ½ teaspoon flour. Repeat layers until all the ingredients are used. Sprinkle the salt-pork dice over the top and add enough cold water barely to cover layers. Simmer over low heat, tightly covered, until tender—about ½ hour.

If preferred, this dish may be baked in a 300° F. oven, in which case it must be cooked a little longer.

SAUTÉED SQUID

Squid, familiar fare in Mediterranean countries, can also be caught and cooked on Martha's Vineyard. Menemsha children introduce their summer playmates to squid jigging in the murky, swirling waters below the docks. Intrepid adults can usually haul in a fair catch with the right combination of patience and luck. Buy a cane pole and some line, wrap a bit of fluorescent orange tape around a treble hook, attach hook to line and line to pole (a half-ounce sinker might be advisable in a swift tide), and lower your line into the water where the children fish. Yank your prey up sharply when he attacks or he may drop off. If you don't catch anything, don't settle for a package of frozen squid. This is for fish, and not for humans.

(continued)

4 portions

4 small fresh squid (do not use frozen)	½ cup olive oil (more if needed)
½ cup flour	2 small eggs, beaten
½ teaspoon salt	Lemon juice
¼ teaspoon black pepper	Lemon slices

Prepare squid for cooking by removing the head and cutting off the tentacles. Slit open the body and clean it well in cold water. Cut body and tentacles into ½-inch rings. Pat pieces with paper towels to absorb most of the moisture on them. Combine flour, salt, and pepper in a paper bag, add squid pieces a few at a time, and shake until well coated with flour mixture. Remove and keep on a plate while heating oil to sizzling hot (use a good-sized heavy skillet). Using a slotted spoon, dip squid pieces into beaten eggs, let drain slightly, then place in hot fat. Cook pieces quickly over moderate heat, turning to brown all sides. Do not overcook or squid will be tough—5 minutes should be the maximum cooking time allowed. Drain cooked pieces briefly on paper towels, sprinkle with a few drops of lemon juice and serve very hot with lemon slices.

Note: The flouring process may be omitted. Simply pat washed squid dry, salt and pepper pieces well, dip into beaten egg and fry as outlined above.

Shellfish

Chapter 3

The fish and shellfish of the great ponds formed the basis of the very sound economy of the Island Indians before the coming of the English. The great ponds, depending on the salinity of the water, will produce variously great quantities of oysters, quahaugs, soft shell clams, scallops and blue mussels. . . . The Indians ate all those shellfish as is indicated by the shell heaps and kitchen middens that mark the sites of their villages. They also ate other shellfish that are no longer generally used for food, such as the little quarterdecks or boatshells which used to be called sweetmeats, and the big whelks which Vineyarders called winkles.

—FROM *An Introduction to Martha's Vineyard,* BY E. GALE HUNTINGTON*

As anyone knows who has ever investigated the insides of a clam or oyster, shellfish are not like other "fish"; they are defined as "aquatic invertebrate animals." The category includes mollusks, such as clams, oysters, mussels, slugs, and snails; and crustaceans, such as lobsters, crabs, shrimp, and—oddly enough—wood lice. Like the rest of us on this increasingly polluted planet, shellfish are at the mercy of their environs. A change in the saline content of the vast, beautiful Great Ponds has often killed off the resident shellfish; and though a mussel can live to a shell-encrusted old age on a jetty at Menemsha Bight, the waters from which he constantly syphons his food may turn him into a live health hazard as a carrier of infectious hepatitis.

Now the Vineyard, like other communities, is concerning itself with the condition of its precious waters, since much of its livelihood is derived in one way or another from the sea. Surely this jewel of an island, to which thousands of people come to escape the filth and frustrations of city life, won't be allowed to succumb to the same ills as more metropolitan areas!

Clamming, scalloping, oystering, crabbing, and museling have been nearly as important as fishing on Martha's Vineyard since the days when the Indians feasted on shellfish cooked in salt steam over sea-

* Dukes County Historical Society, Edgartown, Massachusetts (1969).

weed and hot stones—a custom that evolved into the more elaborate clambake of the white man. In almost every salt-water pond on the Vineyard, summer wanderers still encounter one or another of these intriguing creatures. A scallop may bubble past a young skindiver in Sengekontacket Pond; a crab glide off into the seaweed at the approach of a Sailfish skimming toward him; a steamer clam squirt a watery warning out of his sandhole and withdraw deeper into the black muck as picnickers pass. And once an immense oyster turned up high on the pebbles at Lambert's Cove beach. Though barnacled and worm-burrowed, he was still tight and alive. Carried from his moorings and deposited miles away by some freakish tide, he came nonetheless to a glorious end—chilled, sprinkled with lemon juice, and savored at sunset on a North Tisbury porch.

CLAMS

Though certainly the most popular and familiar bivalve on the Island, clams, for some curious reason, are not included in the 1602 list of "fishes" recorded by the Gosnold expedition. The Indians were using them for food long before that, and their popularity has developed until today clams and clamming are an integral part of the summer scene all up and down the East Coast.

The hard-shelled quahog or little neck (the slightly larger ones are the well-known cherrystones) and the soft-shell or steamer are routed out of their sand beds and used every way from raw to exotic recipes in which they are minced, ground, stuffed, sauced, spiced, or otherwise tampered with. There are other edible clams to be gathered on the Island, if you can find enough of them to make it worth your while. Surf clams, the inhabitants of those huge rounded shells that make such handy ashtrays, have tough bodies, but the muscles that keep the creatures closed against the perils of life in the sea can be cut out and treated like the equivalent muscle in the scallop (the only part of that bivalve that is eaten). Small surf clams can be ground for chowder. And the razor clam, though difficult to capture and extremely perishable, is thought by some to be even more delectable than its more accessible relatives.

STEAMED CLAMS WITH HERBS

If you have friends who are rather blasé about steamed clams, having had them at every New England resort town every summer since early childhood, take them on a clamming expedition along the tidal sands of one of the Great Ponds (or to your own favorite, secret place) and invite them over that night for supper. Or you may want to wait until the next day, and soak your clams overnight in sea water with a handful or so of cornmeal thrown in it. Set the container in a cool place during the soaking period. This rids them of most of their ingested sand. Confronted with a steaming bowlful of this savory blending of seafood and herbs, even the most indifferent diner is likely to forget himself and demand more.

3 to 4 generous portions

1 gallon steamer clams	1 small bay leaf (or 2 dried
1 cup dry vermouth	Vineyard bayberry leaves)
1 cup butter	Freshly ground black pepper,
1 small clove garlic, crushed	a lot or a little
1 teaspoon dried basil (or 2	¼ cup lemon juice
teaspoons chopped fresh	2 tablespoons chopped fresh
basil)	parsley (optional)

Even if you have bought your clams, try to get them as sandless as possible—sand tends to cling in the "necks." (We recommend soaking them overnight as detailed above.) Rinse them gently under cold running water. Use only fresh, live clams. If you have any doubt as to their state of health, smell them. Live clams smell like the sea. Dead ones smell foul, like the black muck they live in.

Place the washed clams in a large, deep 6- to 8-quart kettle with a tight-fitting cover. Combine vermouth, 4 tablespoons of the butter, garlic, basil, bay leaf, and black pepper in a small saucepan and heat until the butter melts. Pour this mixture over

(continued)

the clams and mix in gently with a slotted spoon. Try not to break the clam shells. Cover the kettle and place over high heat until the pot is full of steam. Lower heat and steam about 10 minutes, or until shells fall slightly open. Do not overcook.

While clams cook, combine the remaining ¾ cup butter and the lemon juice in a small saucepan and heat until butter melts. Mix well; keep warm. Ladle clams into a large, warmed bowl. Pour the liquid in the pan through a strainer lined with cheese-cloth into a pitcher and serve it in cups or small bowls as a broth with the clams. Serve the warm lemon butter in several small dishes for diners to dip their clams into. The soup may be garnished with chopped parsley, if desired.

Note: If the clams have been freshly dug, they will not require the addition of salt; if not, you may wish to add salt to taste.

Bayberry

STUFFED QUAHOGS
[*Deviled Clams*]

Almost every Vineyarder who prepares this culinary delight has a different list of essential ingredients. Basically agreed upon, though, are chopped quahogs, bread crumbs, onion, green pepper, and such aromatic seasonings as parsley, sage, or garlic. Considerable preparation is involved before the mixture is placed in the quahog shells and baked. If it is served to appreciative family or friends, however, each heavenly bite is compensation enough for the tedium of preparation. The finished clams may be served as a main course, or be offered as a hot hors d'oeuvre on some special occasion. Vary your starting proportions accordingly.

4 portions

2 cups shucked quahogs and their liquor (save all the shells for later use)

¼ cup minced green pepper

1 cup fresh bread crumbs from day-old French or Italian type, if possible (more may be needed to bind the mixture sufficiently)

½ cup minced onion

1 small clove garlic, finely minced

Suggested seasonings: freshly ground black pepper, Tabasco, sage, Worcestershire sauce

1 egg, lightly beaten

Preheat oven to 375° F.

Chop the quahogs, or put them through the medium blade of a meat grinder. Reserve the liquor. Combine clams, green pepper, bread crumbs, onion, garlic, and any or all of the suggested seasonings to taste. Add the beaten egg and blend thoroughly with the other ingredients. Fill half the quahog shells with the mixture. Lightly oil the insides of the other shells and place one over each filled shell. Tie each filled and covered shell with twine, place in a shallow baking pan and bake for approximately one hour.

Note: The filled shells may be wrapped in foil instead of tied, but in that case they will steam rather than bake and are not quite so good.

QUAHOGS ROCKEFELLER

Specifying clams for this recipe is not meant to deprecate the more traditional choice of oysters, if one is fortunate enough to acquire a mess of the latter from one of the Island's Great Ponds. Quahogs are suggested here because they adapt magnificently in this instance and because they are always in season.

(continued)

4 portions

Rock salt	1 teaspoon dried tarragon (or
24 quahogs, littleneck size,	2 teaspoons chopped
opened and left in the	fresh)
half shell	¼ cup Pernod
¼ pound butter	1 cup chopped cooked
½ cup minced shallots or	spinach
green onions	⅓ cup fresh bread crumbs
4 tablespoons chopped	(use day-old French or
parsley, preferably flat	Italian type, if possible)
Italian type	Salt
½ teaspoon dried chervil (or	Freshly ground black pepper
1 teaspoon chopped fresh)	Cayenne pepper

Preheat oven to 500° F.

Partially fill a shallow baking dish (a rimmed cookie sheet is suggested) with rock salt to provide a bed for the shellfish. Set them in place. Melt 3 or 4 tablespoons of the butter and cook the shallots or onions in it over moderate heat until they are transparent and wilted. Add remaining butter and remove pan from heat as soon as this butter melts. Stir in remaining ingredients except salt, pepper, and cayenne. Top the quahogs with this mixture. Season to taste with salt and both peppers. Bake approximately 10 minutes. The dish may be placed under the broiler for a few moments before serving.

Note: This is an adaptation of the famed New Orleans recipe, which seems to have acquired its name because it was "as rich as Rockefeller." The original version requires twice this much butter; some variations use watercress instead of spinach, others insist on a topping of bacon squares. The Pernod is consistently essential. The reader has the privilege of deleting, substituting, or otherwise improvising on the text as given here.

CLAMS CASINO

Though not exclusively a Martha's Vineyard recipe, here is a wonderfully savory way of using the outcome of a clamming expedition. Proportions given produce a satisfactory prelude to a meal; more, of course, would be needed if clams are to be used as a main course.

4 portions

Rock salt

24 quahogs, little-neck size, opened and left in the half shell

¾ cup soft bread crumbs (use day-old French or Italian type, if possible)

¼ teaspoon freshly ground black pepper

5 tablespoons chopped parsley, preferably flat Italian kind

Pinch of cayenne pepper (optional)

4–6 tablespoons olive oil (or other vegetable oil)

1 clove garlic, minced

Preheat oven to 500° F.

Partially fill a shallow baking dish (a rimmed cookie sheet is suggested) with rock salt. This provides a bed for the quahogs; it prevents them from tipping and losing their juices. Set the half-shell quahogs on the rock salt.

Mix the bread crumbs, black pepper, 3 tablespoons of the parsley, and the optional cayenne pepper. Spoon this mixture equally over the clams. Mix the oil and garlic thoroughly; pour carefully over each clam. Bake for about 10 minutes. If the crumbs have not sufficiently browned, place the dish under the broiler just long enough to achieve the desired browning. Sprinkle clams with remainder of chopped parsley and serve immediately.

Note: Salt has been deliberately omitted from this recipe. If the quahogs have been out of the water only a matter of hours they will be delightfully seasoned with the brine from their natural environment.

(continued)

It is suggested that the quahogs be refrigerated until icy cold; opening them is then a simple matter. The muscle that acts as a hinge, almost locking the two shells in place, will relax considerably when chilled.

RAZOR-CLAM SOUP

These clams are aptly named, and gathering enough of them to prepare this soup could result in far more sliced fingers than a steamer-clam expedition. These elongated, elusive creatures are hard to extricate from their sand burrows, and if you plan to dig for some you'd better equip yourself with spade, tongs, trowel, rake, metal bar, or some other prying instrument and not rely on fingers. Like other clams, razor clams live in colonies, so if you do encounter some when unprepared (they can be easily identified from any seashore guide) you can return another time better equipped for some strategic ploys.

Though not sold fresh in markets—mainly because they are difficult to obtain and are relatively unfamiliar—razor clams are canned and sold as delicacies both here and in other seaside countries. They are generally considered to be the finest of all clams in flavor and texture, though much less common than their familiar soft-shell and hard-shell relatives.

If you do collect some razor clams, be sure to eat them within a few hours. Take some sea water home with you, put the clams in it (first washing them carefully and thoroughly to remove excess sand), add a handful or two of cornmeal, set them in a cool place and let them soak overnight to get rid of ingested sand. The cleaned clams can be eaten in various ways—steamed and dipped in butter, used in spaghetti sauce or chowder, or baked as in Stuffed Quahogs (see page 54) or under a pastry crust. This soup offers one epicurean way of treating them.

4 to 6 portions

About 4 dozen razor clams, cleaned

4 tablespoons white wine

2 cups medium cream (or 1 cup milk, 1 cup evaporated milk)

2 tablespoons butter

Salt and pepper

Paprika

2 teaspoons chopped parsley

Put clams and wine in a large kettle, cover, and bring to a quick boil. Lower heat and steam 10 minutes. Lift clams from kettle with a slotted spoon or tongs, reserving liquid. Let clams cool somewhat, then remove from shells and chop coarsely. Strain clam liquor through a sieve lined with cheesecloth to remove sand. Combine clam mixture, cream or milk, and butter in top part of a double boiler and heat over boiling water until steaming. Add salt and pepper to taste. Serve hot with dash of paprika and garnish of chopped parsley on each bowl.

Note: This soup could be thickened a bit, if desired, by preparing a paste of 2 tablespoons flour and 3 tablespoons cold water and stirring it into the hot clam-and-cream mixture.

CLAMBAKE

No two clambake enthusiasts agree about the ingredients essential in preparing a true clambake. In Rhode Island, white and sweet potatoes, as well as onions, are important. Sometimes chicken or fish is added to the pile. In other lands, both food and procedure vary—the Polynesians, for instance, steam their foods over hot stones in earthen ovens.

New England clambakes—and those on Martha's Vineyard —are conducted more or less as follows: First, a huge pit is dug in the beach and lined with large beach stones. Then a large fire is laid and lighted, and enough cordwood is thrown on to keep the fire going for about an hour and a half. The embers are then raked away and a 4-inch layer of wet seaweed is placed on the stones. Rockweed, a seaweed that is full of

(continued)

"blisters" that break open and contribute additional liquid and flavor, is especially good for this purpose. Then comes the food. Potatoes, if used, go first; then chicken wrapped in cloth. A layer of rockweed follows. Next comes corn, left in the husk, then live lobsters, and last, steamer clams—bushels of them—poured into burlap bags and arranged over the top. Another layer of rockweed is thrown on, then a wet canvas is thrown over the entire pit to confine the steam. The edges of the canvas should be weighted down with stones to form a tight cover; additional seaweed may also be used to hold it down. Sand raked onto the perimeter of the canvas will provide an even tighter seal. The clambake should then be left to steam for about an hour.

When the clambake is opened, the steamed clams are served first, poured out into some huge receptacle and dipped into by each participant, who should be supplied with a paper cup partly filled with melted butter to dunk his clams in. After everyone cleans up a little in the sea (usually getting his feet wet in the process) the rest of the food is hauled out and served. Tomatoes and cucumbers, salt, pepper, more butter are usually set out on a big rock or portable table, and a few cases of cold beer are usually welcome. Big chunks of watermelon provide a suitably messy conclusion to the feast, if anyone has room for it; and a few blankets should be spread around on the perimeter for people to rest on between trips to the pit for seconds or thirds or fourths.

When properly organized, and begun early enough in the day, an old-style clambake can be an experience long remembered with nostalgia. Get to the beach early enough for a swim while the fire burns down, and another while the food cooks. And remember to program everything so that all cleaning up can be done while there's still light. If people want to linger, start a bonfire and sit around it for a while.

MUSSELS

The blue mussel is one of this country's least utilized,* most abundant, and—when properly prepared—most delicious seafoods. Mussels are simple to gather and simple to fix, using only the simplest of seasonings—a little onion and parsley, some pepper, a splash of white wine. And in Massachusetts, at least, one doesn't need a permit to collect them (another indication of their lowly state). Skindivers in the Menemsha area report massive black beds of these beautiful mollusks spreading nearly across the inlet in some places. There are vast beds among the Tashmoo rocks. There is an embryonic colony near Lambert's Cove, and a tremendous breeding ground is trying to hold its own near a South Shore beach. More exact details will not be given here on these latter two sources as most of the mussels in them are still in the "seed" stage and should be left to grow a few more years before humans disturb them. One caution: mussels, like other shellfish, can carry infectious hepatitis, so take a good look at the water they're sieving their food from. If you mussel in Menemsha, you might be wiser not to do so during the weeks those elegant cruisers are tied up at the new marina.

* In contrast, a top-rated European cook book lists nine recipes for mussels, only one for clams!

STEAMED MUSSELS

[*With white wine and aromatic seasonings*]

Irma Rombauer, the personality responsible for the continuing success of the best-selling *Joy of Cooking,* wrote that ". . . in France the mussel is called the oyster of the poor [but] there are many definitions of poverty."

4 portions

3 quarts mussels
1 small carrot, scraped and
cut into ½-inch dice
1 medium clove garlic,
minced

¼ cup green onions, minced
(or finely minced shallots
or onions)
1 cup dry white wine or ⅔
cup dry vermouth

(continued)

½ cup water
¼ teaspoon freshly ground
    black pepper

2 tablespoons parsley,
    coarsely chopped
    (preferably the flat-leaved
    Italian type)

Scrub the mussels thoroughly under running water. Snip beards off with scissors. Don't worry about removing barnacles and other shells—most of them will drop off during the cooking process and add flavor to the broth. Put the carrot, garlic, onions, wine, water, pepper, and 1 tablespoon of the parsley into the pot. Cover and simmer until carrot dice are tender, about 10 minutes. Add the mussels, raise heat to high, and cover pot. Lift and stir mussels occasionally as they cook. Do not have pot too full to manage this. The mussels are ready for the table the moment the shells open. This will take 5 to 10 minutes. Serve the mussels in good-sized soup plates. Spoon the delicious liquid generously over the shells, sprinkle each dish with parsley and serve at once. Do not eat any mussels that are unopened. Try cooking them a little more—they may just be underdone.

Note: While the vegetables are simmering there may seem to be too little liquid in the pot, but the mussels will add their own good juices as they open.

MUSSEL SOUP

A near-relative of Billi Bi, another delicious mussel soup, the following is less rich and not quite so complicated to prepare.

6 generous portions

3 quarts fresh mussels
1 medium onion, chopped
2 tablespoons chopped fresh
    parsley
1 stalk celery, chopped
1½ cups dry white wine
1 quart fish stock (see
    page 8) or bottled clam
    juice

1 cup medium cream
Salt (if needed)
¼ teaspoon freshly ground
    black pepper
3 tablespoons chopped
    chives (optional)

Clean mussels (see page 62).

In a deep kettle cook onion, parsley, and celery in the wine and 1 cup of the fish stock or clam juice over moderate heat until vegetables are tender.

Add mussels to the kettle, cover tightly, and cook over high heat only until mussels open. Lift and stir mussels several times to distribute heat more evenly. Do not overcook. (Mussels are sufficiently cooked when their shells open.) When cool enough to handle, remove mussels from shells. Discard any that seem reluctant to open (or replace in kettle and cook a few minutes more—sometimes they are just not quite done).

To the liquids in the kettle add remainder of fish stock or clam juice. Cook over high heat until liquid is reduced by about one-third. Strain through a fine sieve lined with cheesecloth or a clean dish towel, pressing down on vegetables with back of spoon.

Return liquid to pan, add cream and mussels, and reheat but do not boil, stirring constantly. Add salt if needed, dust with black pepper, and serve. This may also be served cold with chopped chives sprinkled on each serving.

Note: Thicken with a paste of 3 tablespoons softened butter and 3 tablespoons flour before adding the mussels, if desired.

MUSSELS VINAIGRETTE

This is a fine way to use leftover steamed mussels. Strain them, discard the shells, and pour any good French (vinaigrette) dressing over the mussels in sufficient quantity to cover them. Allow the mussels to marinate 4 or 5 hours or overnight. Serve them (drained) as an hors d'oeuvre preceding lunch or dinner or with cocktails. Refrigerated in the dressing, they will keep for days. For Vinaigrette Dressing see page 247. Just before serving, sprinkle the mussels lavishly with chopped fresh parsley.

OYSTERS

Despite the fact that the mature oyster can produce up to sixty million eggs during a single season, the beachcomber who comes across an oyster shell nearly always finds it empty. Oysters, obviously, have a rough time of it. Since 1775, when a disease hit the North American oyster beds, this mollusk has lost much of its vigor and now has to be coddled into maturity by well-researched oystermen, who set out the oyster seed in the backwaters of the Vineyard's salt ponds, then carefully transplant the spat to mature in the sands off Cape Cod. Pollution has hit the oyster as it has every other living thing; but it has other enemies as well. Fish and crabs feed on the defenseless oyster spat as they roam the pond bottoms. Starfish clasp the rough shells with their tentacles and pry them open to eat the soft insides; and the tiny oyster drill manages to burrow through the oyster's protective housing and siphon out the nourishing innards.

Small wonder, then, that the oyster is carefully guarded from ravaging humans. Oysters should not be taken anywhere during the months that lack an "r"; this is not because they are not edible during warmer weather (though their flavor is poorer then), but to allow them to revitalize their colonies. A shellfish permit is required for anyone planning to gather oysters on the Vineyard, and even then the ponds are often closed to oystering, as some of Edgartown's waters were in both the 1969-70 and 1970-71 season, to give the beds a chance to build up.

If you do go oystering, and pick the shells up as they're usually found, in jagged clumps, we offer two precautions. Wear gloves—almost every surface of an oyster seems to have a razor-sharp protrusion that is hard to avoid. And check each shell before you carry it home. A good many of them, you will find, are full not of plump oyster but of nauseating black muck, which makes the unenviable chore of cleaning and scrubbing even less attractive.

OYSTER OR CLAM FRITTERS

Makes 30 to 36 fritters

2 cups oysters or steamer
    clams
2 cups sifted flour
2 teaspoons baking powder
½ teaspoon salt
¼ teaspoon freshly ground
    black pepper
Restrained pinch cayenne
    pepper

½ cup milk, more or less
2 egg yolks, lightly beaten
2 egg whites, beaten until
    stiff
Vegetable oil for deep-fat
    frying (or ½ cup
    vegetable oil for skillet
    frying)
Lemon wedges

Parsley sprigs

Strain the oysters or clams, reserving liquor; chop coarsely.

Prepare the batter by sifting the presifted flour with the baking powder, salt, pepper, and cayenne. Measure reserved shellfish liquor, add enough milk to make 1 cup and add gradually with beaten egg yolks to flour mixture, stirring until batter is smooth. Add chopped oysters or clams and blend well. Stir in 1 or 2 tablespoons of the beaten egg whites, then carefully fold in remainder until no white streaks remain.

In a deep-fat fryer drop batter a tablespoonful at a time into oil heated to 375° F. (There should be at least 3 inches of oil in fryer.) Don't overcrowd the fry kettle. When the fritters are puffed and golden, turn once, cook briefly on other side, remove, drain on paper towels and keep warm in a preheated 200° F. oven until all the fritters are cooked.

If using the skillet method, heat ½ cup oil in a 10- or 12-inch heavy skillet over moderate heat until a light haze forms over oil. Immediately drop in fritter batter, a heaping tablespoonful at a time. Cook until golden, turn, and cook on other side.

Garnish with lemon wedges and parsley sprigs and serve at once.

Note: Frozen oysters or canned minced clams may be substituted; the flavor, however, will not be as robust.

OYSTERS WITH MUSHROOMS

4 portions

½ pound fresh mushrooms,
　sliced
5–6 tablespoons butter
1 pint oysters, undrained
2 tablespoons flour
1 cup milk
½ cup cream
½ teaspoon Worcestershire
　sauce

½ teaspoon salt
¼ teaspoon freshly ground
　pepper (white, if possible)
Pinch of dry mustard
　(optional)
6 slices buttered toast, cut in
　triangular halves
1–2 tablespoons chopped
　fresh chives

Cook the mushrooms in 2 to 3 tablespoons of the butter in a skillet (preferably enamel, cast iron or stainless steel) over moderate heat. Allow the butter foam to subside before tossing in the mushrooms. Stir occasionally; cook 5 to 6 minutes, or until delicately browned. Remove from skillet and reserve.

Add the oysters in their liquor to the skillet and simmer only until edges curl. Remove from pan immediately, drain and set aside. Reserve oyster liquor.

Add 2 more tablespoons butter to skillet. Melt it over moderate heat. Add the flour and blend well. Reduce heat and cook the roux a few minutes longer. Add milk, cream, and reserved oyster liquor and cook over reduced heat, stirring constantly, until mixture thickens and bubbles a little. Add Worcestershire sauce, salt, pepper, and the mustard, if used. (Mix the mustard with the Worcestershire sauce to avoid lumps.) Add oysters and mushrooms; cook only long enough to reheat the mixture. Add the last tablespoonful of butter, swirling it in thoroughly.

Serve immediately on hot buttered toast with chives sprinkled on top.

OYSTER PIE

4 portions

1 pint oysters, shucked
3 tablespoons butter
¼ pound fresh mushrooms,
   sliced
3 tablespoons flour
Approximately 1 cup rich
   milk (half milk, half
   cream)
½ teaspoon salt

¼ teaspoon white pepper
Dash of Worcestershire
   sauce
1 teaspoon lemon juice
Cayenne pepper
Pastry crust, ½ recipe (see
   crust used for Beefsteak-
   and-Kidney Pie, page
   121)

Preheat oven to 425° F.

Drain oysters through a fine strainer; reserve the liquor.

In a heavy skillet melt 2 tablespoons butter over moderate heat; when foam subsides, cook the sliced mushrooms only until lightly browned, about 5 minutes. Remove mushrooms and set aside. Add remaining tablespoon butter to skillet; when it has melted add the flour and stir it until well blended. Cook another minute, then add the strained oyster liquor combined with enough rich milk to make 1½ cups. Reduce heat and cook, stirring constantly, until mixture thickens. Remove from heat. Add the oysters, the salt and pepper, the cooked mushroom slices, Worcestershire sauce, lemon juice, and a restrained dash of cayenne pepper.

Pour the creamed mixture into a round, shallow 8-inch casserole. Cover with the pastry crust, rolled about ¼ inch thick. Seal and crimp the edges, cut slits in the crust (which may be brushed with a little cream), and bake 10 to 15 minutes, or until crust begins to brown. Reduce heat to 375° F. and bake an additional 15 to 20 minutes.

OYSTER CASSEROLE

A small, family-operated restaurant in Edgartown serves this oyster preparation. One of the sons, who shares the cooking honors with his mother, is a true deep-water sailor, having spent considerable time at sea both working sail and in yacht galleys. He therefore is familiar with the shellfish of many islands, far and near, and knows multiple ways of preparing these delicate foods from the sea. The oysters in their casserole, however, are fresh from one of the Island's Great Ponds in proper season, a factor that contributes to the superiority of the dish. Though the use of the oysters is not dissimilar to that involved in scalloped oysters, this young man wisely restrains the use of bread crumbs and seasoning, allowing the flavor and succulence of the plump, fresh oysters to dominate the finished casserole.

2 portions

25–30 small oysters, freshly shucked but undrained (if oysters are large, adjust number proportionately)	¼ teaspoon freshly ground black pepper
	3 tablespoons melted butter
	1 tablespoon fresh lemon juice
4 saltines or common crackers, coarsely crushed	Dash of cayenne pepper (optional)

Preheat oven to 475° F.

Place a layer of half the oysters and half their liquor in a 1-quart ovenproof casserole. Sprinkle half the crushed crackers over them and dust with half of the black pepper. Repeat the layering process. Combine the melted butter with the lemon juice and pour over the ingredients in casserole. Top with a sprinkle of cayenne pepper, if desired.

Bake, uncovered, on top shelf of oven approximately 20 minutes, but only until the edges of the oysters curl. The size of the oyster will determine the baking time.

Note: Salt is deliberately omitted from this recipe. If you are blessed with oysters fresh from one of the Vineyard's Great Ponds, salinity will be at its maximum. If not, add salt with discretion.

SCALLOPS

Most of us living on the Vineyard never encounter the larger varieties of scallops except on a seafood platter in an off-Island restaurant, but we all have admired, sought and, when wading or clamming, even been pinched by bay scallops, the Vineyard's most precious commodity. Flitting through the waters of the salt ponds in their colorful housings, these decorative creatures are usually literally and figuratively out of reach of most of the Island's summer visitors. Anyone caught out of season with even a handful of scallops will be fined a flat and substantial fee; and the season begins long after the vacationers have gone home. In November the licensed Islanders—lone workmen, husbands and wives, sturdy young men—don their hip boots and scalloping gloves and move out onto the cold, still ponds to net their limit of these delicious mollusks. Control laws, the time spent freezing in your boat, the tedium of extracting the edible muscles, the relatively low yield of these per bushel of scallops, and the high demand for these inimitable delicacies all contrive to make scalloping and scallops an expensive taste to indulge. But every Vineyarder should allow himself a few feasts every winter, if only to remind him how vastly varied are the fruits of land and sea that this Island can provide.

It is possible, in these days of quick and careful transportation of perishable foods, to buy bay scallops from good markets in other parts of the country. If you happen to see them during the winter, and they look firm and fresh and show no watery leakage, buy them and enjoy the inimitable sweetness of these fragile sea creatures.

BROILED BAY SCALLOPS

2 generous portions

1 pound bay scallops, drained
¼ teaspoon salt
Pinch of freshly ground black
  pepper
¼ cup (or a little more)
  melted butter
1 teaspoon lemon juice

1 small clove garlic, chopped
  fine
¾ cup fresh bread crumbs
  (use day-old French or
  Italian type, if possible)
Sprinkle of paprika
Parsley sprigs (optional)

Preheat oven broiler, using maximum setting.

Place the bay scallops in a shallow heatproof baking dish; sprinkle them with salt and pepper. Combine melted butter, lemon juice, and garlic; mix into the bread crumbs thoroughly. The crumbs should be quite buttery; add additional melted butter, if desired. Pat the crumbs lightly over the scallops; sprinkle lightly with paprika.

Broil about three inches under the broiler heat for about 10 minutes. Do not overcook; shellfish toughens and shrinks when exposed to too much heat. Serve immediately, garnished with sprigs of parsley, if desired.

Note: It is essential to choose an appropriate-sized baking dish for this recipe. There should be only one layer of scallops and they should be completely contained by the baking dish. A heavy enamel or stainless-steel shallow casserole about 6 by 9 inches is suggested for the quantities given.

SCALLOPS IN MUSHROOM CAPS

4 portions

2 dozen good-sized mushrooms
Salt and pepper
4 dozen bay scallops (or 2
  dozen sea scallops)

6 slices bacon
Chopped parsley for garnish
  (optional)

Preheat broiler, using maximum setting.

Wash mushrooms; pat dry with paper towels. Cut stems off

(save them to use some other way). Place mushroom caps upside down on a cookie sheet large enough to hold them all without touching. Dust each cap with salt and pepper and place 2 bay scallops or one sea scallop on each mushroom. Lay ¼ slice bacon over each mushroom. Broil about 2 inches from heat for 8 to 10 minutes, depending on size of mushrooms. Garnish with chopped parsley before serving, if desired.

SEVICHE

Linked only tenuously with Vineyard cookery—in that Island whalers did stop in South America and their crews probably sampled this strange and exotic treatment of raw fish—seviche is put in this cook book for two reasons: *really* fresh seafood, essential to this dish, can be easily obtained here; and the dish is simple to prepare, unusual to serve, and so good that it deserves much wider usage. It makes a lovely first course for a summer dinner, or can be used as a main dish at lunch. Though good when made with fish, it is far better if prepared with delicate Island bay scallops.

This Peruvian version is traditionally served with a garnish of cooked corn-on-the-cob circles and pieces of cooked yams.

2 generous portions (as a main course)
4 portions (as a cocktail hors d'oeuvre)

1 pound fresh bay scallops
  or 1 pound fillets of any
  white, firm-fleshed fish:
  any flounder type, or
  haddock, halibut, pollock,
  cod, or swordfish
½ cup very thinly sliced
  scallions with tops (or
  sweet Spanish or Bermuda
  onion)
Juice from 3 or more large,
  fresh Persian limes
  (enough to cover fish)

3 or 4 drops Tabasco
⅛ teaspoon freshly ground
  black pepper
½ teaspoon or more salt
Lettuce
Sliced green pepper or hot
  red pepper
Black olives
Sprigs of parsley, dill, and
  watercress

(continued)

Cut fish into thin, narrow strips, about 2 inches long by ¾ inch wide. Use scallops just as they are. Place scallops or fish and scallions (or onions) in a flat glass or enamel bowl and add enough lime juice barely to cover seafood-onion mixture. Add Tabasco, pepper, and salt; mix well, cover dish with plastic wrap and store in refrigerator a minimum of 12 hours, or for 2 or 3 days. The lime juice "cooks" the raw seafood, and scallops or fish slices will be firm, opaque, and aromatically flavored when done.

Serve in lettuce cups. Garnish with strips of cold, crisp green pepper or paper-thin slices of fresh hot red pepper, black olives, and sprigs of parsley, dill, and watercress.

LOBSTERS

A person sitting down to a sumptuous lobster dinner probably doesn't notice that his *pièce de résistance* is "right-handed"—that is, its right pincer is usually much heavier than its left one. Nor does he care that his lobster took at least six years to grow to an edible 1-pound size, is rigidly protected by state and local laws, and has a name derived from an Anglo-Saxon word for spider. He is much more likely to be conscious that, bite for bite, his meal will cost him twice as much as a good steak dinner (as this page was being written fresh lobster meat was selling for $9 a pound in a Menemsha market) and that if he finishes all that extra butter he'll wish he hadn't a few hours later.

People on the Vineyard have various reasons for being interested in lobsters. Not only are lobsters trapped in the offshore waters in pots set out by licensed lobstermen (and often illegally raided by unlicensed ones), but they are hatched by the thousands at the Martha's Vineyard Lobster Hatchery and Research Station, which the Commonwealth of Massachusetts established in 1951 to improve lobster production. Since then, several million *Homarus americanus* (American lobsters) have been hatched, reared, and released by John T. Hughes and his associates. But lobster fry, like many other shellfish, have a host of predators (including their own kind, since they eat each other), and relatively few eggs—only an estimated 60 out of the 60,000 that can be released each season by an adult female lobster—survive the first three stages of growth and are mature enough to drop into the dark, murky depths and begin the defensive, nocturnal existence they are destined for. Small wonder, then, that lobsters are scarce and expensive.

Strangely enough, not only are lobsters scarce but lobster recipes are few as well. Upon reflection, we concluded that people prefer their lobsters in simple style—broiled or boiled. They are so good in these ways they really don't need to be improved on.

BAKED STUFFED LOBSTER
[*A Martha's Vineyard Version*]

4 portions

4 live lobsters, weighing about 1½ pounds each	¼ teaspoon freshly ground black pepper
24 Ritz crackers	½ pound uncooked bay scallops, shrimp, or crabmeat, chopped
½ cup melted butter	
1 tablespoon lemon juice	
½ cup pale dry sherry	Lemon wedges
¼ teaspoon salt	Parsley sprigs

Preheat oven to 450° F.

Prepare each lobster for stuffing by placing it on its back and splitting it lengthwise. (Any good, standard cook book will give detailed and graphic instructions on treating live lobsters for the novice cook.) Reserve the tomalley (green liver) and roe, if any.

Crush the crackers coarsely with a rolling pin. In a mixing bowl combine the melted butter, lemon juice, and sherry; add the crushed crackers, salt, pepper, and the chopped shellfish. Add the reserved lobster liver and roe. Mix these ingredients lightly with a fork, then spoon stuffing into the prepared cavity of each lobster. Bake the lobsters in a shallow pan 20 to 25 minutes, depending on their size. Transfer to a large, heated platter; garnish with lemon wedges and sprigs of parsley.

LOBSTER SAUTÉ

Lobster meat—expensive and elegant at any time—is especially so in this form. A further virtue is that the lobster may be prepared in practically no time, after your guests have arrived, as the procedure is unbelievably simple.

3 portions

5 tablespoons butter

2 small cloves garlic, minced fine (optional but delicious)

1–1½ pounds cooked fresh lobster meat, cut in chunks

½ teaspoon salt

¼ teaspoon freshly ground black pepper

1 tablespoon chopped fresh herbs (a mixture of parsley, chives, basil, and tarragon is very good)

In a heavy skillet, melt butter over moderate heat. When butter foam subsides, add the minced garlic, if used. Immediately add the lobster meat and stir and turn it frequently; sprinkle with the salt and pepper. The lobster is ready to serve as soon as it is heated through. Sprinkle half the herbs over the lobster and mix them well into the lobster meat. Remove skillet from heat, transfer contents to a heated serving platter, sprinkle remainder of herbs on top, and serve immediately.

LOBSTER SALAD ROLLS

A stop in Gay Head at Mrs. Grieder's geranium-decked luncheonette or Manning's Snack Bar for a lobster roll and chowder was for years one of the delights of a summertime tour around the Island. Now, alas, Mrs. Grieder has retired and the snack bar is closed, so it might behoove you to make your own lobster rolls and carry them along for a beachside picnic, if you are fortunate enough to know of an unposted spot.

The secret of her delicious filling, Mrs. Grieder tells us, was to chop the lobster meat very fine—"People don't like chunks in sandwiches." She also emphasized the importance of buttering every bit of the frankfurter roll and of grilling the roll a long time very slowly. Proper preparation was so important to her that she never let anyone else make the lobster rolls but tended to each order herself.

(continued)

*Makes 5 filled rolls (about ½ cup
    salad per roll)*

2 cups finely chopped lobster meat	**Grated onion (optional)**
½ cup finely chopped celery	**Salt**
Sprinkle of lemon juice	**Freshly ground black pepper**
½ cup mayonnaise (approximate)	**Softened butter**
Pinch of curry powder (optional)	**5 frankfurter rolls**
	Shredded lettuce

Combine lobster meat and celery and sprinkle lightly with lemon juice. Mix slightly, then add enough mayonnaise to bind mixture and stir well. Add a pinch of curry powder and grated onion to taste, if desired. (Vineyarders omit these two ingredients, but you may like them.) Add salt and pepper to taste and mix well.

Partially slice frankfurter rolls if necessary, butter the outside surfaces well, heat griddle or heavy skillet and toast rolls slowly on both sides until golden. Put about 2 tablespoons shredded lettuce inside each toasted roll (this makes a bed for the salad) and spoon about ½ cup of the salad on the lettuce, spreading evenly. Keep cool until eaten.

Note: Do not carry unrefrigerated lobster rolls around with you on a hot day. The combination of seafood and mayonnaise is a frequent source of food poisoning.

CRABS

Crab is of Anglo-Saxon derivation, "akin to crawl," says Webster, and anyone who has seen a member of the order Decapoda scuttling for cover, outmaneuvering even the subtlest thrusts of the stalker's net, will appreciate this association. Vineyard winds and waters are too frigid for many of these quaint crustaceans to be attracted to the Island; and blue crabs in particular have behaved erratically over the past ten years or so, appearing, disappearing, and reappearing in Vineyard waters in some mysterious, unpredictable cycle. For several years during the mid-sixties there just didn't seem to be any blue crabs. Now they have come back. When you're exploring the margins of any brackish ponds or creeks during a beach outing, look in the murky, weedy areas for a dark, roundish patch that moves into hiding when you approach. Remember the spot, and come back with a net, a bushel basket floated on an inflated inner tube, a pair of old tennis shoes, and a will to do battle. If you're a poor sport, you can tie chunks of old meat, rotten fish, or almost anything no longer edible on short lengths of string, toss them into the murk or weeds, and lure the creatures into the shallow water where you can block their escape and net them. But a good forthright hunt, human after crab, is fairer and much more exciting. It's also an excellent sport for the 10- to-14 age group who become bored with clamming, are too impatient to fish if it involves waiting, and think beachcombing is sort of a drag. An eye-to-eye confrontation with an 8-inch blue crab, pincers held high and open, ready to battle to the death with the outsize monster that has all the advantages, becomes an experience for child or adult to store away with the other treasured souvenirs of a Vineyard summer.

BASIC STEAMED CRABS

Cooked crabmeat can be used in many delectable ways. Some dishes require a good deal of preparation and a great many ingredients, but the crab recipes in this book are relatively simple, as all summer-resort cooking should be. To obtain the crabmeat needed for them, the crabs may be cooked in the following way.

It will take 4 to 6 large blue crabs to provide a cup of cooked meat, and at least twice that many of the other varieties. Allow at least ½ cup meat for each portion. Cook only live crabs. They can be kept alive for some hours in a cool, shaded place and protected by wet seaweed.

Heat about 6 inches of water to boiling in the largest covered kettle you have. Clean sea water is excellent for cooking crabs or any other seafood. Grab each crab with kitchen tongs, rinse it under cold running water, and plunge it into the kettle of live steam. This is not a chore for the soft-hearted. There is a fair amount of rattling about in the kettle, but the authorities assure us that this level of creature does not feel pain. Keep the flame high and the steam will quickly kill them. Cook the crabs a few at a time, steaming each batch about ten minutes. Stir them around once or twice during this time. Remove cooked crabs from kettle. They can be cooled fairly quickly under running water, or left in the sink until they can be easily handled. If blue crabs are used, lift the little "tail" on the bottom and rip off the top shell. These are male crabs; the females have large "aprons." Discard these tops, along with the feathery "devil's fingers" along each side and the soft pouch under the eyes. Using a nutcracker and nutpick, remove the meat that remains. Crack claws and remove all meat. This meat may be cooled and eaten just as it is, sprinkled with lemon juice and dipped in melted butter. Or it may be reserved for other recipes.

If other varieties of crabs are used, such as rock crabs, use only the meat from the leg sections. There is not enough in the body to bother with.

BLUE CRABS IN BEER

4 or more portions

3–4 quarts beer

1 tablespoon cayenne pepper
(less if desired, or omit)

20–24 good-sized live blue
crabs

1 cup melted butter

2 lemons, cut in slices

A large canning kettle is useful for cooking crabs. If you have nothing big enough to hold them all, cook them in batches, using about 2 cups beer and about ¼ teaspoon cayenne for every 6 crabs. Put beer and pepper in kettle, cover, and heat. When kettle is full of steam, grasp each crab with kitchen tongs, rinse under cold running water and pop into kettle, replacing lid each time. Cook crabs over high heat for 10 to 12 minutes, until they turn red. Remove lid and stir crabs around two or three times during cooking process so all will be cooked. Remove cooked crabs from liquid and cool until they can be handled easily. Serve with melted butter, lobster forks or nutpicks, nutcrackers or lobster crackers, and large bowls of cool water. Float lemon slices on the water for diners to use to clean up their hands and arms from time to time. (Demolishing and ingesting a mess of crabs is not for the fastidious.) Mugs of cold beer help cool the palate if you've been properly lavish with the cayenne.

ROCK-CRAB CAKES

Though too small to be eaten like blue crabs, the Jonah and rock crabs found mainly along the Island's north shore among the rocks and breakwaters are equally as tasty as their larger relatives and make delicious crab cakes. It takes a good many crabs to feed several people, so save this dish for a special small luncheon.

(continued)

4 portions

3–4 cups cooked crabmeat
1 egg, lightly beaten
½ teaspoon salt
About 1 cup dried bread
   crumbs
4–6 tablespoons fat (butter
   or bacon grease is
   especially good)

Black pepper
Small lemon wedges
Parsley or watercress

Prepare crabmeat according to recipe for Basic Steamed Crabs (see page 78). Beat egg lightly, add crabmeat and salt, mix and mash well. Dampen hands and shape mixture into small balls. Roll in crumbs, then refrigerate several hours. Heat fat in a large, heavy skillet. Fry crab cakes, slightly flattened, until golden brown, turning to brown all over. Dust with black pepper and serve at once with lemon wedges and parsley or watercress garnish.

Moors
and Meadows

Chapter 4

In its interiors were valleys with winding streams . . . secret swamps well-hidden from the sea, great thickets. . . . One could find . . . the aromatic bayberry, and the beach plum with its gnarled and windbeaten attitudes. . . . In season the air was perfumed to ecstasy by the wild grape, and Islanders went into the swamps and glades to return with [high-heaped] baskets. . . . On the Great Plain the sweetfern grew, wildflowers in profusion, and, especially after a spring fire, blueberries and huckleberries of large size and succulence.

—FROM *Martha's Vineyard, Summer Resort*, BY HENRY BEETLE HOUGH

The Vineyard, befitting its name, abounds in foodstuffs which any resourceful cook can collect from its roadsides, meadows, woods, and waters. Some of the "edible" things usually listed in books on the subject might be used for survival but really aren't very good, especially when one considers the bother of finding and preparing them. Delicate new fern fronds, for example, treated according to several recipes, invariably turned out fuzzy and acrid, disturbingly suggestive of steamed, buttered caterpillars. Wild greens, unless chosen with care and picked while young, cook up into a stringy, harsh-flavored mess. Milkweed shoots toughen when only a few inches high and can cause nausea when overindulged in or undercooked; and most wild fruits are better left to the wasps, worms, and birds who seem to get at them first in any case.

But a fortuitous encounter with a patch of deep-green upland cress thriving in an abandoned farm garden or the discovery of a mass of tangy, red-brown fox grapes in a thicket off Indian Hill Road should tempt any culinary-minded Vineyarder to transport his find back to the kitchen for the unique enjoyment that can come from eating food from the wild. Leaves, berries, seeds, flowers, roots, stalks, can be brought to the table—some left just as they're picked, others transformed almost beyond recognition, but all retaining to the last taste an ineffable hint of their wild origin.

BEACH PLUMS

The beach plum (*Prunus maritima*) grows rampantly on dunes and coastal plains from Virginia to Nova Scotia, but beach-plum-jelly makers tend to regard their favorite picking places as regional treasure spots, revealed only to close friends or relatives. One young Vineyard housewife who covets her special thicket was quite unhappy when visiting New Yorkers brought her a jar of jelly made out of plums from *their* favorite bushes near their Long Island summer place. All beach-plum jelly should come from the Vineyard, she felt (though she'd heard it was also produced on that unmentionable mainland place, Cape Cod).

Beach Plum

Prunus is a large and important genus of the rose family, which includes all the plums, cherries, and apricots, though oddly enough the peach is usually put in another category. The beach plum is a native American shrub that grows any way from nearly prostrate to a height of 6 feet or so. When picking the fruit, one should investigate the tiny, sprawling varieties, as fruit production is often disproportionate to plant growth, and the biggest, plumpest plums often hide under the scrawniest bushes. In winter, beach-plum bushes are distinctively black-barked and twiggy; in spring clusters of dainty white flowers appear in such profusion that some Vineyard thickets in low-lying sections of the Island look almost as though a small cloud were resting on them. Around Labor Day, the picking begins, so late-staying summer people can usually carry some jelly home with them.

If you plan to start your own beach-plum patch on your Vineyard property, you would be wiser to purchase stock from a nursery than to laboriously transplant wild bushes. There are reasons for this. Beach plums, like many wild-food sources, often thrive in the midst of equally thrifty poison ivy. Wild beach plums love poor, sandy soil, and usually die when moved to more cultivated land. Their roots are deep-growing and brittle, making them hard to dig up. And, furthermore, if you do manage to stagger through the poison ivy and soft sand the several hundred yards back to your car with your by-now bare-rooted and probably broken-rooted prize, get it comfortably established in your own meadow, inspect it anxiously the next spring for signs of life, see it finally put forth a few green leaves and perhaps a feeble cluster or two of blossoms—if your transplanted beach plum survives that long, chances are it will turn out to have plum bladders and leaf spots on its leaves and brown rot on its fruit and be utterly unsatisfactory for either culinary or decorative purposes. Leave beach plums where you can admire them on your way to the beach or the airport (there are masses in that vicinity, but not many are fruit-producing) and purchase a half-dozen young plants. Take heart that one cultivated variety is called Squibnocket. Surely it must have Vineyard sap in it.

BEACH-PLUM JUICE

A tart, tangy breakfast or hot-afternoon drink—a far cry from the bland concoctions arrayed on city supermarket shelves—can be made very simply out of beach plums, sugar, and water. Don't drink it too strong, or too abundantly, as it seems to affect some people's digestive systems adversely.

Pick over a gallon or so of ripe beach plums, discarding any that are bronze-colored, pulpy, or blistered by blight. Don't be too particular—it is almost impossible not to miss a few bad ones. Wash fruit in cold water; remove and throw out any plums that float. Place fruit in large kettle, mash well with potato masher, add enough water barely to show through fruit, bring to a boil, and cook over moderate heat for 10 minutes. Let fruit cool in pan until it can be worked with. Place in cheesecloth bag over a large pan or bowl and squeeze juice through bag until pulp begins to show through cheesecloth. Discard pulp and wash bag thoroughly for future use. Taste juice and add sugar to taste (about ¾ cup per quart of fruit). Let juice cool and store in refrigerator.

This concentrated juice may be canned by the regular steam-bath processing method (see government bulletin, or any canning guide, under fruit juices). Dilute half and half with cold water before drinking.

BEACH-PLUM JELLY

Prepare fruit as in preceding recipe, with two exceptions. If jelly is to be made at once, simply follow the directions enclosed with whatever pectin product you choose for making the jelly. And do not squeeze the juice out of the bag by hand if you want your jelly crystal-clear, but let it drip through (you will get more juice, by far, if you do squeeze the bag). If you are too busy to make the jelly at beach-plum time, can the juice in the approved manner, adding 1 cup sugar per quart and noting this fact on the jar label. When you want to convert juice into jelly, simply open the jar, add the additional sugar, and proceed according to the pectin maker's instructions.

Note: Vineyard housewives who market their jelly usually bottle the plum juice during beach-plum season and convert it into jelly in the spring to sell to summer visitors, claiming it tastes fresher than jelly made during the winter months.

BEACH-PLUM BUTTER

The strong wild-plum flavor of the beach plum in the form of a thick fruit butter is delectable on toast, poured hot over vanilla ice cream, or used in a cottage-pudding recipe. A spoonful or two is delicious with almost any roast meat.

Prepare and cook the fruit as in the recipe for Beach Plum Juice (see page 86), but instead of putting the cooked pulp into a cheesecloth bag, put it a cup at a time through a food mill. The pits make this a bit difficult (and noisy), but if you remove as many as possible as you go along, most of the pulp can be mashed through. Pour a little cold water into the food mill now and then to create additional juice and help wash the pulp through.

Put puréed fruit into a kettle, bring to a boil, and cook slowly until mixture is thick enough to spread like jam. (Let your sample cool a bit before testing it.) Use a large kettle to avoid splattering your stove, and stir often enough to keep the butter from burning on the bottom as it thickens. It may take the mixture several hours to reach the desired consistency. Taste for sweetness and add sugar if desired, while butter is still hot.

This fruit butter can be canned like applesauce, or it may be put up like jelly and sealed with paraffin if it is to be used within a few months.

BEACH-PLUM CHIFFON PIE

6 portions

2 quarts beach plums	2 envelopes unflavored
¼ cup water	gelatin
4 eggs, separated	½ cup water
1 cup sugar	1 baked 9- or 10-inch pastry
½ teaspoon salt	shell

Pick over beach plums, discarding any that are too green or are spoiled (check brownish ones especially carefully). Wash in large amount of water and discard any fruit that floats. Drain plums, place in appropriate-sized kettle, add ¼ cup water and boil 10 minutes. Press pulp through a food mill (the seeds make this a bit difficult, but it can be done, with care). This should produce 1½ to 2 cups pulp.

Beat egg yolks until pale yellow, add ¾ cup of the sugar, the salt, and the plum pulp. Mix well. Pour mixture into top part of double boiler and heat gently over direct heat (do not allow to boil) while bringing approximately 2 cups water to boil in bottom of double boiler. Stir mixture as it heats. When it begins to simmer, place double boiler top over bottom half and continue to cook mixture in the boiling water, stirring constantly, until it thickens somewhat (it will not get as thick as custard). Remove from heat. Soften gelatin in ½ cup water; stir into plum-and-egg mixture and mix well, then pour filling into a large bowl and cool about half an hour, or until mixture holds its shape when stirred. Beat egg whites until they form stiff peaks, then beat in remaining ¼ cup sugar until firm and glossy. Carefully fold whites into fruit mixture. Spoon chiffon mixture into baked pie crust and chill in refrigerator until firm.

Rosa Rugosa

ROSE HIPS

Vineyard roses are not felt by Nantucketers to be nearly as spectacular as those that swarm in colorful profusion over that island's cottages. This is only a minor reflection of the long-standing rivalry between the two neighboring but not particularly neighborly islands. Actually, Vineyard roses can also be awe-inspiring, especially in Edgartown, where carefully tended tea roses and climbers grace borders and white fences and the sides of the neat houses. Along the roads, the old-fashioned single-petaled ramblers sprawl over the stone fences and scent the June air. Up-Island, especially across the Gay Head dunes, the *Rosa rugosa,* of Japanese heritage, thrives on what seems to be pure sand, huge deep-green clumps that in early summer are dotted with pink or white blooms and later will bear hundreds of succulent Chinese-red rose hips, or rose apples.

Actually, only the plumpest and ripest of these fruits could be termed succulent when picked from the bush, but the hips are surprisingly tasty if picked—and eaten—with discrimination. Bite off the pulpy outside, avoiding the seeds; and as you chew remember this is one of the richest known sources of vitamin C.

If you can avoid the insidious poison-ivy stalks that always seem to infiltrate whatever anybody wants to pick, and don't mind pricks and scratches, take home a few quarts of the biggest, ripest rose hips you can find (they should be the size of large cherries) and turn them into jam for breakfast on a cold winter morning in the city—a sweet reminder of the Vineyard summer.

ROSE-HIP PASTE

Derived from a recipe for guava paste, this recipe offers another vitamin-rich delicacy from the fruits of the Island's *Rosa rugosa* bushes. The finished paste is not as compact and chewy as that made from guavas, but has a consistency somewhere between that and a thick jam, perfect, for instance, to serve with cream cheese and crackers at tea or for dessert. Consistency and volume produced may vary somewhat—depending partly on the size and succulence of the rose hips used.

Makes about 1½ cups

3 cups rose hips, sorted and washed

2 teaspoons lemon juice

½ teaspoon grated lemon peel

Sugar as needed

Use only ripe, bright-red fruits. Chill hips slightly, then cut in half and scoop out seeds. Remove furry lining of hips and discard. Set fruit aside. Simmer seeds in water to cover for about 10 minutes. Strain off cooking liquid and save. While seeds cook, measure rose hips into saucepan, add equal amount of water, bring to a boil, lower heat, and simmer about 15 minutes. Do not boil hard or too much water will evaporate. Let fruit cool slightly. Strain liquid off cooked rose hips and reserve this too. Put hips through fine blade of a food grinder or through a food mill. Pour a little of the reserved cooking liquids on them if they seem too dry to grind easily. Add ground or puréed pulp to cooking liquids, add lemon juice and grated peel, measure mixture, and add an equal amount of sugar. Mix well and pour into a 2-quart kettle with heavy bottom (so pulp will not stick to pan). Bring to a simmer over low heat and cook, stirring frequently with a wooden spoon, until mixture is thick and a little placed on an ice cube may be lifted off in one piece. Remove paste from fire. Cool slightly, then beat with wooden spoon for about 10 minutes, or until mixture becomes a heavy paste. Pour into a loaf pan lined with waxed paper and set in cool place or in the refrigerator for 24 hours. Turn out of pan, remove waxed paper and wrap securely in foil to store. Slice as needed.

ROSE-HIP SOUP

People of other countries—especially the Scandinavians—make delectable fruit soups from cherries, peaches, plums, apricots, and all kinds of berries, using the fruits separately or in combination. This is a similar soup, using a wild fruit that is available in season to anyone on Martha's Vineyard who seeks it out. Dressed up with sour cream and a bit of nutmeg, this rose-hip soup is elegant enough to grace any formal dinner menu.

4 portions

3 cups rose hips	2 teaspoons lemon juice
6 cups water	½ teaspoon grated lemon rind
½ cup sugar	½ teaspoon powdered ginger
1 tablespoon cornstarch	4 tablespoons sour cream
1 tablespoon water	More ginger

Pick over rose hips, using only fully ripe but not overripe fruit for measuring. Rinse well, remove stem and bud ends. In a 2-quart saucepan, combine rose hips and water, bring to a boil, and cook over moderate heat for 25 minutes (do not boil too fast or too much water will evaporate). Let fruit cool slightly, then put through a food mill. Measure pulp; if necessary, add enough water to make 3 cups puréed fruit. Put pulp in a smaller saucepan, add sugar, stir well, and bring to a low boil. Mix the cornstarch and 1 tablespoon water thoroughly and stir slowly into fruit mixture. Continue to stir slowly until mixture comes to a low boil again. Cook, still at reduced heat, about 2 minutes, until soup thickens evenly. Turn off heat; stir in lemon juice and rind. Stir in ginger. Let soup cool, then refrigerate until well chilled. To serve, top each portion with a tablespoon of sour cream and add a dash of ginger.

GRAMBS' ROSE-HIP MARMALADE

There are various ways of making rose-hip jam. The standard one involves putting the stewed, deseeded pulp through a food mill or sieve, adding the usual proportions of sugar (1 cup sugar to 1 cup pulp), and boiling the mixture until it is thick enough to use as a spread. Sometimes the jam is made with pineapple. This recipe requires both orange and lemon rind, and suggests adding ginger, which we recommend. If you have never tasted rose hips, try stewing a few in sweetened water before going to the trouble of cutting the seeds out of the rest of the fruit. Most people like the flavor, vaguely reminiscent of quince.

Makes about 3 cups

2 cups prepared rose hips
    (about 1 quart
    unprepared)
1 cup water
Rind of 1 orange, cut into
    julienne strips
Rind of 1 lemon, cut into
    julienne strips

1½ cups sugar
2 tablespoons minced
    preserved or crystallized
    ginger; or same amount of
    cut-up fresh ginger root, if
    available (optional)

Select large, bright-red fruits; chill slightly before using. Cut fruit in half and scoop out seeds with a spoon. Place the seeds in a small saucepan. Add the water. Use just enough to cover the seeds. Cover and cook at a simmer over low heat for about 10 minutes. Put the prepared rose hips, orange and lemon strips, and sugar into a heavy saucepan; strain off the liquid from the seeds and add to the fruit mixture. Stir to combine. Cook mixture slowly over moderate heat until it boils. Add the minced or cut-up ginger, if using. Reduce heat immediately and cook over low heat until fruit is transparent and mixture is thick enough to spread. It will thicken a bit more when cooled. Pour into sterilized jars and seal with paraffin.

THE ELDER—TREE, BERRY, AND FLOWER

The elder, a small tree conspicuous on the Vineyard only when its umbels of off-white flowers appear in June—and to a lesser degree in August when the red-purple berries ripen—has a long, impressive history of service. "Cooked berries, preserves, pies, beverage, soup, breadstuff, pickles, asparagus-substitute, tea" is the list given in one book; another, in quite a different vein, recommends elder canes for "peashooters, blowguns, water pistols, popguns, whistles and flutes." Elder grows almost everywhere, perhaps because it was long thought to be a protection against witches and thus was never cut down. A tisane (medicinal tea) from the dried flowers is said to be delightfully reminiscent of muscatel and is suggested in an English herbal as a "pleasant alternative to aspirin, particularly when mixed with equal parts of lime flowers and chamomile." Dried mint is also good in elder tea. Elderberry juice, rich in vitamin C, is recommended in the same book for chills, neuralgia, and sciatica; and elderberry wine, of course, is an old-time favorite.

Some find the flavor of the elder disagreeable—the berries in particular are bland and slightly rank, but they become very tasty when dried. Since elder is so useful, nutritious, and abundant, it should be tasted in some form or other during your summer stay. There is a lovely display of elder near the West Tisbury millpond, but you'd better leave these for the tourists to enjoy (especially since the town office is only a hundred yards or so down the road) and check some of the swampy areas along Middle Road. A hazard here, however, is one of the few exposed stands of poison sumac on the Island, so be careful.

DRIED ELDERBERRIES

These berries adapt well to drying, taste much better in this form than when fresh, and can be used dried throughout the winter in a variety of ways. Collect the berries when they are fully ripe and remove them from their stems, taking care not to bruise them too much. If feasible, dry your berries in the sun; otherwise, the oven may be used. Outdoors, spread them on an elevated screen in full sun. Be sure to move them indoors before evening moisture begins to collect on them. Repeat this sunning until berries no longer produce a watery juice when squeezed. For oven drying, place berries on shallow racks and place them in the oven. If small pieces of screening are available, they are better, as they allow heat to circulate evenly around the berries. Turn oven to lowest setting, prop oven door slightly open and let berries dry until the same stage is reached as in sunning. This will take some 12 hours or so. They can be stored in clean fruit jars until used (give them a little air now and then to prevent spoilage).

To stew the dried berries cook them in water until tender with a little lemon juice and peel, and sugar to taste. For pie, stew them in a little water until tender, and use the cooked berries in any blueberry-pie recipe. They are also good in Elderberry Chutney (see page 95).

ELDER-FLOWER FRITTERS

A recipe published in London in 1776 says the flowers should be "marinated as the Apples on Pedestals" but gives no hint as to what marinade was used or what Apples on Pedestals were. This more contemporary version makes an unusual, if somewhat esoteric, Sunday breakfast.

Pick the flower heads at the height of their bloom, and use them as soon as possible.

4 portions

16–20 elder-flower heads
1 cup sifted all-purpose flour
2 tablespoons sugar
½ teaspoon salt
1½ teaspoons baking powder
1 egg, well beaten
¾ cup milk
1 teaspoon salad oil

1 teaspoon chopped marigold
   petals (if available)
Nutmeg (optional)
Cinnamon (optional)
Fat or oil for frying
½ cup orange juice
Sugar

Do not wash flower heads. Trim stems to about 1 inch. To make the batter, resift the flour with the sugar, salt, and baking powder. Combine the well-beaten egg in a bowl with the milk; gradually add the sifted dry ingredients. Add the teaspoonful of salad oil; mix well. Stir in the marigold petals, if used. A few shakes of nutmeg or cinnamon may be added.

Heat fat to frying temperature; fritters may be deep-fried in about 3 cups oil or fat, or in a skillet with just enough oil or fat to cover flowers.

Dip flower heads in batter, shake gently to remove excess, and cook about 4 minutes, until light brown. Drain on paper towels, sprinkle with orange juice and a little sugar. Serve at once.

Note: An eighteenth-century Boston housewife made dessert fritters by soaking the flower heads for an hour in brandy before cooking, and adding ½ teaspoon grated lemon peel to her batter.

ELDERBERRY CHUTNEY

Makes about 1 quart

1½ quarts elderberries
¾ cup brown sugar
½ cup white sugar
1 teaspoon ginger
½ teaspoon mixed pickling
   spices

¼ teaspoon cayenne pepper
1 teaspoon salt
1 pint cider vinegar
1 cup chopped crisp apple,
   peeled and cored

(continued)

Put all ingredients except the chopped apple into a saucepan, mash elderberries slightly, mix well, bring to a boil, and cook slowly for 1 hour. Then add the chopped apple, stir in, and cook mixture until it is soft and thick, stirring occasionally. This chutney is especially good with roast fowl. It may be canned according to any regular processing method or stored in clean jars or plastic containers and kept in the refrigerator until used.

Note: Dried elderberries (see page 94) may be used instead of fresh ones, in which case use 1 quart berries and soak them in cold water to cover an hour or so before cooking them.

ELDERBERRY ROB

"Rob," according to Webster, derives from the Arabic word *rubb,* by way of France, and is the "thickened juice of ripe fruits." The mild flavor of the elderberry benefits especially from this melding with pungent spices. When made from undiluted fruit, as our source recipes specify, the rob is more a syrup than a beverage. We give a diluted recipe here because without water the sugar and juice mixture tends to stick and requires careful simmering and frequent stirring. If you want to try it both ways, omit the water specified and use the thick sauce as a topping for cottage pudding or vanilla ice cream. Then add equal parts apple juice or water to the rob if you want to drink some iced on a hot afternoon or warmed and served on a rug by the fire on a snowy night.

Makes about 1 quart (diluted form)

1 quart well-ripened elderberries, removed from stems	1-inch piece stick cinnamon
	12 cloves
	1 scant teaspoon nutmeg
About 1 pint water	(freshly grated is best)
1 scant cup sugar	

Pour about half the elderberries into a good-sized saucepan and crush them with a potato masher. Add more berries and repeat process until all berries are crushed. Bring berries to a low boil, lower heat, and simmer 10 minutes, stirring once or twice to make sure berries cook evenly. Set colander or strainer over a large bowl. Lay a double-folded piece of cheesecloth in the colander and pour berries into it. Let cool until you can work with them, then tighten cheesecloth around berries and strain and press to extract juice until pulp begins to show through cloth. If clearer rob is desired, allow sediment to settle several hours before pouring off juice. Measure juice back into original saucepan and add enough water to give you about 1 quart liquid. Add sugar and spices, place over medium heat, and stir until sugar dissolves. Reduce to a simmer and cook slowly ½ hour. Let juice cool, then strain off into clean jar or pitcher. Store in refrigerator until needed. Serve hot or cold.

Note: Other robs are equally good—try making one with blackberries or grapes.

WINDFALL APPLESAUCE

At the side of many up-Island roads, or sometimes back in the brush or along the dirt lanes used by the earliest colonists, grow half-dead, twig-covered apple trees whose knobby, insect-scarred fruit can be combined with the more shapely but far less tasty products of commercial orchards to make a flavorsome sauce that will delight any apple lover.

Simply gather the best of the windfalls from the ground, adding any usable fruit you can reach or shake down. Take the apples home, wash them, and remove the worst of the blemishes, but do not peel or core. If you overlook a few worms you'll never know the difference. Prepare the store-bought fruit in the same manner. Cut smaller apples in half, larger into quarters. Using half wild and half regular apples, put cut fruit into a saucepan and add cold water until it shows around the fruit. Make whatever quantity you wish—you will get about 2 quarts applesauce from 3 quarts prepared fruit. Cook fruit at a medium boil, stirring and turning now and then, until all pieces are fairly mushy. This will take about 20 minutes. Let mixture cool. (For a richer sauce,

(continued)

add 1 tablespoon butter per quart while fruit is still warm.) Put mixture through a food mill, a cup or so at a time. Season to taste with sugar, a dash of salt, and any desired spice. Nutmeg or ginger makes an enjoyable change from the more conventional cinnamon. A little grated lemon peel may also be added. Serve sauce at room temperature to appreciate the full flavor.

FRIED WILD APPLES*

Since one author of this book is by heritage a Southerner, some of the recipes, like this one, depart from traditional New England styles and tastes, principally in the use of bacon and bacon fat for frying or seasoning. This dish does need the Southern touch, and is delicious for an early-fall lunch or for your teenagers' breakfast, especially if served with hot, freshly baked cornbread.

4 portions

3 quarts wild apples or 1½ quarts regular apples (these never taste as good)
3 slices bacon
½ teaspoon salt

¼ to ½ cup brown sugar (or to taste)
Cinnamon, cloves, or nutmeg (optional)

Wash apples, cut into halves or quarters, remove cores and the worst of the wormholes and bruises, but do not peel. Some may have to be thrown away entirely—thus 3 quarts are specified to start with. In a large frying pan fry bacon until crisp, remove from pan, and add apples to the hot fat. Lower heat, sprinkle apples with salt and brown sugar and fry until tender—about 15 minutes. Spices may be added if you like them. Turn the fruit frequently so it will cook evenly. Add a small amount of water or apple juice if the pan seems too dry. When apples are done, crumble bacon over the top of them and mix well. Serve while hot.

* By "wild" apples we mean fruit from an abandoned orchard or from one of the many roadside seedling trees on the Vineyard (also referred to as "windfall" apples).

WILD-APPLE BUTTER

Makes about 1½ quarts

1 gallon cut-up apples
1 quart apple cider or juice
Sugar as needed
1 tablespoon cinnamon

1 tablespoon ginger
1 tablespoon nutmeg
1 teaspoon cloves

Prepare apples as for Windfall Applesauce (see page 97), but work with a large quantity—at least one gallon of prepared apples—as mixture will cook down considerably. Cook apple pieces in a large kettle, uncovered, until tender, using apple cider or juice instead of water (the frozen brands are convenient and good). Stir and lift food to speed cooking. Let pulp cool until it can be put through a food mill. Return pressed pulp to pan, and add one cup sugar per quart of pulp. Stir in spices and cook mixture over low heat for several hours, until butter is thick and dark. Stir now and then so butter will not burn, or place an asbestos mat or other heat diffuser under the kettle.

This butter is also surprisingly good with no added sugar—the natural sugars become more concentrated as the mixture cooks down. Much depends, of course, upon how sweet your wildling apples are to begin with. The butter may be canned according to standard directions for canning applesauce.

OLD-ORCHARD PEAR BUTTER

If you are lucky enough to know the location of one of the Vineyard's old homesites, way back off the main roads, you probably know where there's an old pear tree—winter, Seckel, or even Bartlett—whose branches droop heavy with pears every September, years and years after the householders have died or moved away. Pears don't store as well as apples, but they can easily be converted into a wonderful sort of butter that can double as a dessert sauce. Plan to can some of this butter—it really takes very little time, and the jars will be waiting for summer break-

(continued)

fasts when you come back to the Island the next summer.

Gather as many pears as you think you will use, take them home, wash them, and cut them up, removing the cores. Don't bother to peel them; and don't worry about the size or shape of the pieces, as they will be reduced to pulp in no time. Add enough water* to the cut pears to enable them to boil, and cook them, stirring and lifting the fruit to facilitate the cooking process, until they are soft and mash easily. Remove from heat and allow to cool in pan until you can work with them. Put pulp through a food mill, removing the cores and seeds from the mill if it becomes clogged. Replace pulp in kettle (use a large one as the mixture will splatter as it thickens) and cook slowly until desired thickness is reached. Stir well now and then to prevent sticking. You don't really need sugar if the pears are sweet enough to eat raw; otherwise, add sugar to taste. Stir in about ½ teaspoon each nutmeg and ginger per quart of butter; or season with whatever spices you like. The butter does need something to spruce up the bland pear flavor, but don't overspice.

If mixture is to be canned, follow processing instructions for applesauce as given in any canning guide.

SPICED WILD-GRAPE JELLY

Plain wild-grape jelly may be prepared by following any recipe for regular grape jelly, but here are the directions for a tart, spicy garniture for roast meat or poultry, from a 1963 collection of Vineyard recipes published by the local hospital auxiliary.

Makes about 12 jelly glasses

4 quarts wild grapes, removed from stems	¼ stick of cinnamon, broken up
1 pint vinegar	3 pounds sugar
¼ cup whole cloves	(approximately)

---

* Cider or apple juice may be used instead of water.

Do not wash grapes. Place in a large kettle, crush with a potato masher, add vinegar and spices, mix, and crush again. Cook mixture 15 minutes. Pour off juice, pressing out as much as you can from the grapes. Then, either (a) let juice drip through a regular jelly bag; or (b) let juice settle in bowl overnight, then dip out or pour off carefully, leaving sediment in bottom. Measure juice and add sugar cup for cup. Heat to boiling, stirring sugar to help dissolve it. Cook fairly rapidly until jelly thermometer registers 220° F. Cool slightly, skim, and pour into clean hot containers. Seal at once.

BLACKBERRIES WITH OR WITHOUT CREAM

If you disdain blackberries as being "too sour," "too full of seeds," or for any other reason, sensory or otherwise, you are missing out on one of the finest fruit flavors there is. It is a humble berry and is best served in a humble way. Seek out the brambles that grow in damp places; and remember that the best berries ripen in the shade of the leaves and canes. Those along dry sunny roadsides are apt to be tiny and tasteless. Beware the ubiquitous poison ivy—it masquerades as a bramble. Long sleeves and long pants and a pair of tongs for pulling the out-of-reach canes closer are all recommended. A good way to find all wild fruits is to watch for the blossoms when you're traveling round the Island in June, then check for fruit late in the summer. Blackberries abound on Chappaquiddick, if you can find them; and

(continued)

there are fairly good patches along Moshup's Trail which are easily accessible.

Pick your blackberries either early or late in the day. Use two containers—one for the plumpest and ripest, the other for all the rest. Use these less perfect specimens for pie, pudding, juice, jam, or jelly. Treat the prize berries carefully. Don't bruise them, wash them, refrigerate them, or drop them in the sand. Keep them fairly cool and out of the sun until you are ready to eat them, then roll them into a bowl and serve them just as they are. Some people insist a sprinkle of sugar improves their flavor; and most enjoy them more with cream than without. The cream melds with the tart berry juice to produce a different taste—undeniably delicious, but the purist will still prefer his blackberries unadorned.

Common Barberry

BARBERRY JELLY

These fiery-red berries, dangling in prickly splendor along so many Vineyard driveways and house fronts from fall into winter, seem an uninteresting food source, but we found so many references to barberry jelly in old cookery books that we donned gloves, managed to collect a quart of berries, and were rewarded with some of the tastiest and most colorful jelly we've ever had. Tart, suggestive of both plum and currant, barberry jelly fulfills the usual breakfast requirements, but is also wonderful spooned onto vanilla ice cream, pancakes, or cornbread, or served as a side dish, like cranberry sauce, with a roast meat or fowl. In gathering the berries, wear cotton gloves and strip the heaviest-laden sprigs toward you, holding a pan underneath to catch the berries. You can't avoid a few imbedded barbs, but the hazards are minimal compared to the treats in store once the filled jelly jars are safely on the shelf.

Gather the barberries before they freeze; otherwise they lose their flavor. Pick out the most obvious twigs and any berries that are obviously spoiled. Rinse under cold water. Place in a saucepan and add 1 cup cold water to each quart of berries. Bring to a boil and cook slowly about 5 minutes, stirring to mix berries well. Line a colander with a double thickness of cheesecloth, place over a large kettle, and pour cooked berries into cheesecloth. Allow to drain thoroughly. If more jelly is desired, fold cheesecloth around berries and squeeze out remaining juice. The finished product will not be so clear but the flavor will be improved. Boil this plain juice five minutes, then measure, and add 1 cup sugar for each cup of juice. Bring to a boil again and cook until jelly is 8° F. above the boiling point of water (on jelly thermometer), or until mixture sheets from a metal spoon. Turn into hot clean glasses and cover with paraffin while hot, if to be stored for later use.

Day Lily

DAY-LILY BUDS

In mid-July, great, grasslike clumps of green along the Vineyard's roads burst almost overnight into spectacular bloom. These are the blossoms of the orange day lily (*Hemerocallis fulva*), one of our loveliest wildflowers, escaped long ago from cultivated gar-

(*continued*)

dens and now naturalized throughout our countryside. Though day lilies are almost as familiar to summer vacationers as daisies or goldenrod, few of them know that the buds of these slender plants are good to eat. Euell Gibbons, in his fascinating book on using wild plants for food, *Stalking the Wild Asparagus,** details the importance of lily buds—both fresh and dried—in the cuisine of the Far East. We tried steaming the fresh buds, and agree that they are delicious—in flavor and texture somewhere between green beans and okra. Pick with discrimination, if you want to try them, leaving a succession of new buds for you and other summer people to enjoy in flower.

2 portions
Vegetable steamer	½ teaspoon salt
24 day-lily buds	Freshly ground black pepper
2 tablespoons butter	

Pick buds that are somewhat swollen and tinted with orange. Place them in a steamer over 1 inch of boiling water, cover, and steam 5 minutes. Remove carefully with tongs into a small, warmed bowl, add butter, salt, and pepper, mix gently and serve at once.

SORREL SOUP

This common weed is infuriatingly familiar to gardeners, as its roots creep underground like vine roots, and when one plant is pulled up five others seem to crop up overnight. Furthermore, it presumably thrives in poor, overly acid soil and thus reflects adversely upon the condition of one's garden! The sorrel family, genus Rumex, has, however, long enjoyed culinary status in Europe, particularly in France, where *crème d'oseille* is a cherished soup in the cuisine of many households and restaurants. We write at this length because our weedy sorrel (*Rumex acetosa*) is quite different from the more highly cultivated, broad-leaved French variety that is described in an English cookbook as "a slender

* David McKay Company, Inc., New York, 1962.

perennial plant about 2 feet high with spikes of reddish green flowers." This need not dismay you in your search, however, as in a particularly delinquent garden area American sorrel (which also produces spikes of reddish-green flowers) produces succulent leaves 3 to 4 inches long, and enough for a quart of soup can be yanked up in a few minutes.* (We suggest using scissors or a knife instead, or cutting the roots off the plant at the source, to avoid having to wash them.) Consult a wildflower guide or other authority if you aren't familiar with the leaves. The plant likes moist, loose soil (it grows in almost everything, including sandy gravel paths and undernourished lawns, but in such locations the leaves are useless as food), and can be gathered from early spring to the first hard freeze of winter. The greens can be cooked up like a rather stringy spinach (it is sometimes described as a "sour spinach"), or a few can be chopped into salad, but we think the soup pot is far the best place to transform this ubiquitous pest into a *potage extraordinaire*.

Sorrel was used by Greek and Roman doctors as a diuretic, is considered good for the blood and an appetite stimulant, and has been recommended in times past as a cure for kidney stones. We don't vouch for any of this, but we do know there is nothing better for lunch on a hot summer day than a bowl or two of chilled sorrel soup, served out in the shade, with perhaps a good Camembert, some crackers, a fruit salad, and a cold bottle of Chablis.

4 to 6 portions

2 cups sorrel leaves, firmly packed
3 tablespoons butter
1 medium onion, chopped fine (or ¾ cup finely chopped green onions)
1 tablespoon flour
3 cups chicken stock (canned stock may be used)

½ teaspoon salt
Freshly ground black pepper
2 egg yolks
1 cup medium cream
2 tablespoons chopped parsley (or 2 tablespoons chopped chives)

(continued)

---

* Seeds for the French sorrel (*oseille*) can be purchased from several seed specialists or obtained from France, if you want to try growing the more civilized variety.

Prepare the leaves by trimming off the stringy parts. Rinse them and drain thoroughly on paper towels. Chop fine, or use scissors to cut the leaves. Melt the butter in a heavy 2-quart saucepan, add the onion and cook over low heat until golden and transparent. Stir in the flour thoroughly. Stir in the chopped sorrel and cook until the leaves are wilted. Add the chicken stock and salt and pepper and cook until mixture comes to a simmer. Cook an additional 5 minutes. Beat the egg yolks; gradually beat in the cream. Then slowly beat in 2 cups of the hot soup. Return this mixture to the soup pot and cook carefully over very low heat, stirring constantly, for another moment or two. Do not boil. Additional salt and pepper may be added. Serve hot or very cold. Garnish with chopped chives or parsley, or both.

Beach Pea

BEACH PEAS

This decorative relative of the garden-grown green pea forms pods after its magenta-pink blooms have faded. Beach peas are rampant across the road from the Menemsha docks, and equally common though less accessible along most of the South Shore sand dunes and banks. If you can find enough pods to gather a basket while the peas in them are still bright green and before they have hardened—and if you have the time and patience to shell them—they make a very tasty vegetable. Since they are smaller than the cultivated pea they take an inordinate amount of time to prepare, but both picking and shelling would provide a worthy afternoon project for the children on a poor beach day.

3 to 4 portions

Vegetable steamer
2½ cups shelled beach peas
½ teaspoon salt
1 teaspoon sugar
4 tablespoons butter

½ cup medium cream
Freshly ground black pepper
1 tablespoon chopped fresh
  chives (optional)

Place the steamer and about an inch of water in a saucepan, cover, and bring water to a boil. Put peas in steamer, cover pot, and steam about 10 minutes. Remove strainer and peas from pan, pour out water, replace peas and add all other ingredients except chives, if to be used. Simmer over low heat for 5 minutes, stirring once or twice. Do not boil. Serve hot with chives sprinkled on top if desired and an additional dusting of black pepper.

Note: You might like to try cooking beach peas like snow peas —leaving them in the pod for steaming. In this case, the tedium of shelling would be eliminated, but peas would have to be gathered when very young.

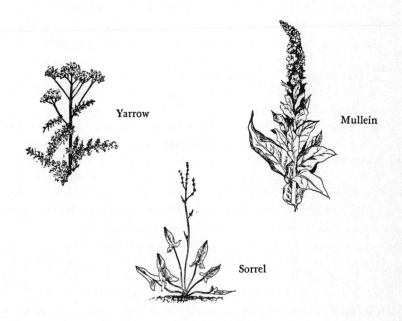

Yarrow

Mullein

Sorrel

WILD GREENS

Spring is the best time for greens, except for a few like upland cress and sorrel which are equally good in fall. By the time the summer people arrive, many of the edible wild plants are already in bloom. The second-cycle plants produced from these seeds will lack the succulence of the spring-growing ones, which thrive on the Island's cool, damp spring days. In old garden plots or near damp roadside areas, delicious greens can be gathered in the fall until frost; upland cress may even winter over from one year to the next. A free mimeographed circular called "Wild Greens or Potherbs in Massachusetts" is obtainable from the Extension Service of the University of Massachusetts in Amherst. It will tell you what to look for and where you may find it.

Dandelions, watercress, milkweed, wild mustard (which flourishes, as do many wild flowers, on burnt-over ground and is usually rampant at the Island dumps), lamb's-quarters, and sorrel are some of the most familiar greens. Dock, peppergrass, pigweed, purslane, and chicory (this plant with its lovely purple-blue flowers grows by the acre on the undeveloped land between Oak Bluffs and Vineyard Haven) are less familiar but can be identified from any wildflower guide. All are cooked in the same manner. Young leaves—or, in the case of milkweed, tender short roots—are washed, trimmed, drained slightly and cooked a little longer than spinach, with a little added water and salt to taste. They are usually better in combination, in the true, rural "potherb" style. A bit of bacon or fatback may be put in with the raw greens and the mess may be simmered a long time, Southern fashion. And, again like their cultivated counterparts, wild greens may be served with bits of brown bacon, slices of hard-boiled egg, lemon slices, a pitcher of vinegar. Or they may be added to soup. The best way to tell when they are done is simply to taste them. Cooking times vary—as do individual tastes.

Do not, under any circumstances, go about gathering whatever wild greenery may take your fancy. Some are acutely poisonous; many can cause severe stomach disorders. Pick and use only what you are sure of. Even poison ivy looks delectable at some stages of growth.

DANDELION BUD OMELET

2 portions

12 dandelion buds	4 eggs
About 3 tablespoons butter	½ teaspoon salt
Freshly ground black pepper	

Pick dandelion buds just about to open; wash them if necessary, and toss in paper towels to dry. Melt 2 tablespoons butter in small skillet or omelet pan, add dandelion buds, and cook them slowly 2 or 3 minutes, stirring carefully so they will cook on all sides. Remove pan from heat. Take out dandelion buds and reserve. Beat eggs gently only until mixed; stir in salt. Heat pan with additional butter (about 1 tablespoon) over moderate heat until butter foams. Pour eggs into pan and cook slowly, lifting around edges to allow uncooked mixture to run under omelet. When eggs are almost done, spoon dandelion buds onto one half of omelet. Fold omelet. Dust lightly with pepper and serve at once.

Irish Moss

IRISH MOSS BLANC MANGE

When you're ambling along the ocean some summer day at low tide, collect some pastel-hued fronds of Irish moss, or sea moss, as the old-timers named it. Sort it over at home and put your best specimens outdoors on a clean board or similar surface (a flat slab of Island granite is ideal) to dry in the sun. It looks pretty stored in a decorative glass canister, and will keep for years. Use bits of it to thicken stews or gravies, or to produce this delicate pudding.

(*continued*)

4 to 5 portions

¼ cup sea moss bits (it may be
presoaked 15 minutes,
then drained, before
measuring)
3 cups milk
2 tablespoons sugar (or to
taste)

½ teaspoon grated lemon or
orange peel (optional but
recommended)
¼ teaspoon salt
1 teaspoon vanilla or lemon
extract
Fruit for garnish

Combine sea moss, milk, and sugar in a saucepan; simmer
about 20 minutes, stirring occasionally. (The grated lemon or
orange peel, if used, should be added during the simmering.)
Strain mixture through a fine-meshed sieve lined with cheesecloth. Add salt and vanilla or lemon extract; mix well. Pour into
individual molds and chill thoroughly. The pudding will thicken
as it chills. Unmold and top with sweetened crushed fresh strawberries or raspberries, or with slightly sweetened oranges.

MEADOW TISANE

A fascinating lore—and an ancient one—exists that suggests herb
tea of one sort or another to cure almost anything. Horsetail is
diuretic. Lady's-mantle is "a woman's best friend." Goldenrod
is anti-inflammatory; verbena, sedative; yarrow, a digestive. Be
all this as it may—and we like to believe they all do what they're
said to do—a pleasant, country, summery sort of tea can easily
be made from almost any of the following, in whatever combination you fancy or can find to pick. (If you include wild strawberry leaves, be sure that they are well-dried before use.) Take
along a basket when you stroll through the lovely up-Island meadows, but pick only things you know. Some leaves—laurel, for
instance, and some evergreens—are poisonous enough to make
you very ill if you chew up a few. We suggest: yarrow (leaves
and flowers), red clover (leaves and flowers), elder flowers, mullein flowers, goldenrod (leaves and flowers), wild strawberry
leaves, chicory leaves, sweet fern leaves and almost any leaves
from your herb garden, especially mint, but also borage, sage,

chamomile, lemon balm, marjoram, thyme, and lemon verbena. Dry the leaves and flowers well on screens, remove stems and twigs and store the mixture in a canister. To make the tea, use fresh boiling water and allow 1 teaspoon leaf-flower mixture per cup and 1 for the pot. A few dried roses may be added for color (though the color fades when the leaves are placed in hot water!). This meadow-herb mixture is an inexpensive and nostalgia-producing memento to take back to your city apartment and enjoy during your months off-Island.

Sassafras

SASSAFRAS TEA

People ought to drink more sassafras tea. They used to. Children went out with their fathers into the springtime woods and grubbed for the aromatic roots, brought them home and scrubbed them, boiled them for about half an hour in plenty of water, and everyone gathered for the first sassafras tea of the year. This pleasant ritual has all but died out in our ridiculously urban-oriented society, but it—like many others—can easily be revived on the Vineyard, where "sassafras trees great plenty all the island over," as an early seventeenth-century account says, make most woods a source of the red-brown roots.

A relative of cinnamon, sassafras has been used medicinally for centuries, one of its presumable virtues being to make people thin. It certainly produces a prettier and more palatable spring

(*continued*)

tonic than the strangulating mixture of molasses and sulfur that some of us choked down each year. Though many feel sassafras roots are more flavorful in spring before the sap rises, they may be gathered at any time; and as the trees usually grow in prolific clumps, the saplings can be pulled up or dug out without harming older trees. You can distinguish the young trees in winter by the soapy taste of the twigs and the rich, deep green of the bark. At other times, it is one of the few trees that bears several patterns of leaves—as many as three types, including the familiar "mittens and gloves," may be found on one twig.

To make tea, use 3 or 4 short chunks of scrubbed roots per quart of cold water. Cover the pot and let the roots simmer for 20 to 30 minutes. The brew can be drunk at any strength, from a delicate rose-pink (but not *too* delicate, or you miss the essence of the flavor) to a rich orange-red. Try it different ways, including iced. Add sugar if you prefer a sweetened drink. The used roots may be dried and reused several times. Well-dried chunks may be stored in lightly closed containers almost indefinitely, though they lose much of their strength after a year or so.

Dried young sassafras leaves, by the way, have long been used for thickening food and are the traditional *filé* of Creole gumbos. Sift the powdered, dried leaves through a large-screened sieve, and use about one tablespoon of the powder to thicken a quart of hot cooked stew or soup. Keep the dried powder in tightly capped jars, like spices.

Meat,
Game, and Poultry
Chapter 5

MEAT

Rev. James Freeman, who visited the Island in 1807, reckoned that there were 15,600 sheep, 400 horses and colts, 2,800 neat cattle and 800 swine. . . . Figures for 1855 are almost identical, but by 1872, they begin to show a decline. . . . The reasons for the gradual abandonment of farming were several: tired land, erosion of salt meadows, falling wool prices, lack of demand for homemade butter and cheese, but most of all, the exodus of farm boys to sea or to jobs on the mainland.

—FROM *A Short History of Martha's Vineyard,* ELEANOR R. MAYHEW, ED., DUKES COUNTY HISTORICAL SOCIETY, EDGARTOWN, MASSACHUSETTS, 1956

Our townsman, Mr. David N. Look, has the honor of having the largest herd of cattle in the county, thirty-two head. . . .

—FROM WEST TISBURY ANNUAL REPORT, 1894

The faced stone walls that border so many Vineyard fields were not built for the purpose they so often serve today—to discourage trespassers and enhance the beauty of the high-priced land they outline. Rather, the walls—and hedges, ditches, and miles of post-and-rail fences that have almost entirely disappeared—were meant to confine the Island's livestock. As far back as the 1660's there were hogs, horses, and goats; and some of the fine sheep and cattle had bloodlines tracing back to the English animals that were driven down from Boston by the "Bay Path" and ferried across to the Vineyard on sailing ships. So numerous were these creatures that one account reports there were "seventeen gates and twenty-one pairs of bars which had to be opened and closed by the traveler" within a distance of ten miles. But little by little the pastures were cut up into building lots (as they continue to be today, to the regret of most Island residents), and now only a few dozen head of cattle and some small flocks of sheep remain. Several farmers still slaughter their own sheep and beef cattle; one has a few hogs left. So if you know the right people you may feast on a roast of salt-hay-fed lamb or a Vineyard-produced steak some winter night.

BEEFSTEAK AND OYSTERS

This old-fashioned dish—Victorian and opulent—suggests a hearty midwinter dinner before the fire after a bone-chilling expedition in the gray silence of a Great Pond on a lowering January day. The succulent delicacy of the oysters is balanced by the solid texture and taste of a good hunk of beef. With it you might serve baked potatoes, slices of sweet red onion, a cooked green vegetable, and a bottle of zinfandel or some other light red wine.

4 generous portions

Boneless steak (preferably sirloin) weighing about 3 pounds after fat is trimmed
Freshly ground black pepper
½ teaspoon salt
Approximately 1 pint fresh oysters, drained

3 tablespoons melted butter
Maître d'Hôtel Butter (see page 248)
1 teaspoon chopped fresh parsley

Preheat broiler.

Season both sides of the steak with a few grindings of black pepper and the salt. Broil on a greased rack about 3 inches from heat until brown. Turn steak. Remove from broiler about 5 minutes before cooked to your preference. Reduce oven heat to 375° F.

Place steak in a shallow, heatproof baking dish, cover it with the drained oysters, pour the melted butter over the oysters, and bake only until the oysters are plump, about 5 to 10 minutes. Serve immediately with Maître d'Hôtel Butter and the chopped parsley sprinkled over all.

YANKEE POT ROAST

6 to 8 portions

⅛ pound salt pork, cut in
½-inch dice

4–5 pounds boneless beef
chuck, round, or rump
(fresh brisket is a good
choice)

1 teaspoon salt (or to taste)

¼ teaspoon freshly ground
black pepper (or to taste)

1 cup coarsely chopped onions

2 or more cups beef stock (or
canned beef bouillon)

½ bay leaf

3 or 4 sprigs parsley, with
stems

6–8 young carrots, peeled

6–8 medium onions, peeled

6–8 small potatoes, peeled

1 yellow turnip, peeled and
cut into 1-inch squares
(optional)

1 tablespoon flour mixed to
smooth paste with 2 tablespoons water

In a heavy 5- to 6-quart iron pot or Dutch oven cook salt-pork dice over moderate heat until crisp and golden. Remove from pan, drain on a paper towel, and reserve. Dry beef thoroughly with a paper towel or clean cloth; rub some of the salt and the pepper into it. Brown the meat in the hot fat over moderate heat, turning so that all sides are evenly browned. Remove meat from pan and cook onions in the fat until golden and transparent, reducing heat sufficiently so that the onions cook slowly. Return beef to pan. (It may be necessary to pour off accumulated fat.) Add enough beef stock barely to cover beef; add bay leaf and parsley. Cover tightly, bring to a simmer over moderate heat, then cook at a gentle simmer about 3 hours or until beef is tender. It is done when a sharp-pronged fork pierces it easily.

For the last half hour or so of cooking, add the reserved salt-pork dice, carrots, onions, potatoes, and turnip (if used); sprinkle the vegetables with a little salt. When the vegetables are tender, remove them and the beef to a heated serving dish and keep warm. Remove the parsley from the pot and discard it.

Over high heat cook liquids down to concentrate flavor until about 1½ to 2 cupfuls remain. Season carefully to taste, adding

(continued)

additional salt and pepper if needed. Reduce the heat, and thicken the sauce with the flour-and-water paste, stirring it in gradually until the proper consistency is reached. The liquid should coat the spoon lightly. Simmer a few moments longer. Spoon a little of the sauce over the meat and vegetables and serve the remainder in a pitcher or bowl.

For the sake of variety, try replacing the beef stock with cider, adding a tablespoon or 2 of brown sugar or to taste. Or prepare a pot roast with cranberries, using the required amount of beef stock but replacing the vegetables with 2 cups fresh cranberries. In this case, add the cranberries for the last half hour of cooking.

Note: This meal may be placed in a preheated 275° F. oven to cook instead of being simmered on the stove top.

SPICED BEEF

An old favorite, this—reminiscent of Germany's sauerbraten. It could be that a Hessian soldier, brought here during the American Revolution, settled in New England after hostilities ended and passed along the recipe. A more prosaic suggestion is that the marinade used in the preparation of this dish acted as a preservative, a considerable boon to both the European cooks and the colonists, who managed their kitchens admirably without benefit of refrigeration.

6 to 8 portions

MARINADE

2 cups cider vinegar	2 teaspoons salt
2 medium onions, sliced thin	1 teaspoon whole black
1 teaspoon ground cinnamon	peppercorns
1 teaspoon ground cloves	½ bay leaf
½ teaspoon ground allspice	1 clove garlic

Combine marinade ingredients in a saucepan, bring to a boil, and simmer 5 minutes. Meanwhile, place beef in bowl of appropriate size, then pour the hot marinade over it. Leave beef in marinade at least 12 hours, turning occasionally. It will not require refrigeration.

4–5-pound boneless beef chuck, rump, or fresh brisket	1 stalk celery, coarsely chopped
2 cups beef stock (or canned beef bouillon)	4 carrots, peeled and cut in ½-inch dice
2 tablespoons each butter and vegetable oil (or ¼ pound salt pork, cut in ½-inch dice)	1 medium-sized yellow turnip, cut in ½-inch dice
	1 tablespoon cornstarch mixed to a smooth paste with 2 tablespoons water
2 onions, coarsely chopped	

Remove meat, reserving marinade, and place meat in a heavy flameproof casserole. Strain marinade, combine half of it with the beef stock, place in a small saucepan, and bring to a boil. Pour it over the beef. Cover casserole tightly. Bring to a simmer over moderate heat, then place casserole in a preheated 275° F. oven and cook 3 hours, or until beef is tender. Turn beef at least once during the cooking period. It is done when a sharp-pronged fork pierces the meat easily.

While the beef is cooking, heat the butter and vegetable oil in a skillet until the butter foam subsides; add the chopped onions and celery and cook over moderate heat, stirring occasionally, until lightly browned. Add to casserole. If using salt pork, cook the diced pork in the skillet until crisp and golden, remove from pan, drain on a paper towel and reserve. Use fat from pork to cook the onions and celery. About half an hour before the beef is done, add the carrots, turnip, and salt-pork bits (if used) to the casserole and cook until vegetables are tender.

Remove beef and vegetables to a heated serving dish and keep warm.

(continued)

Bring liquid in casserole to a boil over high heat, reduce heat, and simmer 5 minutes. Add the cornstarch-and-water paste, using only enough to achieve the desired thickness. The sauce should coat the spoon lightly. Adjust seasonings, if necessary. Pour a little of the sauce over the meat and serve the remainder in a pitcher or bowl.

Note: A tablespoon of brown sugar may be added to sauce just before serving and stirred in until dissolved.

BEEFSTEAK-AND-KIDNEY PIE

The whaling wives of days past needed substantial concoctions like this one to send their men off well fortified for the long months—and even years—of eating salt pork and salt beef (called "Salt Horse" by the sailors). It is indeed an old-fashioned dish, but an honorable one, and one that should be brought again into the winter cuisine of the Vineyard. What more auspicious aroma could greet young skaters and iceboaters returning from an afternoon outing on Squibnocket Pond?

The English mother of one author of this book lives in a fairy-tale "gingerbread" house overlooking Sunset Lake and its swan-dwellers, at the edge of the Oak Bluffs campground. In her tiny kitchen, she still concocts a beefsteak-and-kidney pie worthy of one of London's finest chophouses. This is how she makes it.

4 generous portions

1 beef kidney, trimmed of fat, cut in 1-inch squares
Salt
1½ pounds beef chuck, cut in 1½-inch squares
1 teaspoon salt
½ teaspoon freshly ground black pepper
2 tablespoons butter
2 tablespoons vegetable oil

1 large onion, coarsely chopped
2 cups or more beef stock (or canned beef bouillon)
3 or 4 small carrots, peeled and cut in ½-inch circles
1 tablespoon flour mixed to a smooth paste with 2 tablespoons water
Pastry crust (see below)

Soak the kidney squares for 1 hour in water to cover, adding 1 tablespoon salt per quart of water, then drain and dry them thoroughly with paper toweling. Season beef and kidney with 1 teaspoon salt and the pepper. In a heavy kettle or flameproof casserole, heat butter and oil until almost smoking, and quickly cook the beef and kidney pieces until brown on all sides. Do not overcrowd pan; if necessary do a few pieces at a time and set aside.

Cook onion, reducing heat to moderate, until golden and transparent. Add beef stock to onion in kettle; cook, stirring and scraping up coagulated juices until dissolved. Simmer a few more moments. Add beef and kidney squares. The liquid should almost cover the meat; if it doesn't, add additional beef stock. Cover tightly and cook at a gentle simmer about 1½ hours.

Add the sliced carrots and cook an additional half hour, or until the carrots are done and the beef is tender. With a slotted spoon transfer beef, kidneys, and vegetables to a casserole or baking dish of sufficient size to hold all ingredients. Over high heat bring liquid in kettle to a full boil, then add the flour-and-water paste, stirring constantly, using only enough paste to achieve the proper thickness. The sauce should coat the spoon lightly. Adjust seasonings if necessary. Pour the sauce over the beef and kidney mixture.

Preheat oven to 450° F.

Prepare pastry crust as follows:

PASTRY CRUST

2 cups sifted flour	¼ cup milk
1 teaspoon salt	1 egg lightly beaten with 1
½ cup vegetable oil	tablespoon milk

Resift the flour with the salt into a mixing bowl. Combine oil and milk without stirring and add all at once to flour. With a 4-tined fork stir lightly until well mixed. Form into a smooth ball. Roll out between two 12-inch squares of waxed paper. (The paper will not slide during the rolling-out process if the work counter is slightly dampened.) Use short, very gentle strokes until circle reaches appropriate size for baking dish; the pastry

(continued)

should be approximately ½ inch thick. Carefully peel off top paper. Position the circle carefully over the pan, paper side up, then peel off remaining paper. Crimp the edges of the pastry onto the dish to seal the casserole. Cut 3 or 4 slits in the pastry so steam can escape, brush with the egg-and-milk mixture to glaze (using about 2 tablespoons) and bake 15 minutes, or until crust is lightly browned. Reduce heat to 350° F. and bake 20 to 25 minutes more. Serve immediately.

NEW ENGLAND BOILED DINNER

Having survived more than two hundred years of culinary tradition, the celebrated New England boiled dinner is still prepared in much the same way as it has always been.

The corned beef may require presoaking; ask your butcher about this. If advised to do so, soak the meat for several hours, then discard the water.

6 to 8 portions

4–5 pounds corned beef

8 medium beets

12–16 small potatoes, peeled (new potatoes are recommended)

8 or more small white onions, peeled (if a cross is pierced in the root ends, the onions will not burst during cooking)

6–8 carrots, peeled or scraped

1 head of cabbage (about 2 pounds), cored and cut into 6 or 8 wedges

Freshly ground black pepper

1–2 tablespoons freshly chopped parsley (optional)

Horseradish (optional)

Mustard (optional)

Pickles (optional)

In a 6- to 8-quart pot cover the corned beef with sufficient cold water to rise about 2 inches above the meat. Bring to a boil, skimming off any scum that appears on the surface. Reduce heat so that the liquid barely simmers, cover the pot, and cook from 4 to 6 hours, or until tender. Add boiling water to the pot during the cooking process if the water level drops below the meat.

Scrub beets thoroughly, trim tops. Cook beets in a separate pot in boiling water to cover until tender, about ¾ hour. Slip off their skins. Keep warm.

Add the potatoes, onions, and carrots to the meat; cook about 15 minutes. Add the cabbage and cook another 15 minutes. Cover the pot again while the cabbage is cooking.

When cabbage is added, lift the meat out of the pot so it will "rest" and be easier to slice.

To serve this traditional meal, slice the beef and arrange the slices in the center of a large heated platter. Dust lightly with the pepper. The vegetables may be arranged attractively around the meat and chopped parsley may garnish all. Horseradish, an aromatic mustard, and a variety of pickles may be offered as accompaniments.

BRAISED OXTAILS

[*Oxtail Ragout*]

Until only a few years ago, it was possible for the day tourist visiting Gay Head to cross the road from his parked bus and have his picture snapped with a yoke of oxen and their Indian owner. In the more glorious days of the Vineyard's history, this visitor's grandfather might have docked in the *Monohansett,* a paddlewheel steamer that used to tie up at the Lobsterville wharf, and been driven to the top of the famed Gay Head clay cliffs in an ox cart, hanging tightly to his bowler hat as he jolted along.

Although many people tend to think of the ox as a rather bizarre creature often mentioned in the Bible, an ox is not born an ox but is an "adult castrated male bovine"; and as a mode of conveyance he has long since been superseded, though there are still two yokes on the Vineyard, handsome animals that can usually be seen at the annual Agricultural Fair. One pair of these is still used by their West Tisbury owner to work the fields. Male bovines are more profitably left to grow up as bulls these days, or killed and sold as food before they reach maturity.

Oxtail, therefore, is merely beef tail, but as it is hardly a best seller at the meat counter, food purveyors have wisely stuck to

(continued)

the old name in offering this item to the housewives who do search it out. Whatever one calls it, oxtail is one of several specialty meats that deserve to be used more often.

4 portions

3 pounds oxtails, cut into
    joints
1 teaspoon salt
¼ teaspoon freshly ground
    black pepper
Flour for dredging
2 tablespoons butter
2 tablespoons vegetable oil
1 small onion, chopped
    coarsely
2 cloves garlic, chopped fine
2 cups red wine

1 cup beef stock or canned
    beef bouillon, or more
Additional salt and pepper,
    if needed
8–12 small whole white
    onions, peeled
½ cup diced carrots
¼ cup diced celery
1 tablespoon chopped fresh
    parsley
2 tablespoons flour (optional)
3 tablespoons water (optional)

Preheat oven to 300° F.

Roll the oxtail sections in flour seasoned with the salt and pepper. In a heavy skillet, heat butter and oil over high heat until butter foam subsides. Add the oxtail pieces, reduce heat to moderate, and brown them thoroughly on all sides. Remove them from pan. Add to the pan the chopped onion and garlic and cook until lightly browned. Add the red wine and 1 cup beef stock to the pan, stirring well; allow it to come to a full rolling boil. Add additional salt and pepper at this time, if required. Reduce heat and allow liquids to simmer for 10 minutes. Transfer oxtail pieces to an ovenproof casserole; pour liquids from skillet over them. The liquid should just barely cover the meat; it may be necessary to add a little more beef stock. Cover tightly and place in the preheated oven; bake approximately 3 to 4 hours, or until meat is fork-tender. Add, for the last ½ hour of cooking, the onions, carrots, and celery. Serve with a garnish of chopped parsley.

If desired, the sauce may be thickened slightly by carefully stirring in a smooth paste of 2 tablespoons flour mixed with 3 tablespoons water, a little at a time, until the proper consistency is reached.

ROAST LEG OF VINEYARD LAMB
WITH FRUIT GLAZE

Vineyard lambs—and a few farmers still raise them—are fed for a time during their rearing on salt hay; they are taken to the salt meadows and there they graze. The flesh acquires an indefinable flavor, much like the French lamb *pré salé*. Such lamb provides a memorable meal. The following recipe is suggested as a some-what sophisticated treatment; though it is simple to prepare, the results are singular.

6 to 8 portions

1 teaspoon salt
¼ teaspoon freshly ground
    black pepper
Small leg of lamb, 5–6 pounds
    preferably
1 cup orange juice
1 cup apricot purée (combine
    syrup with pitted apricots
    from a small can and
    whisk in electric blender
    or put through a food mill)

4 tablespoons cognac
Sliced oranges (optional)
Whole canned apricots
    (optional)

Preheat oven to 300° F.

Rub salt and pepper thoroughly over surface of meat. Place meat in a roasting pan, using a rack if desired. Pour the juice, purée, and cognac over it. Roast, uncovered, about 30 minutes per pound, or, if a meat thermometer is used, until internal heat reads 175° to 180°. Baste occasionally with the pan juices while meat is roasting.

Remove pan from oven and set oven to broil position. Broil lamb sufficiently for surface to be nicely glazed, basting during the process.

If a fruit garnish is desired, add slices of orange and whole canned apricots to the pan before the broiling process, then garnish with these fruits at serving time.

ROAST LOIN OF PORK WITH BEACH-PLUM-JELLY GLAZE

4 to 6 portions

4–5-pound center cut of pork loin (a fresh ham or pork shoulder may be used instead)

Salt and freshly ground black pepper

1 cup beach-plum jelly (see page 86)

1 tablespoon flour (or 1½ teaspoons cornstarch)

1 cup stock (or water with a beef or chicken bouillon cube dissolved in it)

Preheat oven to 350° F.

Rub pork (which should be removed from refrigerator at least ½ hour before cooking) with salt and pepper. It may be necessary to trim surplus fat before seasoning the meat. Place meat, fat side up, on a rack in a roasting pan and cook it approximately 30 to 35 minutes to the pound, or until it reaches an internal heat of 185°, if using a meat thermometer.

While meat is roasting, melt the beach-plum jelly over low heat in a small pan. Remove from heat. When the roast is thoroughly cooked, skim off all but several tablespoons of the fat in the roasting pan. Carefully coat the roast with most of the beach-plum jelly and return it to the oven, basting every 10 minutes with the pan juices. The remaining jelly may be used as additional basting liquid. When the roast is nicely glazed, after 20 to 30 minutes, remove it from the roasting pan and keep it in a warm place on a heatproof platter.

Carefully blend flour or cornstarch into the pan juices and jelly remaining in the roasting pan. Gradually add stock, stirring constantly. Strain into a sauce boat and serve with the sliced roast pork.

KIDNEY "STREW"

From a summering Chilmark cook, born and reared in China, came a family recipe devised and proudly copied out by hand in his new English by their Chinese cook. As set down by Chou Lin on a now-stained and faded half sheet of rice paper, here are the instructions:

½ lb. kidneys sat pepper ¼ lb. mushroom 1 cup stook
½ ib. onion ¼ butter green pepper 1 tablespoon flour
　　Clean the kidneys frist and cut to slices, fried them in butter with flour. Put the onion, green pepper, sat, pepper, mushroom and stook in, strew them in every slowly fire about one hour.

The Chilmarker who donated the recipe has noted at the bottom: "Any sort of wine improves this. Also garlic."
　　We would amend Chou Lin's instructions as follows:

2 portions

2 tablespoons butter	1 tablespoon flour
2 small veal kidneys, trimmed of fat and filament	½ cup beef stock (or canned beef bouillon)
1 medium onion, sliced	4 tablespoons good dry red wine
¼ pound fresh mushrooms, sliced	Salt and freshly ground black pepper to taste
½ small green pepper, coarsely chopped	1 teaspoon chopped fresh parsley
1 clove garlic, chopped fine	
Butter, if needed	

In a heavy skillet over moderately high heat, melt butter. When foam subsides, brown the whole kidneys quickly on both sides, about 10 minutes. Remove them from pan and keep warm. Reduce heat; cook onion in same skillet until transparent. Add mushrooms, green pepper, and garlic; cook 5 minutes or so. Add a little butter if needed. Stir in the flour, blending it in well. Gradually stir in the beef stock and the red wine, stirring constantly. Let this mixture simmer over low heat. Meantime, rapidly

(continued)

cut kidneys into ½-inch slices. Add salt and pepper to taste to the skillet liquids, then the kidney slices. Stir carefully only long enough to reheat the kidneys and serve immediately with a garnish of chopped parsley.

Note: After fat and filament are removed, kidneys should be wiped clean with a damp, clean cloth, never washed. Nor do we believe in sautéing them sliced because they tend to toughen.

RULLEPØLSE
[*A Scandinavian Christmas dish*]

This traditional Norwegian dish is prepared each Christmas season by the Larsen families of Menemsha, who from that tiny fishing village carry on a seafaring heritage that goes back many generations. *Rullepølse* can be made in various ways—with veal instead of lamb, for instance; or tied up in cloth bags instead of sewn. But this is the way the Larsens—the children enjoy helping too—make this seasonal treat. Like many traditional or holiday foods, it takes a good deal of time to prepare. And it has to season a week before it is cooked. But, according to Carol Larsen, who gave us this recipe, it is fun to make and brings joy to the household when it is served up on Christmas Eve.

The recipe below allows for two servings each for twenty people, and should be adjusted to your family's needs. Leftover *rullepølse*—and there probably will be some—is delicious sliced and served cold or warmed up. The dish must be started about ten days before it is to be eaten.

40 to 45 portions

20 pounds lamb flanks	About 3 pounds rock salt
2 whole legs of lamb, meat sliced from the bone and cut into 1-inch cubes	25 medium potatoes, peeled and halved
12 large onions, chopped	25 medium onions, peeled
Salt and pepper	25 medium turnips, peeled
1 box poultry seasoning (not all will be used)	25 carrots, cut in half lengthwise

Work on a large cutting board or a clean counter. Place a lamb flank on the counter and put a proportionate amount of the lamb cubes on top of it (the flank will be gathered and sewn around the cubed meat) . Sprinkle on the cubed meat a tablespoon or so of the chopped onion, ½ teaspoon salt, ½ teaspoon pepper, and ½ teaspoon poultry seasoning. Roll the flank tightly with all ingredients inside, tucking in the ends neatly. Then sew flank together all the way around the open part. Prepare all flanks in this manner.

Place a layer of rock salt in bottom of a large earthenware crock or similar receptacle (do not use metal). Cover salt with a layer of *rullepølse,* then add a layer of salt. Repeat this process until all meat flanks are used. Cover crock and set in a cool place. Leave the *rullepølse* in this brine (do not add water—they will produce their own liquid) for at least a week. The night before they are to be eaten, remove the sewn flanks from the brine and soak in cold water overnight. The next day remove and drain the *rullepølse,* rinse under cold water, then place in a large kettle (or two kettles, if needed—leave plenty of room for the vegetables). Cover meat with fresh, cold water, bring to a boil, lower heat and simmer about 2½ hours, until the meat is tender. Taste the cooking water at least once during this period; if it seems quite salty, pour it out and replace it with fresh water. Repeat this process until cooking water is only slightly salty.

When meat is tender, add the potatoes, whole onions, turnips, and carrots. Cook until vegetables are tender, about ½ hour. Lift out vegetables and meat, drain slightly, and serve meat in one dish and vegetables in another.

GAME

The rest of the day was spent in trading with them for furs,
"which are Beavers, Luzernes, Marterns, Otters, Wild-Cat
skinnes . . . blacke foxes, Conie skinnes . . . Deere skinnes
very large, Seale skinnes, and other beast skinnes to us un-
knowen."

—FROM BRERETON'S JOURNAL, QUOTED IN
BANKS, *History of Martha's Vineyard*

You aren't likely to encounter a marten or a wildcat as you drive
around Martha's Vineyard nowadays, but one motorist did count
34 conies (or Eastern cottontails) on the 3- or 4-mile stretch of road
between the youth hostel and the airport during a misty, nighttime
drive. Through September and October the squirrels frenziedly stock
up on acorns and hickory nuts, and a birdwatcher making his way
through the brush surrounding a quiet inland pond may startle an
otter sunning himself on the warm mud. Both red and fallow deer
are numerous, often materializing magically out of the dark woods,
leaping stiff-legged across the road in front of an oncoming car, and
disappearing before the driver even slows down.

Game animals, as well as others, find the Vineyard a tranquil
haven during most of the year. Some creatures are less popular than
their edible brethren, like the wharf rats and the recently introduced skunks. Skunks apparently thrive on the Vineyard, and now
plague country households with nightly forages into the garbage
cans and compost heaps or odoriferous encounters with the family
dog. But deer, rabbits, pheasants, quail, and other potentially delectable wild creatures are hunted and killed during certain seasons of
the year, and used for food as they have been by Vineyard inhabitants
since it was first settled.

ROAST LEG OF VENISON

Authorities differ about the length of time required to age venison, assuming, that is, there is a hunter in the family who proudly brings home a deer. Consensus seems to be that at least a week is required for aging and that the carcass should be hung in a cool, airy place with temperatures ranging between 38° and 43° F.

Cuts from the hindquarter—in this case the leg—don't really require tenderizing in a marinade. This recipe suggests it, nevertheless, for the marinade conveys a subtle flavor to the meat, and the addition of a small quantity of the reserved marinade to the finished pan juices is a splendid enhancement.

6 to 10 portions, depending on size of roast

MARINADE

3 cups good red Burgundy or claret
½ cup vegetable oil
½ teaspoon freshly ground black pepper
1 teaspoon salt
1 bay leaf (optional)
2 cloves garlic, minced

1 small onion, chopped
2 teaspoons chopped fresh herbs, mixed (parsley, basil, tarragon, chives, etc.) or 1 teaspoon dried herbs
1 cup each celery and carrots, diced

Combine marinade ingredients. Place half the marinade in a container of sufficient size to hold the meat. Place the meat in the marinade, then ladle the rest of the marinade over the meat, including the vegetables and herbs. Cover and let stand at least 6 hours. Turn the meat every 2 hours. If the meat is refrigerated, it may marinate 12 to 24 hours.

Leg of venison, properly larded (see below)
½ teaspoon salt

¼ teaspoon (or a little more) freshly ground black pepper
¼ pound salt pork, thinly sliced

(continued)

Preheat oven to 325° F.

Remove meat from marinade; pat it thoroughly dry with a paper towel. Rub the salt in. (Not too much salt; the salt-pork slices, if used, contribute saltiness.) Dust with the black pepper. Reserve the marinade.

Most cooks agree that venison requires larding before it is cooked to preserve its juiciness. Ideally, lardoons (thin strips of salt pork) cut ½ inch thick and 3 to 4 inches long are inserted in the meat at 2- or 3-inch intervals. If you lack a larding needle, an ice pick or a thin-pointed knife will force the lardoons into the meat. Or thin strips of salt pork or bacon may be placed over the top of the roast so that each slice nearly overlaps its neighbor.

Cook in an uncovered roasting pan 15 to 20 minutes to the pound, or to an internal temperature of 140° F. for rare, if a meat thermometer is used.

Remove the finished roast to a heated platter and keep warm. Pour or skim off all fat from roasting pan except for about 2 tablespoons, and proceed with the following sauce:

1 tablespoon flour	Salt and freshly ground black
1 cup of the reserved	pepper, if required
marinade	¼ cup sour cream (optional)
1 cup beef stock (or canned	
beef bouillon)	

Add the flour to the remaining fat and juices in the roasting pan, place over moderate heat and blend thoroughly, then add the marinade and the beef stock, stirring constantly, scraping up all the coagulated juices. At this point additional salt and pepper may be added, if needed. Strain the sauce into a serving bowl. Serve very hot.

Optional: The sour cream, if it is to be used, is stirred slowly into the sauce over gentle heat. Do not let sauce boil or it will curdle.

VENISON POT ROAST

Before using the less-tender cuts of venison—any portion of the forequarter, for instance—it is almost essential that the meat be marinated overnight in the refrigerator (or at least 4 to 6 hours at room temperature) for maximum flavor and tenderness. The marinade tenderizes and adds an additional dimension of flavor as well.

6 to 8 portions

Marinade (see page 131)
4–5-pound piece of venison
2 tablespoons butter and 2 tablespoons vegetable oil (or ¼ pound salt pork, cut into ½-inch dice)
½ teaspoon salt, or more
¼ teaspoon freshly ground black pepper, or more
2 medium onions, coarsely chopped

2 small garlic cloves, finely chopped
2 teaspoons flour
1½ cups beef stock (or canned beef bouillon), more if needed
About 1 tablespoon beach-plum jelly (optional)

Marinate venison 4 to 6 hours at room temperature or over night in the refrigerator, turning it occasionally.

Remove meat from marinade; dry with paper towels. Reserve the marinade.

Heat butter and oil over moderate heat in a heavy 6-quart kettle or a flameproof casserole until butter foam subsides. If using salt pork, cook over moderate heat until crisp and golden; remove pork bits, drain them on paper towel, and reserve. Brown meat on all sides in the hot fat, remove it from pan, and sprinkle with the salt and pepper.

Add onions to the pan and cook slowly until transparent and golden. Add chopped garlic and cook a minute or two longer. If using salt pork, drain off all but 2 or 3 tablespoons of the fat. Add the flour to the pan, blending it in thoroughly with the fat,

(*continued*)

onions, and garlic. Add the beef stock and ½ cup of the reserved marinade and allow the liquids to come to a simmer over moderate heat. If using salt pork, add the reserved, cooked dice. Place the meat in the pot, cover tightly, and cook at a gentle simmer until the meat is tender. Cooking time will vary considerably according to the age of the animal. If you prefer, the pot roast may cook in a 275° F. oven. If additional liquid is required, add a little more beef stock. Turn the meat at least once during the cooking period.

When tender, remove meat from pan, transferring it to a heated platter.

If necessary, add more salt and pepper to the liquids in the pot or casserole. Stir in the beach-plum jelly, if desired. Then strain and pour into a heated sauce boat.

Slice the meat, spoon a little of the sauce over the meat slices and serve with the additional sauce.

Note: Lean meat such as venison is improved by larding. See comments about this contained in recipe for Roast Leg of Venison (see page 131).

VENISON MEAT LOAF

Here on Martha's Vineyard, the hunters, in the proper season (and a few in the improper season), stock their freezers with venison roasts, steaks, and chops, but just as important a freezer item is the ground meat obtained from the trimmings and from the shoulder and neck. The ground venison makes such a deliciously different meat loaf that some of us rank it in importance with the venison roasts and steaks.

6 to 8 portions

2 slices white bread, crusts removed

½ cup beef stock (or canned beef bouillon)

3 pounds ground venison

or

2 pounds ground venison and 1 pound ground beef (preferably chuck)

¼ pound salt pork, ground (optional)

1 small onion, chopped fine

1 small clove garlic, chopped fine

¼ teaspoon freshly ground black pepper

½ teaspoon salt (if ground salt pork is used, omit salt)

1 tablespoon chopped fresh parsley (or 1 teaspoon dried parsley)

1 teaspoon prepared mustard (preferably Dijon type)

2 tablespoons catsup (or 1 teaspoon tomato paste)

1 teaspoon Worcestershire sauce

3 or 4 thin slices salt pork or bacon (optional)

Preheat oven to 350° F.

Soak bread in the beef stock. Combine all other ingredients except whole slices of salt pork or bacon, then add the soaked bread. Stir everything thoroughly, being sure that the bread combines completely with the other ingredients. Shape into a loaf and place in a shallow baking pan. A black iron skillet is recommended. If desired, place slices of salt pork or bacon on top of the loaf. Bake for approximately 1½ hours, basting occasionally with pan juices.

(continued)

Note: A little additional beef stock, about ½ cup, may be added to the pan juices after removing the cooked meat loaf. (If using salt pork, pour off excess fat before adding stock.) Stir the added stock thoroughly over moderate heat, then simmer for about 10 minutes, strain, and pour over the meat loaf.

RABBIT STIFLE

3 to 4 portions

1 or 2 rabbits (2½–3 pounds net weight), skinned, cleaned, and cut into serving-size pieces

Salt

¼ teaspoon freshly ground black pepper

Flour for dredging

2 tablespoons butter and 2 tablespoons vegetable oil (or ¼ pound salt pork, cut in ½-inch dice)

4 medium-sized onions, cut in ½-inch slices

2 cups beef stock (or canned beef bouillon)

1 teaspoon tomato paste

1 tablespoon flour mixed to a smooth paste with 2 tablespoons water

¼ cup sour cream (optional)

1 tablespoon chopped fresh parsley

1 teaspoon chopped fresh dill (or ½ teaspoon dried dill weed)

Soak rabbit for 2 hours in water to cover, adding 1 tablespoon salt per quart of water. (Recommended for freshly killed rabbit as an aid in extracting any traces of blood.) Dry thoroughly with paper towels. Rub the rabbit pieces with ½ teaspoon salt and the pepper; dust thoroughly with flour, shaking off the excess.

Melt the butter and oil in a heavy 5- or 6-quart kettle or flame-proof casserole over moderate heat. If using salt pork, cook the diced bits until crisp and golden; remove them and drain on a paper towel. Reserve them. Brown the rabbit pieces on all sides in the hot fat. Remove the rabbit pieces, reduce heat, and cook the onion slices until golden and transparent.

Pour off excess fat, then add beef stock to pan and bring to a full boil over high heat; cook for 5 minutes, stirring occasionally.

Reduce heat to low; add the tomato paste, continuing to stir for a moment or two. Additional salt and pepper may be required at this point.

Add the rabbit pieces and salt-pork bits to the pan, cover tightly, and cook at a very gentle simmer until rabbit is tender. Cooking time will vary depending on the age of the creature; it should take approximately 1 hour. The kettle—or casserole—may also be placed in a slow oven, 250° to 275° F.

Transfer rabbit pieces to a heated serving bowl; keep warm. Add the flour-and-water paste to the liquids in the pan, stirring constantly over moderate heat until the mixture thickens and bubbles. Turn off heat and carefully stir in the sour cream, if used.

Pour a little of the sauce—about ¾ cup—over the rabbit pieces, sprinkle with the parsley and dill. Serve the remainder of the sauce in a separate bowl.

RABBIT WITH RED-WINE SAUCE
[*Rabbit Fricassee*]

Vineyarders claim we are overrun with these swift members of the hare family. It has to do with an imbalance of population among our wild creatures, a phenomenon explained more satisfactorily by ecologists than by cook-book writers. Suffice it to say that there are insufficient predators to maintain the proper ratio of rabbits. If the men in your family hunt in the proper season, rejoice and enjoy the following:

3 to 4 portions

1 or 2 rabbits (2½–3 pounds net weight), skinned, cleaned, and cut into serving-size pieces
Salt
1 clove garlic, minced fine
½ teaspoon powdered ginger (optional and delicious)

¼ teaspoon freshly ground black pepper
Flour for dredging
2 tablespoons butter and 2 tablespoons vegetable oil (or ¼ pound salt pork, cut into ½-inch dice)
1 medium onion, chopped fine

(*continued*)

1 cup beef stock (or canned
   beef bouillon)
1 cup any good red wine
   (Burgundy, Beaujolais, or
   Bordeaux)
2 tablespoons chopped fresh
   parsley plus 2 or 3 parsley
   stems (or Bouquet garni:
   5 or 6 parsley sprigs, a bay

leaf, 4 or 5 thyme sprigs,
   and a small piece of celery
   tied together with string)
½ pound fresh mushrooms,
   sliced
Additional butter and oil
2 tablespoons flour mixed to a
   smooth paste with 3 tablespoons water

Soak rabbit pieces for 2 hours in water to cover, adding 1 table-spoon salt per quart of water. (Recommended for freshly-killed rabbit as an aid in extracting any traces of blood.) Dry thoroughly with paper towels. Rub the rabbit pieces with ½ teaspoon salt, the garlic, ginger, and pepper; dust thoroughly with flour, shaking off the excess.

Heat butter and vegetable oil over moderate heat in a heavy 5- or 6-quart kettle or flameproof casserole. When the butter foam subsides, add the rabbit pieces and brown on all sides. Remove from pan.

If using salt pork, a wonderful substitute for the butter-vegetable-oil mixture, cook the diced bits over moderate heat until crisp and golden, remove them and drain on paper towel. Reserve them, and use the fat in browning rabbit.

Cook the chopped onion in fat remaining in kettle, stirring over moderate heat until golden and transparent. Pour off all but 2 tablespoons of fat in pan. Add beef stock, red wine, 1 table-spoon of the chopped parsley and the parsley stems (or the bouquet garni, if used). Over high heat stir the liquids constantly while scraping up the coagulated pan juices until they dissolve. Lower heat, add rabbit pieces and the reserved salt-pork bits (if used), cover tightly, and allow to simmer very gently until rabbit is tender, about 1 hour. Or place in a flameproof casserole and cook in a preheated 250° to 275° F. oven.

While the rabbit is simmering, cook the sliced mushrooms in a heavy skillet with additional butter and oil, about 1 tablespoon of each, over moderate heat until lightly browned, about 5 minutes. Remove from skillet and reserve.

Transfer cooked rabbit to a heated serving dish. Keep warm. Remove parsley stems, or bouquet garni if used. Over high heat bring sauce to a full boil; cook a few minutes, stirring occasionally. Reduce heat, add the flour-and-water paste gradually until the sauce thickens; the mixture should coat a spoon lightly. If too thick, stir in additional beef stock.

Add the reserved mushrooms to the sauce; reheat briefly. Spoon the mushrooms and approximately 1 cup of the sauce over the rabbit; sprinkle with the remaining tablespoon chopped parsley. Pass the additional sauce in a heated serving bowl.

ROAST PHEASANT WITH APRICOT SAUCE

Few connoisseurs of game agree about the length of time game birds should be cooked. Nor is there an area of agreement concerning the length of time wild birds should be hung. Pheasant, for example, is hung, incredibly enough, for as long as six months by some. For the average palate, two or three days should be enough. Hang the birds in a cool, dry place (38° to 48° F.) before they are drawn or plucked. Wild duck and pheasant—birds with dark meat—are usually served rare; white-fleshed birds such as partridge or quail are usually served well done. Wild birds have little fat and this lack must be supplemented by the addition of butter, bacon, salt pork, or larding.

Allow at least 1 pound of bird per person

1 ready-to-cook pheasant, weighing 2½–3 pounds	1 small whole apple
1 tablespoon melted butter	1 small whole onion, peeled
Salt and freshly ground pepper to taste	1 slice lemon
½ cup celery leaves	1 clove garlic (optional)
	4 slices salt pork, cut thin
	Apricot Sauce (see below)

Preheat oven to 350° F.

(continued)

Rub the cavity of the bird with the melted butter, then with a little salt and pepper. Place the celery leaves, apple, onion, lemon slice, and garlic clove (if used) inside the bird. Truss the bird, place the salt-pork slices over the breast, and roast, uncovered, from 15 to 30 minutes per pound, depending on one's preference. Baste the bird frequently with the pan juices while it is cooking.

Remove bird from its baking pan. Discard string and salt-pork slices. Strain or pour off fat in roasting pan. Set pan aside. Transfer bird to heated platter and keep warm.

Serve with Apricot Sauce.

APRICOT SAUCE

4 to 6 portions

1½ cups chicken stock (or canned chicken broth)

1 cup canned pitted apricots, drained (reserve juice)

1 teaspoon grated orange rind, orange part only

¼ cup port or sherry

½ cup apricot juice

Liver from the pheasant, coarsely chopped (uncooked)

Salt and freshly ground black pepper to taste

1 teaspoon cornstarch or arrowroot mixed with 2 teaspoons water (optional)

Add stock to roasting pan. Stir over moderate heat, scraping up all coagulated juices until dissolved. Cook down until about ¾ cup liquid remains. Rub apricots through a coarse sieve or food mill; add to roasting pan with the orange rind, port or sherry, apricot juice, chopped liver, and salt and pepper. Reduce heat and simmer 5 minutes. Spoon a little of the sauce over the pheasant and pass the remainder in a pitcher or bowl.

The sauce may be thickened very slightly by mixing the cornstarch or arrowroot with water to a smooth paste and adding it gradually to the simmering sauce until the desired thickness is achieved.

ROAST WILD DUCK

4 portions

2 wild ducks, weighing approximately 2½ pounds each, ready to cook (reserve livers)
2 tablespoons melted butter
1 teaspoon salt
½ cup celery leaves
2 small whole apples

2 small whole onions, peeled
2 slices lemon
2 cloves garlic (optional)
¼ teaspoon freshly ground pepper
6 slices salt pork, cut thin, or additional melted butter
Madeira Sauce (see below)

Preheat oven to 350° F.

Rub cavities of birds with melted butter, then with about ½ teaspoon of the salt. Place the celery leaves, apples, onions, lemon slices, and garlic cloves (if used) inside the birds. Sprinkle on remaining salt; dust with the pepper. Truss the birds, place the salt-pork slices over the breasts (or rub with additional melted butter) and roast them in an uncovered roasting pan from 15 to 30 minutes per pound, depending on one's preference. Baste the birds frequently with the pan juices while they are cooking.

Transfer birds to a heated platter, discarding trussing string and salt-pork slices. Strain or pour off fat in roasting pan. Set pan aside. Serve a half duckling per person.

Serve with Madeira Sauce.

MADEIRA SAUCE

4 to 6 portions

2 cups chicken stock (or canned chicken broth)
½ cup Madeira or port
2 duck livers (uncooked), coarsely chopped

Salt and pepper to taste, if needed
1 tablespoon cornstarch or arrowroot
2 tablespoons water

(continued)

Add stock to roasting pan; stir over moderate heat, scraping up all coagulated juices until dissolved. Add the Madeira or port and cook until liquids are reduced to about 1½ cups. Add the chopped livers and simmer over reduced heat another 5 minutes. Add salt and pepper if needed. Make a smooth paste with the cornstarch or arrowroot and water; mix into sauce a little at a time until desired thickness is achieved. The sauce should coat the spoon lightly.

ROAST WILD GOOSE WITH CHESTNUT STUFFING

6 to 8 portions

6–8-pound young wild goose, ready to cook (reserve liver)
Juice of 1 lemon
1 teaspoon salt
¼ teaspoon freshly ground black pepper

4 tablespoons melted butter (or 6 slices salt pork, cut thin)
Chestnut Stuffing (see below)
2 or 3 juniper berries
½ cup gin
¾ cup water

Preheat oven to 350° F.

Sprinkle the cavity of the goose with half the lemon juice and half the salt and pepper. Rub the melted butter, if used, over the goose, sprinkle it with the remainder of the lemon juice, then with remainder of the salt and pepper. Fill the cavity lightly with Chestnut Stuffing, close the opening with small skewers, and truss the bird. If using salt pork instead of melted butter, cover the breast with the salt-pork slices. Roast, breast side up, in an uncovered roasting pan, until tender, 2 to 3 hours. Combine juniper berries, gin, and water and baste the bird frequently with this mixture.

Transfer goose to a heated platter. Spoon or pour off accumulated fat in roasting pan, add ½ cup water to pan juices and cook over moderate heat, stirring frequently, until coagulated pan juices are dissolved. Strain, then spoon some of this sauce over the goose just before serving and put the remainder in a pitcher or bowl.

CHESTNUT STUFFING

2 pounds chestnuts
½ cup melted butter
½ cup finely chopped onion
Goose liver
3 cups soft bread crumbs
(from day-old French- or
Italian-type)

½ cup cream (or chicken
stock)
2 tablespoons chopped fresh
parsley
¼ teaspoon freshly ground
black pepper
1 teaspoon salt

½ teaspoon powdered ginger

With a small paring knife, cut slits in flat side of each chestnut. Place in a saucepan of cold water; bring to a boil. Cook several minutes, then remove pan from heat. Peel the outer shell and the inner skin from chestnuts. Remove only a few from the water at one time—chestnuts peel a bit better while they are warm. Return the peeled chestnuts to the saucepanful of water; cook 10 minutes longer, or until they are tender. Put them through a coarse sieve or a food mill.

In a heavy skillet, heat a little of the melted butter and cook the onion and the goose liver for about 5 minutes. Chop the liver coarsely. Combine all ingredients, including remaining butter and chestnuts, tossing lightly with a fork until well mixed.

POULTRY

Be kind to poor hens in every way, and not let them suffer with hunger and cold; cruelty not in any way. . . . Hens must not have fish, it physics them. Hens must not have anything relaxing. . . . Be clever to them. They must not be affrighted. They can never get over it.

HEN'S GRAVESTONE
Poor little heart, ADA QUEETIE,
O my heart is consumed
In the coffin underground,
O how I feel for her,
She and I could never part,
She was my own heart within me,
She had more than common love,
And more than common wit.

—*The Works of Nancy Luce* (1888)

Though few people become as enamored of hens as Miss Luce did,* those of us who have raised, known, and loved hens can never think of them as mindless and uninteresting. Like people, hens can be stupid or smart, curious and affectionate or ill-tempered and unmanageable. They love to help with the gardening, and will murmur to you incessantly while laying their eggs, if there is a rapport between you. Fortunately for henlovers, no such nonsense precedes the selection of a plump roasting chicken or tender broiler at the meat counter, for there is no denying that chicken is one of the most satisfactory meats we can eat. Relatively inexpensive, endlessly adaptable, delicious plain or fancy, hot or cold, chicken appears frequently on most American tables and is one food that almost everybody loves to eat.

* For more on this incredible, hen-loving woman, consult the West Tisbury library, or see the material about her in Walter M. Teller's *Cape Cod and the Off-Shore Islands*, Prentice-Hall, New York (1970).

ROAST CHICKEN WITH
HERBS AND LEMON

4 portions

4-pound roasting chicken
(remove from refrigerator
1 hour before roasting)
1½ lemons
½ teaspoon salt
¼ teaspoon freshly ground
black pepper
2 tablespoons butter, melted
1 teaspoon chopped fresh
tarragon or ½ teaspoon
dried

1 teaspoon chopped fresh
parsley
½ teaspoon dill weed (dried
may be used)
¼ teaspoon crushed coriander
seed
⅛ teaspoon powdered ginger
½ cup chicken stock (or
canned chicken broth)
½ teaspoon grated lemon rind
½ cup sour cream

Preheat oven to 350° F.

Rub inside of chicken with juice from ½ lemon and some of the salt and pepper. Rub the melted butter over the chicken; sprinkle with remaining salt and pepper. Truss the bird. Mix the herbs and spices and sprinkle over the chicken. Place in roasting pan, uncovered. Roast until the leg bone turns easily in its socket, or about 1 hour and 15 minutes; baste occasionally with pan juices. Remove chicken to a heated platter.

To the pan juices add the chicken stock and the juice from the remaining lemon. Cook over moderate heat, stirring thoroughly, scraping up the coagulated roasting juices to incorporate into liquids in pan. Add additional salt and pepper if necessary. Cook 5 to 10 minutes. Add the lemon rind. Turn off heat and blend in the sour cream. Pour into a sauce boat and serve immediately with the chicken.

Note: Paper-thin slices of lemon, about 8 of them, may be substituted for the lemon rind. Add the slices to the sauce just before blending in the sour cream.

CHICKEN BAKED WITH RUM AND HONEY

Rum, a sugar-cane product distilled chiefly in the semitropical West Indian islands, has long figured in the Vineyard scene. Clipper ships carried the "red rum of St. Thomas" home to New England; later, during prohibition, rum running was a lively business and Vineyard seamen who knew their way around the local bays and channels were in great demand.

This recipe was developed by Louise Tate King some years ago when she was in charge of a mountainside restaurant in Charlotte Amalie, St. Thomas, during the winter months. It was so successful that she incorporated it into the menu of her Martha's Vineyard restaurant, where it is still featured.

4 portions

2 broiler chickens, about 2¼ pounds each, split, backs and necks removed

2 tablespoons butter, melted

1 teaspoon salt

¼ teaspoon freshly ground black pepper

½ cup rum—any kind, although the New England type is best

½ cup chicken stock (the stock may be made by simmering the backs, necks, etc., with 1 carrot, ½ small onion, 1 small stalk of celery with a little water until chicken pieces are tender)

½ cup honey

Preheat oven to 400° F.

Rub the chicken pieces with the melted butter; sprinkle with salt and pepper. Place them, skin side down, in a shallow roasting pan or flameproof baking dish of the appropriate size. Bake 20 to 25 minutes, or until skin is golden. Turn them and bake another 20 minutes.

Combine rum, chicken stock, and honey; baste the chicken with this mixture at frequent intervals for about another 20 minutes. The chicken is done when the leg turns easily in its socket. Transfer chicken to a heated serving dish and keep warm.

Place the roasting pan over direct heat and simmer the sauce slowly, scraping up the coagulated pan juices until dissolved. Continue to cook, stirring, until the sauce is reduced to about 1 cup. Strain the sauce, pour over broilers and serve.

Note: Brandy, about ¼ cup, may be gently heated for a few moments, ignited, and poured over the chicken just before serving, either at table or in the kitchen, depending on one's flair for the dramatic.

CHICKENY CHICKEN

Somewhere in the process of mechanizing and "improving" poultry production, the flavor of chicken seems to have disappeared. If you are cooking an Island-raised, honest-to-God hen, allow it to generate its innate flavor by cooking it simply, without embellishments or camouflage. This recipe is for the chain store's weekend special.

Chickeny chicken was developed by a partially blind octogenarian cook in West Tisbury who can no longer see well enough to make anything fancy but still sets an enviable table. In other circumstances, in earlier days, she disdained "prepared" foods such as canned soups (as we still do); forced now to use them, she does so with a flourish.

A big pot of this chicken is usually ready when her family arrives on a late-night ferry for an out-of-season visit (they begin anticipating dinner as far away as Providence). Simple and delicious, it delights everyone and is practically foolproof.

4 to 6 portions

4-pound roasting chicken, cut up
1 can cream of chicken soup (concentrated type)
1 teaspoon mustard, preferably Dijon type
½ cup water
¼ teaspoon freshly ground pepper

(continued)

Wash chicken pieces well and remove extraneous fat. Place pieces directly in a large, heavy saucepan or flameproof casserole without preliminary browning. Combine soup, mustard, and water. Pour over chicken. Sprinkle pepper over chicken pieces. Cover saucepan or casserole and cook chicken over very low heat for about 2 hours, until meat is almost falling off the bones. Lift and turn the pieces once or twice during the first 10 minutes to prevent their sticking to the pan.

The dish may also be cooked in a 250° to 275° F. oven for about 2½ hours. Prepare it the same way, using an ovenproof casserole with a good, tight cover.

Salt may be added to finished casserole, if needed. For most tastes it will be salty enough.

BAKED CHICKEN WITH OYSTERS

4 portions

2 two-and-one-quarter-pound broiler chickens, halved, necks and backs removed
2 tablespoons melted butter
1 teaspoon salt
¼ teaspoon freshly ground black pepper

1 pint (containing at least 20) freshly shucked oysters, drained
1 teaspoon chopped fresh parsley
Maître d'Hôtel Butter (see page 248), optional

Preheat oven to 400° F.

Rub the chickens on both sides with the melted butter, then with the salt and pepper. Place chickens skin side up in the baking dish. Bake without turning for approximately 1 hour. (Chicken is done when the leg turns easily in the socket.) Remove dish from oven. Distribute the oysters evenly over the chickens, allowing 5 or 6 per serving. Spoon the pan juices over the oysters and return the dish to the oven only long enough for the edges of the oysters to curl. Serve immediately with the chopped fresh parsley sprinkled over all.

A teaspoonful of Maître d'Hôtel Butter may garnish each serving.

CHICKEN AND EGGPLANT CASSEROLE

This is an excellent casserole to prepare in the morning before going off to the beach for the day; it can be reheated for dinner when you get home. Turn off the oven before you leave for the beach and let the casserole sit there. If you are in a hurry, you need not brown the chicken pieces first; in that event, bake the casserole at a higher oven temperature.

4 to 6 portions

1 cup flour
1 tablespoon salt
½ teaspoon freshly ground black pepper
4–5-pound roasting chicken, cut into 10 pieces
2 tablespoons butter
2 tablespoons vegetable oil
Medium-sized eggplant, unpeeled, cut into ¾-inch half circles
1 large can Italian tomatoes, drained (or 3 cups fresh tomatoes, cut in chunks)
2 cloves garlic, minced fine
1 green pepper, coarsely chopped

1 large onion, coarsely chopped
¼ pound fresh mushrooms, sliced
½ teaspoon dried orégano
½ teaspoon dried basil
4 tablespoons chopped fresh parsley
Additional salt and freshly ground black pepper, if desired
2 to 3 tablespoons grated Parmesan or Romano cheese (optional)
4 tablespoons olive oil, vegetable oil, or melted butter (optional)

Preheat oven to 325° F.

Put the flour, salt, and pepper in a heavy brown paper bag, drop in the chicken pieces and shake vigorously until each piece is well coated with flour. Remove chicken from bag and shake off excess flour.

In a large, heavy skillet melt butter with the oil over moderate heat. When the butter foam subsides, brown the chicken pieces, skin side down first; don't overcrowd the skillet. Set chicken aside. Transfer half the chicken to a heavy ovenproof casserole,

(continued)

about 4-quart capacity. Arrange half the eggplant, tomatoes, garlic, green pepper, onion, mushrooms, dried herbs, and parsley over the chicken. Sprinkle with additional salt and pepper, if desired.

Repeat, reserving remaining tomatoes and chopped parsley. Arrange the tomatoes and parsley on top, sprinkle with additional salt and pepper, and grated cheese if desired.

Bake, covered, for 2 hours. Reheat 10 to 15 minutes in a preheated 300° F. oven at serving time.

If you elect to eliminate browning the chicken pieces, bake the casserole, covered, in a preheated 425° F. oven, pouring the optional 4 tablespoons oil or melted butter over all ingredients. Cook for 1 hour, turn oven heat off and leave casserole in oven until needed.

The grated-cheese topping (optional) will produce a golden-brown crust if the hot casserole is placed in a moderately hot broiler for a moment or two.

PICNIC CHICKEN

[*Chicken Baked with Crumbs and Herbs*]

Here is a splendid chicken recipe, good either hot or cold, and admirable because it can be done ahead of serving time. Cooled, it may be taken to the beach for a picnic supper or served on the patio. If it is to be presented hot, it is a simple matter to reheat it in the oven.

4 to 6 portions

2 broiler chickens, 2¼ pounds each, split, backs and necks removed (use the latter to make a little chicken stock)

8 tablespoons melted butter

½ teaspoon salt

4 tablespoons strong prepared mustard (Dijon type, preferably)

½ cup chicken stock (or canned chicken broth)

Pinch of cayenne pepper

1 teaspoon Worcestershire sauce

⅛ teaspoon Tabasco

3 cups fresh bread crumbs
(use day-old French or
Italian type, preferably)

1 tablespoon chopped fresh
parsley (or 1 teaspoon
dried parsley)

½ teaspoon chopped fresh
tarragon (or ¼ teaspoon
dried tarragon)

¼ teaspoon chopped fresh
basil (or a pinch of dried
basil)

4 tablespoons finely chopped
scallions (use some of the
green stems, too)

¼ teaspoon freshly ground
black pepper

Preheat oven to 450° F.

Brush the chicken halves with 3 to 4 tablespoons of the melted butter (or use half butter, and half vegetable oil). Sprinkle with the salt. Bake in a shallow baking pan, skin side down, about 20 to 25 minutes, or until skin is golden. Baste several times. Turn the halves and continue to bake another 20 to 25 minutes; baste occasionally. The chicken is done when the leg turns easily in its socket. Remove chickens from pan; set aside.

To juices in baking pan add remaining butter, the mustard, chicken stock, cayenne, Worcestershire sauce, and Tabasco. Cook over moderate heat until the mixture comes to a simmer, stirring and scraping up the coagulated pan juices until they are dissolved. Cook another few minutes. Remove from heat.

Preheat oven broiler to moderately hot.

Combine remaining ingredients in a mixing bowl, mixing thoroughly, then add to the liquids in the baking pan, lifting and stirring with a fork to allow the crumbs to absorb the liquids evenly.

Pat and press the crumb mixture onto the chicken halves so that the flavored crumbs adhere to both sides.

Brown the chicken halves in the broiler, 5 to 6 inches from the heat source. Watch carefully; the crumbs will brown quickly.

Remove chickens from broiler and cool them. If the chickens are to be served several hours later, it is not necessary to refrigerate them.

(*continued*)

Note: If you prefer to serve the chicken hot but wish to do your cooking in advance, prepare it up to and including the crumb-coating process. About 15 minutes before serving time, place in a preheated 450° F. oven, allowing chicken to reach serving temperature. Regulate the oven heat, if necessary, to avoid overbrowning the crumb coating.

CHICKEN LIVERS WITH
SHERRY AND CREAM

Featured at Louise Tate King's restaurant, this recipe is suggested here because its preparation is simple, and it may be prepared advantageously an hour or so in advance of dinner.

4 portions

1 pound chicken livers, preferably fresh	1 tablespoon flour
Flour	¼ cup dry sherry
½ teaspoon salt	¼ cup chicken stock (canned chicken broth may be substituted)
¼ teaspoon freshly ground black pepper	
2 tablespoons butter	½ cup cream
2 tablespoons vegetable oil	½ teaspoon fresh thyme, chopped (or ¼ teaspoon dried thyme)
½ pound fresh, firm mushrooms, sliced	

Wipe the chicken livers dry. Cut large ones in two. Roll them in flour seasoned with the salt and pepper.

In a heavy skillet over moderate heat melt the butter with the oil. When the butter foam subsides, add the livers and cook until brown on one side, then turn them, but do not overcook—5 to 8 minutes in all is sufficient. Remove from skillet. Cook the mushrooms in the same skillet about 5 minutes. Remove them from skillet.

To the pan juices add the 1 tablespoon flour and blend carefully. Let simmer a few moments, then add sherry, chicken stock, and cream, and simmer until thickened. If sauce seems a trifle thick, dilute with a little additional chicken stock or cream.

Just before serving, return livers to the sherry sauce and reheat briefly without allowing the sauce to boil.

Sprinkle with the thyme and serve.

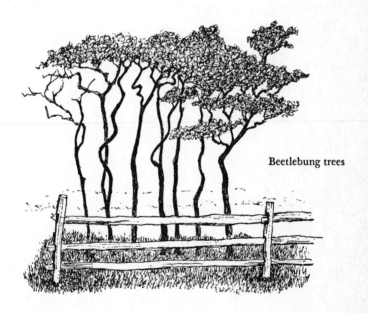

Beetlebung trees

Vegetables

The vegetable departments were well represented, comprehending every variety and size to be found in the category. It is useless to waste adjectives in vainly attempting to portray the enormity of the squashes, the stupendity of the pumpkins and the giganticity and general outrageousness of the turnips and beets.

—FROM THE ACCOUNT OF THE FIRST DUKES COUNTY AGRICULTURAL FAIR, QUOTED FROM THE *Vineyard Gazette,* OCTOBER 21, 1870

Vegetables grown on the Vineyard seem, at least to Vineyarders, to taste better than vegetables brought over on the ferry. Traditional upon arrival for many summer people is a visit to Farmer Greene's place in North Tisbury. Here they may pick up a box of the gigantic, luscious strawberries or tiny new potatoes that are his specialty; or perhaps some fresh-pulled corn to roast while the swordfish broils, or a head of ruby lettuce almost too beautiful to eat.

Spring is the Vineyard's least appealing season—many residents, in fact, say there is none, we just go from winter into summer. A garden record for May 24 notes: "Cold and damp still; lots of rain," and for May 31: "Still windy and chilly every day—nothing up yet but lettuce." Yet slowly the icy waters warm, the wind softens, and the sun and the soft sea air nurture the crops all over the island. And each August, as they have since 1870, gardeners and homemakers bring their finest, their ripest, their biggest—whether it be fifteen carefully matched string beans or two quarts of garden relish—to the West Tisbury Agricultural Fair to compete for the blue ribbons.

Though Vineyard gardens are slow to come up, they bear on and on and on into the bright, bracing days of October. A few sturdy plots are still producing in November—some nubbins of broccoli, a few handfuls of stunted but tasty beans, some hard-skinned, sweet-fleshed cherry tomatoes, and of course the important fall crops of squashes, rutabagas, and turnips and various hardy greens, to be eaten on into winter and even spring.

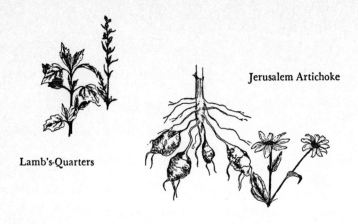

Jerusalem Artichoke

Lamb's-Quarters

STEAMED JERUSALEM ARTICHOKES

The Jerusalem artichoke, a vastly underrated and undercon-
sumed vegetable, was an important food source, along with corn,
beans, and squash, for the Vineyard Indians of earlier days. It
flourishes in the Island's sandy soil, and we are including several
ways of using this obscure vegetable to encourage local gardeners
to start growing artichokes again.

As far as we know, the Jerusalem artichoke has no connection
with either Jerusalem or artichokes. Rather, it is a somewhat
weedy member of the sunflower family. Its profligate growth and
prodigious appetite (it will dwarf everything else in the garden
and drain the soil of the nutrients you are trying to feed your
other vegetables) make it a hazard in the family garden, but if
you can confine the plants to one section or border they will yield
as many as you can use of these adaptable, strange-looking tubers.
Artichokes shrivel quickly and thus are seldom sold in vegetable
markets. You can leave your crop in the ground quite late—almost until the first heavy freeze; then dig them, store, covered
with damp sand, in a box in the garage or basement, and remove
your artichokes as needed. They can be stored for a few days in
a plastic bag in the refrigerator or wrapped in a damp towel in
the vegetable bin.

4 portions

Vegetable steamer (optional)	1 teaspoon salt
12–16 Jerusalem artichokes	1 tablespoon chopped parsley
2 tablespoons butter	Freshly ground black pepper

Wash artichokes well. If dirty from garden, soak in cold water before scrubbing. Trim off tiny rootlets, but do not peel. If disparately shaped, cut into pieces of approximately the same size. Place in steamer over 1 inch of boiling water and steam until tender—15 to 20 minutes; or boil them in water to cover approximately the same length of time. They will suddenly get mushy; test them with a fork from time to time and try not to overcook them. Remove artichokes and steamer (if used) from pan and pour out water. Replace artichokes, add butter, salt, parsley, and pepper. Cut into smaller pieces if desired. Reheat slightly and serve warm. Delicious with roast meat.

GREEN BEANS IN CREAM

This recipe comes from a Nebraska cook, but since Vineyard gardens, like mainland ones, tend to produce masses and masses of green beans—until cooks grow tired of cooking them and diners tired of eating them—here is a slightly different preparation that might be welcome in bean season.

4 portions

1 quart green beans	1 cup medium or heavy cream
	1 teaspoon salt

Prepare beans for cooking—either leave whole or cut up. Place in saucepan and add cream and salt. Over moderate heat bring to a simmer, then lower heat at once and simmer for about ¾ hour, until most of the cream has boiled away. Beans will be "cooked to death" but delicious.

THREE-BEAN SALAD

4 portions

1 cup cooked fresh lima beans
1 cup cooked green beans, cut in 1-inch slices
1 cup canned red kidney beans, drained
3 scallions (green onions), cut in ½-inch pieces
½ cup sliced green pepper
2 whole pimientos, diced or chopped

2 tablespoons chopped fresh parsley
2 teaspoons chopped fresh chives
½ teaspoon salt
¼ teaspoon freshly ground black pepper
Vinaigrette Dressing (see page 247), to taste

Combine all ingredients and mix well. Allow salad to season an hour or so in the refrigerator before serving. Serve chilled but not too cold.

BABY BEETS

[*With Dill and Sour Cream*]

The Indian Hill section of West Tisbury is now all private property, with the exception of a mile-square area in Christian-town, where the tiny chapel and graveyard of the "praying Indians" are located, memorial land that now belongs to the county. Farmland, small ponds, early homesteads and lovely lichen-covered stone walls that ramble way back into the wood-lots characterize this charming area.

An Indian Hill resident with a good old Vineyard name, Mrs. Charles Norton, who lives way down past Norton Circle, told us of an interesting way to prepare the tiny baby beets you can pull out of the row in your garden or buy from Indian Hill's Arrow-head Farm each summer season.

4 portions

12–16 baby beets, depending on size (or 4 or 5 medium beets)	1 teaspoon lemon juice
1 teaspoon salt, or more	½ teaspoon grated lemon rind
2 tablespoons butter	⅓ cup sour cream
1 tablespoon flour	2 or 3 flowerets of fresh dill
1 tablespoon honey	(if not available, use ½
1 teaspoon vinegar	teaspoon dill seed—or dill weed, if preferred)

Cook beets, unpeeled, with the salt in water barely to cover until beets are tender. (Cooking time will vary with size and freshness of beets.) Drain them, reserving ½ cup of the beet liquor, and slip off skins. If tiny leave whole; otherwise cut in slices or chunks. Set prepared beets aside.

In a small saucepan melt the butter, add flour, and stir to a smooth paste. Simmer over low heat for 3 or 4 minutes. Add honey, vinegar, reserved beet liquor, lemon juice, and lemon rind. Bring to a simmer and cook for several minutes. If additional salt is needed, add it at this point. Return beets to this sauce (which will be quite thick) and simmer only long enough to bring up to serving temperature. Remove saucepan from heat; stir in the sour cream and the dill. Serve immediately.

CARROTS, POTATOES, AND ONIONS

One Island family has happily eaten this combination for over forty years, since it was first "invented" as a midwinter solution to the problem of what vegetables to serve with dinner. When this dish is served with a simple meat, such as braised pork chops, a good cabbage slaw, and ice cream for dessert, the preparation of dinner becomes a simple matter for a tired cook.

(continued)

4 to 6 portions

6 medium-sized potatoes,
  peeled and cut in half
6 medium-sized carrots, cut in
  pieces
6 medium-sized onions, peeled
  and halved
2 tablespoons butter (more if
  desired)

½ teaspoon salt
Freshly ground black pepper
  (or cracked black pepper)
1 tablespoon chopped fresh
  parsley (optional)

Combine vegetables in a saucepan with a small amount of water. Try to have the carrots and potatoes more or less the same size, so all three vegetables will cook evenly. Add butter and salt, bring vegetables to a boil, cover tightly, and cook over moderate heat until all are tender but not mushy—about 20 minutes. Check saucepan once or twice to be sure water has not boiled away—add a bit more if needed, but use a minimum of water. (The vegetables can be steamed, but the flavors do not blend so well as if they are cooked in liquid.) When vegetables are cooked, remove saucepan from heat, add pepper (the coarse grind is good), and stir in parsley, if desired. More butter may also be added when dish is served.

GREEN CORN PUDDING

Mrs. E. W. Foote of West Tisbury contributes this splendid offering. The recipe appears in the Martha's Vineyard Hospital cook book, *Vineyard Fare;* it has also been printed in *Yankee* magazine and in Imogene Wolcott's delightful *Yankee Cookbook.* It is so delicious it bears constant repetition.

Fresh ears of corn are urgently recommended. The starchy liquids vary according to the freshness and type of the corn used, therefore the exact amount of milk to be added to the custard cannot be specified. The consistency, when the dish is ready for the oven, should resemble that of a cornbread mixture. For stripping the kernels from the cob, follow the procedure suggested in the Corn Chowder recipe (see page 16).

8 portions (as a main course—see note below)

12–18 ears of corn (about 6
cups kernels—frozen corn
may be used)

3 eggs, well beaten

2 tablespoons melted butter

1 teaspoon salt

1 tablespoon sugar (more if
desired)

Milk or cream

2 teaspoons additional butter
(optional)

Preheat oven to 250° F.

Strip kernels from corn ears; combine with all other ingredients except milk or cream. Then add milk or cream until the mixture is the consistency of a cornbread or corn-muffin batter. Pour into a greased large, shallow baking dish. If desired, dot the top of the batter with 2 teaspoons additional butter. Bake 2 to 3 hours. The pudding should be nicely set and browned on top, and dry enough to cut easily into squares.

Note: Vineyarders sometimes serve this dish as a dessert. Additional sweetening may then be used. Also, the eggs should be separated, yolks and whites well beaten, and the stiff egg whites folded into the batter as the final addition.

OVEN-ROASTED CORN

[*Or Charcoal-Grilled*]

Leaving husks on ears, soak ears in sea water, if possible, for an hour before cooking. Then pull down the husks, remove the silk, and tie the husks back in place with string. Soak another 10 minutes. Place on a rack in a preheated 375° F. oven for at least half an hour. The corn may be sprinkled with additional water during the baking process.

Follow the same procedure if the corn is to be grilled over charcoal outdoors, sprinkling the corn much more frequently with water (preferably from the sea) and turning a number of times so that it cooks evenly on all sides.

Cooked in this way, corn has much the flavor of the corn served at clambakes.

EGGPLANT CASSEROLE

This recipe was developed by a summer Vineyard cook as a low-calorie version of a more elegant (but fattening) dish.

4 portions

1 medium eggplant (un-peeled), cut in ½-inch slices
½ teaspoon salt
½ cup sliced, pitted ripe olives
6 scallions, cut fine

2 tablespoons olive oil
1½ cups tomato or mixed vegetable juice (more may be needed)
½ teaspoon orégano
¾ cup grated Parmesan cheese

Preheat oven to 325° F.

Wash and slice eggplant, discarding stem end. Salt slices and arrange them in one layer in a large, shallow ovenproof dish. Do not overlap. Scatter sliced olives over eggplant. In a large skillet, sauté cut-up scallions in olive oil for about 2 minutes over moderate heat. Add tomato or vegetable juice and orégano, lower heat, and simmer for about 20 minutes. Pour sauce over eggplant slices. If it doesn't quite cover them, add a bit more tomato juice. Sprinkle grated cheese over the top of the sauce and bake 35 to 45 minutes, or until most of sauce has been absorbed.

NEW POTATOES WITH HERBS

Several local farmers sacrifice quantity for quality each summer by rooting around their still-growing potato plants and detaching tiny new potatoes, the size of large marbles, to sell to their customers. Baby potatoes have a delicate, fresh flavor and are marvelous just steamed until tender, dipped in salt and popped into the mouth. Some people boil them with fresh peas. This is another suggestion.

4 portions

3 cups tiny potatoes

1 cup chicken stock (or 1 cup
water and 1 chicken bouillon cube)

1 teaspoon chopped fresh
chives (optional)

1 tablespoon chopped fresh
herbs (almost any combi-
nation of dill, parsley,
chervil, summer savory,
thyme; or dill or chervil
alone)

2 tablespoons butter

Salt to taste (if needed)

Freshly ground black pepper

Wash and scrub potatoes gently but do not peel. Put chicken
stock or water and bouillon cube in a saucepan and heat until
cube is dissolved. Add potatoes and bring to a boil, then cover
and cook over moderate heat about 20 minutes, until potatoes
are tender. Shake pan several times to move potatoes around so
they will cook evenly (if stirred with a spoon or fork their skins
may be torn). Remove from heat, drain, and add chives if desired, other herbs, butter, salt if needed, and pepper. Shake or
mix gently; replace over low heat until butter is melted and
potatoes are well coated.

CREAMED NEW POTATOES
AND FRESH PEAS

4 generous portions

1 pound tiny new potatoes

1 cup water (or chicken stock)

Salt to taste

Freshly ground black pepper
to taste

1–1½ cups fresh peas (frozen
may be substituted)

1 tablespoon butter

1 tablespoon flour

½–1 cup milk (or half milk,
half cream)

(continued)

Wash and scrub the little potatoes gently; do not peel them. Cook them with salt and pepper to taste in the water or chicken stock in a small saucepan over moderate heat until tender, about 20 minutes. Add the peas; cook them until tender. (This will depend on the freshness of the peas, but do not overcook them. Frozen peas, if defrosted first, cook so quickly they are ready practically by the time the cooking liquid comes back to a simmer.)

Drain the vegetables. If using chicken stock, reserve it. Transfer vegetables to a heated serving bowl. Melt the butter in the saucepan over moderate heat; blend in the flour until a smooth roux is obtained. Add 1 cup milk (or ½ cup of the reserved chicken stock and ½ cup milk). Cook slowly until mixture bubbles; extra salt and pepper may be added. Pour the sauce over the vegetables and serve immediately.

PEAS WITH CELERY AND MUSHROOMS

There really is no better way to prepare fresh garden peas—or almost any other freshly picked vegetable—than steaming or boiling them until just tender and seasoning them with butter, salt, and pepper. For those who like fancier dishes, this recipe, served at Louise Tate King's Edgartown restaurant, offers an alternative.

4 portions

1 cup finely chopped celery
1 cup chicken stock (or canned chicken broth)
2 cups fresh garden peas
⅛ pound fresh mushrooms, sliced

¼ teaspoon salt, or to taste
1 whole canned pimiento, chopped or diced

Cook celery in chicken stock over moderate heat for 10 minutes. Add peas and mushrooms, reduce heat, and simmer uncovered 5 to 10 minutes, cooking only until peas are tender. Salt to taste. Garnish with the diced pimiento.

SUCCOTASH

The Vineyard's early settlers discovered the pleasures of this vegetable combination from the Indians. The Indian name for the dish seems to have been *m'sickquatash* (meaning "the grains are whole," thus distinguishing this use of corn from the more common meal form). It is a delight when made from fresh corn, cut from the cob, and freshly shelled baby lima beans. Try cooking the vegetables with a small chunk of salt pork.

6 portions

½ cup water
2 tablespoons butter (or about ⅛ pound salt pork)
2 cups hulled baby lima beans
1 teaspoon salt (less if salt pork is used)

Freshly ground black pepper
½ teaspoon sugar
2 cups fresh corn, cut from cob (see page 16)
⅓ cup rich milk or light cream

Bring water and butter or salt pork to a simmer in a saucepan, then add beans (frozen beans—and frozen corn—may be used, but their flavor is inferior), salt, pepper, and sugar. Simmer until beans are tender, about 10 minutes. Add corn and simmer another 5 minutes. Stir in the rich milk or cream (the water should have been absorbed by now; if not, pour it off first). Let heat but do not allow to boil. Check seasonings and serve immediately. If salt pork is used, remove it before serving the succotash.

Sweet Fern

ARROWHEAD SUMMER SQUASH
[*Two Versions*]

In the service shed at Arrowhead Farm, along with the artistically laid-out young vegetables that were their proud offering, the Fergusons used sometimes to set out a blackboard with a customer's recipe chalked on it—a practice which luckily their young successors have continued. One of the customers carried the instructions for cooking yellow summer squash home in her head and happily made it with basil for several years, until a dinner guest who had taken the time to copy the recipe down advised her it was supposed to be made with mint. We think it is delectable either way.

6 portions

Vegetable steamer (optional)
8–10 yellow summer squash,
   3–4 inches long
½ teaspoon salt
1 tablespoon butter

½ cup sour cream
¼–½ cup chopped fresh basil
   or mint leaves
Freshly ground black pepper
   (if desired)

Wash squash, cut off stem and blossom ends. If steamer is used, place it in large saucepan, add 1 inch water. Add whole squash and steam over moderate heat until fork tender, 10 to 15 minutes. If preferred, squash may be placed in large saucepan with sufficient water to cover bottom of pan, covered tightly, and cooked 10 to 15 minutes, until fork tender. Try not to overcook as this destroys much of their delicate flavor. Remove squash and steamer; discard water. Replace squash in saucepan, slice with fork and knife or mash lightly with masher. Sprinkle with salt; stir in butter and sour cream; stir in mint or basil. Add pepper if desired (this recipe is good without it). If necessary, heat just enough to warm to serving temperature. Do not simmer or sour cream will curdle.

SQUASH BLOSSOMS AND
SCRAMBLED EGGS

3 portions

2 tablespoons butter
1 green pepper, minced
½ medium onion, minced
6 eggs, beaten
1 cup minced squash blossoms
½ teaspoon chopped fresh
    basil (or ⅛ teaspoon dried
    basil)

Salt to taste
Freshly ground black pepper
    to taste

Melt butter in a heavy skillet over moderate heat, sauté green pepper and onion 3 or 4 minutes, then add remaining ingredients and scramble in the usual manner. Additional butter may be needed in pan before eggs are added.

FRIED SQUASH BLOSSOMS

[*From an Old Recipe*]

4 portions

24 fresh squash blossoms (pick
    male ones unless you are
    overrun with squash)
1 cup sifted all-purpose flour
1 teaspoon baking powder
½ teaspoon salt
¼ cup sugar

1 egg, well beaten
½ cup milk
½ teaspoon vanilla extract
2 teaspoons salad oil (not
    olive)
Fat for frying
Dash of cinnamon or nutmeg

Pick squash blossoms early in the day and float them in cold water in a cool place until ready to cook them. Avoid picking blossoms that show tiny squashes forming at their bases—these can be seen even before the buds open and are the ones that will

(continued)

bear fruit. Remove blossoms from water and allow them to drain in a colander or on a sink drainer half an hour before frying them.

Sift flour with baking powder, salt, and sugar into a 1-quart bowl. Combine beaten egg, milk, vanilla, and salad oil and stir into dry ingredients. Mix until batter is smooth. Heat skillet with enough fat to cover bottom of pan (butter, margarine, bacon fat, or vegetable oil may be used). Remove stamens and pistil from each blossom, flatten blossom slightly, dip in batter, and fry about 1 minute in hot fat, then turn and fry the same way on the other side. Drain briefly on paper towels, dust with cinnamon or nutmeg, and serve at once.

ZUCCHINI WITH FRESH HERBS

4 portions

10–12 young zucchini, not longer than 3–4 inches
1 or 2 cloves garlic, minced
1 tablespoon chopped chives
½ teaspoon salt
3 tablespoons olive oil
Freshly ground black pepper
12 short sprigs of fresh herbs (almost any combination will do but include parsley, basil and dill, if possible)

Wash zucchini and slice it very thin. Place in skillet and add garlic, chives, salt, olive oil, and pepper, then with kitchen shears cut fresh herbs over squash slices. Cover tightly and cook over moderate heat about 10 minutes, then lower heat and cook about 5 minutes more, until slices are tender. Stir slices once or twice during cooking time. The steam and oil should cook the vegetables if they are tightly covered, but if necessary add a tablespoon or so of water.

Any leftover squash may be served without reheating. Mix about ½ teaspoon lemon juice or vinegar into each cup of squash before serving.

SUMMER SPAGHETTI SAUCE

6 to 8 portions

1 quart stewed fresh tomatoes (or 1 large can Italian tomatoes)
1 six-ounce can tomato paste
½ cup olive oil
6–8 good-sized garlic cloves, minced or put through press

1 large green pepper, coarsely chopped
1 cup chopped parsley, loosely packed
1 teaspoon salt

Combine all ingredients in a 3- or 4-quart kettle (a large one is needed because sauce will splatter). Stir to mix, bring to a boil over high heat, then lower heat and cook sauce slowly for at least 1 hour, stirring occasionally to prevent sticking. It is important to use the full amount of both garlic and parsley; the more garlic, the better the sauce (a French chicken recipe calls for 40 cloves). This sauce keeps well; in fact, it is better if allowed to sit in the refrigerator a day or two before use. Serve hot over hot, freshly cooked spaghetti; sprinkle with freshly grated Parmesan or Romano cheese before serving.

A GARDEN CASSEROLE

This is a marvelous dish—a simplified version of the famed Mediterranean concoction, ratatouille. Once the ingredients are assembled, it can be prepared for the oven in 5 minutes; it can be cooked at one time and warmed up sometime later; eaten cold; or left, ready to cook, all day on top of the stove and popped in the oven in late afternoon. It is delicious with both fish and meat; served with either and followed by a green salad and cheese or fruit, it makes a nourishing meal. It is equally good at subsequent meals. Proportions of the vegetables can be adjusted to accommodate whatever the gardener brings in; and people who

(continued)

think they don't like eggplant eat it with murmurs of delight. Made in a handsome white or bright-colored serving dish, this casserole is beautiful to look upon both before and after it is cooked.

8 portions

4 zucchini squash, about 5 inches long

1 large eggplant, unpeeled

2 medium-sized onions, peeled

4 large, ripe tomatoes, un-peeled (a large can of Italian tomatoes, drained of excess juice, may be substituted, but is not as good)

1 large green pepper, with seeds and membranes removed

3 cloves garlic, chopped

1 tablespoon salt

½ teaspoon cracked black pepper, more if desired (or a pinch cayenne pepper)

4 sprigs parsley, chopped

½ cup olive oil

Preheat oven to 300° F.

Slice the washed vegetables and arrange them more or less in layers in a 2-quart ovenproof casserole. Cut the eggplant into ½-inch circles, the other vegetables a bit thinner. Sprinkle some of the salt and whichever pepper you use on the sliced vegetables as you go along. Arrangement is not too important, but do try to make the vegetables look pretty. When the vegetables (including the garlic, which need not be chopped too fine) are all used up, sprinkle the rest of the salt and pepper and the chopped parsley over the top and pour the olive oil over everything. Bake, cov-ered, for 1½ hours, or until all vegetables are soft when pierced with a fork. Let cool a bit before serving. If time is short, you may cook the casserole at 425° F. for half an hour, then lower heat to 300° F. and cook another half hour or so.

Blueberries
and Cranberries

Chapter 7

BLUEBERRIES

The small bush creepeth along upon the ground, scarce rising
half a yard high, with divers small dark green leaves set in the
green branches . . . [the flowers] pass into small round berries
. . . of a purple, sweetish, sharp taste; the juice of them give a
purplish colour to the hands and lips that eat and handle
them. . . .

—Culpeper's Complete Herbal (1640)

Whatever name you call them by—high-bush, low-bush, early
sweet, late low, or sour-top blueberries, whortleberries, huckleberries,
dangleberries, whorts, hurts, bilberries—the fruit of the twenty or
more species of *Vaccinium* and *Gaylussacia* are popped into almost
every mouth on the Vineyard during blueberrying time. Discriminat-
ing pickers tend to seek out one variety and pass up the others, but
most of us just drop anything that's within reach and ripe into our
pans and serve them all up together. The black huckleberries—the
dark-colored berries that lack that lovely dusting of soft blue—have
tiny, hard seeds, but their spicy flavor overbalances this slight flaw.
High-bush blueberries in full fruit are a spectacular sight—ten feet
high and laden with ripe berries. There are acres of them on the
Vineyard, but don't expect a berry picker to tell you where they are.
He probably guards his secret jealously, because there is a sort of
magic about blueberrying alone or with one special friend in a high,
rock-studded Vineyard meadow on a blue-skied summer afternoon
that is too precious to share at random.

BLUEBERRY PUDDINGS

[*One old, one adaptation*]

From *The Dinner Cookbook*, published by Scribner's in 1878 and reproduced here from its reprint in the *Vineyard Gazette* some years later, comes this intriguing recipe for a blueberry dessert:

BLUEBERRY PUDDING WITH SWEET SAUCE

1 pint of milk

2 eggs

1 quart of flour (or enough
   for thick batter)

1 gill baker's yeast

1 saltspoonful of salt

1 teaspoon soda dissolved in
   boiling water

1 quart of blueberries,
   dredged in flour

Make the batter and let it rise in a warm place for four hours. When very light, stir in the berries lightly and quickly; pour into a buttered dish and bake one hour, covering with paper should it "crust" over too fast. Turn out and eat with Sweet Sauce.

SWEET SAUCE

3 tablespoons of powdered
   sugar

2 cups of cream

2 teaspoons of rosewater

Sift sugar into cream and add the rosewater.

Confusions arise when one starts to prepare this dish. "1 gill of baker's yeast" becomes ½ cup; if today's dried yeast were used, the batter would rise to heroic proportions. How much boiling water is needed to "dissolve the teaspoon of soda"—enough to make a paste, or more? And how is the gill of yeast treated? If it is dissolved with the soda, the boiling water would of course destroy the leavening capacities of the yeast organisms. How much is a "saltspoonful of salt"? And, most important of all, if one were to "stir in the quart of berries dredged in flour" four hours after preparing the yeast-risen batter, the berries would be a sodden, pasty mess, a sad aftermath to the pleasant time spent picking them in a breeze-swept Vineyard pasture.

Today's recipes, formulated in more precise terms for the busy cook, promise successful results. Here is a contemporary version of a blueberry pudding that should please any cook, whether novice or expert.

STEAMED BLUEBERRY PUDDING

4 generous portions

2 cups sifted flour
4 teaspoons baking powder
½ teaspoon salt
3 tablespoons sugar
3 tablespoons butter
1 tablespoon lemon juice
2 tablespoons molasses (optional but very good)

⅞ cup milk
2 tablespoons flour
1½ cups blueberries, leaves and stems removed
Hard sauce or Foamy Sauce I or II (pages 248–49)

Resift the 2 cups flour with baking powder, salt, and sugar. Work in the butter with a pastry blender or the fingertips. Combine lemon juice, molasses if used, and milk and add to flour mixture. Sift the 2 tablespoons flour over the blueberries and add them to other ingredients. Avoid overmixing. Grease a 1-quart mold or a 1-quart earthenware bowl, fill two-thirds full with the pudding mixture. If your pudding mold has no cover, or earthenware bowl is used, cover with foil or a clean dish towel and tie to the sides with string. Place either bowl or mold in a large pot; pour in enough boiling water to come three-quarters of the way up the bowl or mold. Cover the pot tightly and cook over low heat 1½ to 2 hours. Replenish the water as needed. A small rack or trivet may be used to support the mold while it is steaming.

Turn out the pudding on a serving platter. Serve with hard sauce or Foamy Sauce I or II.

BLUEBERRY GRUNT

[*Sometimes called Blueberry Pot Pie or Blueberry Slump*]

4 generous portions

BLUEBERRY SAUCE

2 cups fresh blueberries   1 cup water
½ cup sugar   1 tablespoon lemon juice

Remove stems and leaves from berries, if any. Wash the berries. Combine them with sugar, water, and lemon juice in a heavy 4-quart saucepan, cover tightly, and cook over moderate heat until the berries are barely tender. (They will finish cooking with the dumplings.) Remove from heat.

DUMPLINGS

1 cup sifted all-purpose flour   ½–¾ cup milk
2 teaspoons baking powder   Heavy cream or whipped
¼ teaspoon salt   cream (optional)
1 teaspoon sugar (optional)

Resift the flour with the baking powder, salt, and sugar (if used). Stir in sufficient milk so that the dumpling dough will drop readily from a spoon.

Return blueberry sauce to stove; over low heat bring to a gentle simmer. Drop the dough from a tablespoon over the blueberry sauce—the dumplings should measure 1½ to 2 inches. Cover pan tightly and cook about 15 to 20 minutes.

Spoon the dumplings into shallow soup plates, covering them with the berry sauce. Serve with heavy cream or slightly sweetened whipped cream, if desired.

A salty Chilmark acquaintance remarks that the dumplings are to be "bailed out of the pot" at serving time.

BLUEBERRY CRISP

About 6 portions

3 cups fresh blueberries
(frozen or canned may be
substituted)
½ cup sugar
¼ teaspoon mace or nutmeg
¼ teaspoon cinnamon
1 tablespoon lemon juice
½ teaspoon grated lemon rind
¾ cup sifted all-purpose flour

½ cup sugar (brown sugar
may be substituted)
6 tablespoons butter, softened
¼ teaspoon salt
¼ cup nut meats, chopped
(optional but recom-
mended)
Whipped cream or vanilla ice
cream (optional)

Preheat oven to 350° F.

Remove stems and leaves, if any, from blueberries. Wash and drain the berries and place in a mixing bowl. Add sugar, spices, lemon juice and rind; mix lightly. Place the mixture in a shallow 1- to 2-quart casserole or baking dish.

Prepare the crumb topping as follows:

Combine in a mixing bowl the flour, sugar, butter and salt. With the fingers or a pastry blender, work these ingredients to a crumbly consistency. Sprinkle over the berry mixture, with the nut meats, if they are used.

Bake 30 minutes, or until the topping is nicely browned and the fruit is tender.

Serve with sweetened whipped cream or a scoop of vanilla ice cream, if you wish.

BLUEBERRY–COTTAGE CHEESE PIE

CRUST

1½ cups graham-cracker crumbs
¼ cup sugar

½ cup melted butter
⅛ teaspoon nutmeg

Preheat oven to 350° F.

Mix graham-cracker crumbs, sugar, melted butter, and nutmeg thoroughly in a bowl, pressing with a fork to blend well. Put mixture into a 9-inch pie plate and shape into crust. Chill in refrigerator while preparing filling.

FILLING

½ cup light cream or evaporated milk
1 pound dry-curd cottage cheese
⅓ cup sugar
½ teaspoon salt
3 eggs, well beaten

Juice and grated rind of 1 lemon
2 tablespoons melted butter
1 cup blueberries (if using frozen or canned berries, drain well)

Blend cream or milk, cottage cheese, sugar, and salt in a blender until thoroughly combined (do only half of mixture at a time). Put blended cheese mixture in a large bowl and add beaten eggs, lemon juice and rind, and melted butter. Mix well, then fold in blueberries. Pour mixture into chilled crust. Allow pie plate to warm slightly before putting in oven, if using ovenproof glass. Bake for 1 hour.

BLUEBERRY PANCAKES WITH ORANGE SAUCE

Makes about 1 dozen 4-inch cakes

1½ cups sifted all-purpose
    flour
1 teaspoon salt
3 tablespoons sugar
2 teaspoons baking powder
1 cup milk
2 eggs, lightly beaten (you
    may separate them, add-
    ing the lightly beaten yolks
    to the milk; the stiffly
    beaten whites then are
    folded into the batter just
    before baking)

3 tablespoons melted butter
1 cup blueberries (if using
    frozen or canned, drain
    well)
Orange Sauce (see below)

Preheat a griddle or heavy skillet over moderate heat; it will be ready for use when a few drops of water sprinkled over it sputter, bounce around and evaporate almost instantly. When the cakes are ready for the griddle, brush it lightly with an oiled brush. Repeat the oiling as necessary.

Resift the flour with the salt, sugar, and baking powder in a mixing bowl. Make a well in the center of these ingredients; pour into it the milk and beaten eggs (or only the yolks if the whites are to be folded in later). Stir these ingredients only long enough to blend them, then add the melted butter and blend briefly. Ignore the lumps in the batter; the cakes will be lighter if the batter is not overmixed. Fold the stiffly beaten egg whites, if used, into the batter only until no white streaks appear.

Pour the batter onto preheated griddle, forming 4-inch cakes. (A pitcher or ladle is best for pouring.) Immediately sprinkle a tablespoon or so of the blueberries onto the cakes. Bake until a number of bubbles appear on the surface—about 3 minutes.

(continued)

Immediately turn the cakes with a pancake turner or spatula; bake another minute or two.

Transfer to a heated platter and proceed with next batch. The platter may be kept in a 150° to 200° F. oven but these cakes are best when served promptly and as successive batches leave the griddle. Serve with Orange Sauce.

Note: It is not desirable to fold the fruit into the batter before baking; the berries are liable to stick to the griddle.

ORANGE SAUCE

Makes about 1½ cups

½ cup softened butter
1 cup sifted confectioners' sugar

1 teaspoon grated orange rind
¼ cup orange juice

Beat the butter until it is very soft. An electric mixer is best for this. Add the confectioners' sugar gradually; continue beating at high speed until the mixture is light and fluffy. Add orange rind and orange juice and continue to beat until well blended.

BLUEBERRY MUFFINS

Home from a berrying expedition, a lovely conflict arises. What shall be done with these fruits of the summer? Shall it be blueberry pancakes served with orange sauce, blueberry pie, a steamed or baked pudding? Or blueberry muffins, bursting with fruit, made by the following recipe?

Makes about 2 dozen 2-inch muffins

2 cups sifted all-purpose flour
1 teaspoon salt
4 teaspoons baking power
½ cup sugar, sifted
2 eggs, well beaten
¾ cup milk

⅓ cup melted butter
1 cup blueberries (if frozen or canned berries are used, drain well)
⅓ cup flour
1 teaspoon cinnamon

Preheat oven to 425° F.
Butter muffin tins or insert paper liners.

Resift the 2 cups flour with the salt, baking powder, and ¼ cup of sugar. Combine the beaten eggs, milk, and melted butter; stir quickly into the dry ingredients only until ingredients are moistened. Unnecessary handling of the mixture results in tough, grainy muffins. Do not try to smooth out the lumps.

Sprinkle the ⅓ cup flour over the berries and combine quickly and lightly; stir immediately into the batter, lifting and mixing just long enough so that the berries combine with the batter. (If using frozen or canned berries, after draining them, sprinkle the flour over them, making sure they do not stand long enough for the flour coating to become pasty.) Fill muffin cups about ⅔ full. Combine the remaining ¼ cup sugar and the cinnamon and sprinkle a little over each muffin.

Bake 20 to 25 minutes. Remove the muffins immediately from the tins or turn them on their sides in the tins while they are cooling.

BLUEBERRY CORNBREAD

6 to 8 portions

2 cups sifted all-purpose flour	2 eggs, lightly beaten
½ teaspoon salt	1 cup yellow or water-ground
4 teaspoons baking powder	(white) cornmeal
½ cup softened butter (or	1½ cups milk
half butter, half	1 cup blueberries, preferably
margarine)	fresh
1 cup sugar, sifted	¼ cup flour

Preheat oven to 425° F.

Butter thoroughly a 9-by-14-inch glass or heavy metal baking dish. Resift the 2 cups flour with salt and baking powder. Cream butter or butter-margarine mixture until light and fluffy. Add sugar gradually, beating into creamed butter. Add beaten eggs and mix thoroughly. Add half the flour mixture, half the cornmeal, and half the milk. Blend only until mixture is moistened. Add remainder of flour mixture, milk, and cornmeal. Blend throroughly but do not overmix. Flour blueberries lightly

(continued)

and quickly with the ¼ cup flour and fold them into batter. Pour batter into baking dish, spread evenly, and bake about 30 minutes.

Cut into squares and serve.

DURGIN-PARK'S BLUEBERRY TEA CAKE

Makes 15 to 20 squares

3 cups sifted all-purpose flour	2 tablespoons melted butter
¾ teaspoon salt	1½ cups milk
4 teaspoons baking powder	1½ cups blueberries (if frozen
¾ cup sugar	or canned are used, drain
2 eggs, well beaten	them well)

¼–⅓ cup flour

Preheat oven to 400° F.

Butter a baking dish 9 by 14 by 3 inches; flour it lightly and tap off excess flour.

Resift the 3 cups flour with the salt and baking powder.

Mix sugar with the eggs, combining well. Add dry ingredients and the melted butter and milk. Mix only long enough to moisten all ingredients. Ignore any lumps; they will smooth out while baking.

Sprinkle the ¼ to ⅓ cup flour over the blueberries, less if using frozen or canned berries. Immediately add the floured berries to the batter; mix lightly, lifting and stirring only long enough to combine the berries in the batter.

Pour the batter into the baking pan, spreading it evenly. Bake about 30 minutes, or until a cake tester or toothpick inserted in center of cake emerges clean.

Note: Some minor liberties have been taken with this famous restaurant's recipe. More berries, for instance, are used, assuming that one's berrying expedition to Chappaquiddick or elsewhere was a rewarding one. (A Chappaquiddick friend, when asked to elaborate on that island's status regarding blueberries, replied: "Loaded! High bush, low bush, home-canned, home-frozen!")

CRANBERRIES

Tuesday was Cranberry Day in the town of Gay Head and the majority of inhabitants turned out, visiting the wild bogs to harvest the berries after the manner of their Indian ancestors. . . . The berries grow on common land, for Gay Head is the only Island town to preserve its "common," and all inhabitants have rights to the crop, and even descendants of Gay Head people who live elsewhere are granted whatever rights that may be theirs by inheritance.

—FROM THE *Vineyard Gazette*,
OCTOBER 16, 1953

Cranberries, like blueberries, are another long-used fruit with somewhat confusing early appellations. The herbalist John Josselyn referred to cranberries as "bear berries" because bears "use much to feed upon [them]." The true bearberry, however, is an entirely different plant, whose bright red berries are of no use as food but were recommended by Gerard, the best known of the early writers on folk medicine, as good for "burning agues."

On the western end of the Island, in the low-lying land behind the towering Gay Head cliffs, wild cranberry bogs still thrive on the peat beds formed by remains of the preglacial forests that once covered the Vineyard. The low-growing evergreen plants blanket the spongy soil, dwarfed and protected from the sweep of the sea winds by thickets of beach plum, bayberry, and bush poison ivy.

The rich-red berries have been used as food for hundreds of years; a local record from 1755 refers to their use by the early settlers, and of course the Indians gathered cranberries long before that. There is still token celebration of Cranberry Day in Gay Head, and though cranberries are no longer grown commercially on the Island, the industry is still enormously important on Cape Cod, and is credited with rescuing that entire area from economic disaster in the lean years following the Civil War.

Long associated with Thanksgiving and other festive occasions,

(continued)

the cranberry is actually widely adaptable for use in cakes, muffins, stews, pies, and puddings; and cranberry juice is a tart and delightful beverage.

There is also a high-bush "cranberry" that flourishes on the Vineyard. This is no relation to the true cranberry, but a species of viburnum and more closely related to the elderberry. Though not included in this book as a food source, high-bush cranberries have long been used medicinally, and quite acceptable jelly and juice can be made from its clusters of brilliant red fruits.

WILD CRANBERRY RELISHES

[*One Cooked, One Raw*]

Louise Aldrich Bugbee, whose cognizant comments on the local scene in the *Vineyard Gazette* may well become legend, makes these tart, tasty relishes each fall from wild Island cranberries given her by some Gay Head friends. "The 'trick' to both these recipes," says Mrs. Bugbee, "is to use the wild berries which are small and sweeter and have more of the cranberry flavor than the cultivated berries."

COOKED RELISH

Cook an equal amount of wild cranberries and sugar in a small amount of water until the skins pop on the berries. Let cool, then chill before serving. Less sugar may be used, if desired.

RAW RELISH

Grind about a pound of raw wild cranberries and one California orange, with the skin but without the seeds, if any. Sweeten to taste with a mild honey, such as clover or orange blossom, and allow to stand several days. This relish will keep a month or six weeks in the refrigerator or can be heated and sealed in jars to keep as long as desired. The cooking does not improve the flavor, and the relish that is allowed to stand for months only ferments a little and is still delicious. (*Authors' note:* With a little adjusting, this sounds like the making of a delicious homemade wine. The reader might consult a wine-making manual and experiment.)

SPICED CRANBERRIES

Makes about 3 cups

1 cup water	½ teaspoon ground allspice
1½ cups brown sugar	½ teaspoon ground cloves
½ teaspoon ground cinnamon	½ teaspoon ground ginger
1 pound cranberries, washed	

Combine all ingredients except cranberries in a heavy sauce-pan. Bring to a boil, then simmer over low heat for 20 minutes. Add cranberries (discard imperfect fruit). Cook over very low heat for 2 hours, stirring occasionally. Pack immediately into hot sterilized jars and seal. The spiced berries may also be kept in a covered container in the refrigerator.

Recommended as a relish for roast pork or cold meats.

STEAMED CRANBERRY PUDDING WITH FOAMY CRANBERRY SAUCE

6 to 8 portions

1 cup sifted all-purpose flour	1 cup coarsely chopped cranberries
½ teaspoon salt	1 egg, lightly beaten
2 teaspoons baking powder	⅓ cup milk
⅓ cup brown sugar, lightly packed in cup	Foamy Cranberry Sauce (see below)
½ cup fresh bread crumbs	
⅔ cup finely chopped suet (may be put through food chopper)	

Grease a 1-quart pudding mold with lid, or a 1-quart earthen-ware bowl (or even a 1-pound coffee can).

Sift the flour again with the salt and baking powder. Combine in a mixing bowl with the brown sugar, bread crumbs, suet, and chopped cranberries. Combine the beaten egg and milk, and add.

(continued)

Stir just enough to moisten and combine all ingredients. Turn into the greased mold. Mold should not be more than ¾ full. If lacking a lid, cover tightly with a piece of foil or a clean dish towel and tie securely.

Place the mold on a rack in a kettle of sufficient size. Fill kettle with boiling water until water comes three fourths of the way up the sides of the mold; place over high heat until steam forms, then reduce heat to a simmer, cover, and cook two hours. Add more water to kettle as needed.

Unmold pudding onto a heated platter, spoon a little Foamy Cranberry Sauce over the pudding and pass remainder of sauce in a separate bowl.

FOAMY CRANBERRY SAUCE

Makes about 1½ cups

6 tablespoons butter	1 egg yolk
¾ cup sifted confectioners' sugar	⅓ cup cranberry juice
	Grated rind of ½ orange
1 egg white, stiffly beaten	

In an electric mixer, preferably, work butter until soft, gradually adding confectioners' sugar. Beat well, then add egg yolk and beat at high speed until mixture is fluffy. Beat in cranberry juice and orange rind.

Fold in stiffly beaten egg white just before serving.

CRANBERRY UPSIDE-DOWN CAKE

6 tablespoons butter	¼ teaspoon salt
2¼ cups sugar, sifted	4 egg yolks
2 cups cranberries, washed	1 teaspoon vanilla
1 cup sifted cake flour	4 egg whites
1½ teaspoons baking powder	Whipped cream

Preheat oven to 350° F.

In a 9- or 10-inch skillet with ovenproof handle melt 4 tablespoons of the butter over moderate heat, add 1¼ cups of the sugar and stir the mixture well. Add the washed cranberries (discard imperfect fruit). Cook slowly about 5 minutes, stirring frequently. Remove skillet from heat.

In a small saucepan melt remaining 2 tablespoons butter over moderate heat and set aside to cool.

Resift the flour with the baking powder and salt. Beat egg yolks until thick and pale yellow, gradually adding all but 2 tablespoons of the remaining sugar. Continue beating until mixture is very thick. Beat in the vanilla.

In another bowl beat the egg whites until they form soft peaks, then beat in remaining 2 tablespoons sugar until egg whites form stiff peaks. Spoon half of the egg-white mixture over the egg-yolk mixture, sift on about half of the flour mixture and delicately fold in until partly blended. Add remaining egg-white mixture, sift on remainder of flour mixture, repeat folding-in process, and just before mixture is fully blended, gradually add remaining 2 tablespoons melted butter. Avoid overmixing or the egg whites will collapse.

Spoon the mixture over the prepared berries in the skillet. Bake 30 to 40 minutes. Cool slightly. Cover skillet with a plate of proper size, invert and turn out cake. Serve with whipped cream.

CRANBERRY NUT BREAD

1½ teaspoons baking powder
½ teaspoon baking soda
½ teaspoon salt
1 cup sugar, sifted
2 cups sifted all-purpose flour
1 cup washed cranberries, cut in halves
½ cup chopped walnuts or pecans

1 egg, well beaten
Juice of 1 orange, plus sufficient warm water to make 1 cup
3 tablespoons melted butter
1 teaspoon grated orange rind

Preheat oven to 350° F.

Grease a 4-by-8-inch loaf pan; coat it with flour; shake off excess flour.

(*continued*)

Sift the baking powder, soda, salt, and sugar with the sifted flour. Add cranberries and nutmeats and mix lightly. Combine beaten egg, orange juice, melted butter, and orange rind. Combine these ingredients with the flour mixture; stir only long enough to moisten. Fill the loaf pan.

Bake approximately 1 hour or until a cake tester or a toothpick, inserted in center of cake, emerges clean. Invert cake over rack and cool about 1 hour.

CRANBERRY CONSERVE

Makes about 5 eight-ounce glasses

4 cups cranberries
1½ cups water
3 cups sugar
½ cup seeded raisins (the plump, muscat type)
2 apples, preferably tart ones, coarsely chopped (cored but not peeled)
1 orange, put through largest blade of food chopper (reserve juice)

1 lemon, put through largest blade of food chopper (reserve juice)
2–4 tablespoons crystallized ginger, coarsely chopped
1 cup walnut meats, coarsely chopped
½ cup brandy

In a large kettle, at least 8-quart capacity, cook the cranberries in the water over moderately high heat until their skins pop open. Add the sugar, raisins, apples, chopped orange and juice, and chopped lemon and juice. Stir and mix all ingredients thoroughly. Bring to a boil and cook over moderately high heat, stirring frequently, until the mixture is thick and clear. (Cooking times vary. As the mixture thickens, place a small amount in a spoon, cool it slightly and let it drop back in the pan from the side of the spoon. When two large drops form on the edge of the spoon, one on each side, the conserve may be removed from the heat.)

Add 2 to 4 tablespoons of the crystallized ginger, depending on one's taste, the walnuts, and the brandy.

Pack in hot, sterilized jars; seal with melted paraffin.

CRANBERRY-APPLE RELISH

Makes about 2 to 3 cups

1 large apple, cored and
    chopped (may be put
    through medium blade
    of food grinder)
1 cup cranberries, chopped
    (may also be put through
    medium blade of food
    grinder)

¾ cup sugar
Pinch of salt
1 tablespoon crystallized
    ginger, chopped (optional
    and very good)

Combine all ingredients thoroughly. Let stand at least 1 hour before serving to allow flavors to develop.

CRANBERRY PUDDING

In a Victorian house set high on a Chappaquiddick knoll, surrounded by blueberry bushes and with a long view across the Katama sandspit and the ocean, Virginia and Vance Packard spend many pleasant months each year. While he writes, she works on her paintings (for some years a professional artist, she has had many canvases exhibited at shows), beachcombs, decorates the house, plans dinner parties, and does other enjoyable, creative things.

Cooking is one of her many pleasures; and this dessert is a favorite at Packard dinner parties. Described as one of her "treasured recipes," it was given to her by a very special friend. The finished pudding has a cakelike bottom and a crisp, meringue-type topping.

6 portions

2 cups fresh cranberries,
    washed and picked over
¾ cup sugar
¼ cup coarsely chopped
    walnuts

6 tablespoons melted butter
1 egg, well beaten
½ cup flour
Vanilla ice cream (optional)

(*continued*)

Preheat oven to 350° F.

Place cranberries in a well-buttered 8-inch pie plate. Mix ¼ cup of the sugar with the nuts and 4 tablespoons of the melted butter and pour over the cranberries. To the beaten egg add the remaining ½ cup sugar combined with the flour, then add the remaining 2 tablespoons melted butter. Beat a bit more. Pour over berry mixture. Bake 45 minutes.

The pudding is at its best when served warm with a scoop of vanilla ice cream on top of each serving.

ETHEL'S CRANBERRY CONSERVE

While she rested on her sofa in her tiny, snug West Tisbury cottage under a handsome striped blanket woven many years ago out of wool from Farmer Whiting's sheep, the elderly lady who makes this delicious preparation described it as "sort of rehashed Fanny Farmer." She studied her tattered and bespattered 1924 edition of that most venerable of cook books and then read out her version of this excellent conserve. The main change is the addition of extra raisins and the omission of nuts because they get "all gooey."

Makes about 8 standard jelly jars

1 quart cranberries, washed	3¼ cups sugar
⅔ cup water	⅔ cup boiling water
1 scant cup seeded raisins	
1 California orange, thinly sliced and chopped into tiny pieces	

Combine cranberries and water in a saucepan, bring to a boil over moderate heat and cook until the skins split. Allow to cool slightly, then put cranberries and cooking liquid through a food mill. Replace in saucepan and add all other ingredients. Bring to a boil, then reduce heat to a simmer and cook about 25 minutes, or until quite thick. Pour or spoon into clean hot jars and seal at once with paraffin.

Cakes,
Cookies, and Breads

Chapter 8

General Directions for Making a Cake: Do not use the hand to make a cake, but a wooden spoon or spad. Earthern is best to make a cake in. In receipts where milk is used, never mix sweet and sour milk . . . even when either alone would not do it. . . . Try whether cake is done by piercing it with a broom splinter and if nothing adheres it is done.

—FROM THE *Vineyard Gazette,*
JUNE 29, 1848

Baking seems to have been a favorite occupation of early Vineyard housewives, as it was of most New England homemakers. Cakes in particular—along with pies, of course—have long lured the ungodly as well as the godly to church suppers and other community affairs. And, for several decades, various groups of civic-minded ladies have set up tables several times each summer under the magnificent linden tree on Vineyard Haven's Main Street and raised funds for worthy causes by selling to vulnerable passersby cakes oozing with rich-brown chocolate or similarly irresistible home-baked goodies. Bake shops flourished, as they do now. In 1945 the Meiklehams' little shop in Edgartown, the Seagull and the Whale, advertised "Delicious FFV [Finest Food Value] Cake Squares, Penoches, MV Square Deals, Crisp Cookies, Nutritious Date Nut Bread." One of this book's authors remembers nostalgically a summertime experience of long standing—the first trip of the season to Argie Humphries' North Tisbury bakery, where one could munch on a freshly baked, still-warm date square and savor the air while waiting for Argie to count out the cookies.

Cook books—old ones and new ones—seem stuffed with recipes for baked goods, many traditional, some relying on mixes and other shortcuts. This being so, we have chosen only a few recipes to represent the cakes, cookies and breads of the Vineyard. Most are special favorites, family favorites, from local cooks. One or two, however, will look—and taste—familiar to the summer people who like to stop in the little local bake shops and choose a bag of goodies for the weekend.

CHILMARK CHOCOLATE CAKE

This true chocolate fudge cake, rich and delicious, has long been a favorite at ladies' gatherings up-Island. It should satisfy, at least temporarily, the most rabid chocolate addicts. Don't be alarmed if the batter seems too thin. This is characteristic of the cake.

4 squares unsweetened baking chocolate	1¾ cups milk
2 tablespoons butter	¾ teaspoon salt
2 cups sifted sugar	1 teaspoon vanilla
4 egg yolks, beaten until light	1 teaspoon baking soda
	2 cups sifted cake flour

Preheat oven to 350°.

Grease and flour two 9-inch round cake pans.

In a heavy saucepan, melt chocolate and butter over low heat. Pour into mixing bowl and add sugar, egg yolks, and 1 cup of the milk, then beat until smooth. Add salt, vanilla, ½ cup of the milk, and soda dissolved in the remaining ¼ cup milk and beat some more. Then add, about ⅔ cup at a time, the sifted cake flour. Beat slowly while adding the flour (use low speed if using an electric mixer). Bake 30 to 35 minutes. Cool cakes in pans for 5 minutes, on racks. Run a knife around sides of pan, invert each on a plate, then turn right side up on a rack. Cool completely before frosting.

Frost with Soft Chocolate Frosting (see page 249).

ENGLISH LEMON CAKE

The grandmother of a Vineyard cook used to serve this cake in England; it now is a special favorite in several Island and off-Island households. It is as lemony as the Chilmark Chocolate Cake is chocolatey.

Makes 1 loaf

1⅓ cup sugar	½ teaspoon salt
1 scant cup butter, softened	1 teaspoon baking powder
2 eggs	½ cup milk
1½ cups flour	Juice of 1 large lemon

Grated rind of ½ lemon

Preheat oven to 350° F.

Grease a standard-sized loaf pan.

Cream 1 cup sugar and the butter together. Add eggs, one at a time, beating in well until mixture is light and fluffy. Resift flour with salt and baking powder; add to first mixture alternately with milk, beating in well. Pour into the pan and bake 45 minutes.

Mix the remaining ⅓ cup sugar, lemon juice, and lemon rind in a small saucepan, heat until sugar is dissolved, and pour over cake in pan while cake is still hot. Let cool to room temperature before removing cake from pan.

DAFFODIL CAKE

A Vineyard favorite for generations, relished for its marble-cake effect of angel-food and sponge cake. An electric mixer is almost essential in making this cake.

THE ANGEL-FOOD CAKE

8 egg whites	½ cup sifted cake flour
¾ teaspoon cream of tartar	¾ cup sugar, sifted
⅛ teaspoon salt	1 teaspoon almond extract

(continued)

Preheat oven to 325° F.

Beat egg whites until foamy; add cream of tartar and salt, and continue beating until mixture holds a point and has a slightly glazed appearance. Resift flour with sugar, sifting it slowly over egg whites and folding it in gradually until no flour shows. Fold in almond extract.

THE SPONGE CAKE

8 egg yolks
⅛ teaspoon salt
¾ cup sugar, sifted
¾ cup sifted cake flour
¼ teaspoon baking powder

¼ cup boiling water, slightly cooled
Grated rind of 1 small orange (or 1 teaspoon orange extract)

Beat egg yolks until light and foamy, add salt, and beat in sugar gradually, continuing to beat until the mixture is thick and forms a slowly dissolving ribbon when it falls back onto itself. Resift flour with baking powder, then gradually fold into egg mixture, alternating with the boiling water. Fold in the orange rind or extract.

Place these two batters, about 1 cup at a time, in an ungreased tube pan, alternating the colors. Bake 50 to 60 minutes.

Invert over a cake rack for at least 1½ hours before removing from pan.

ORANGE KISS ME CAKE

There must have been good reason for tacking such a ridiculous name onto such a delectable concoction as this old-time favorite cake. Whatever it is, we failed to uncover it. But the cake was the topic of a good deal of pleasant banter in Louise Bugbee's *Gazette* columns not long ago, and since one of this book's authors also "grew up on it" we include it in spite of its name.

Orange Kiss Me Cake, by the way, is even better the second day after baking than it is when freshly baked, if one can resist cutting into it that long.

THE CAKE

1 large navel orange
1 cup seeded raisins (muscat type)
2 cups sifted flour
1½ teaspoons baking soda
1 teaspoon salt
½ cup shortening (half butter, half margarine is suggested)

1 cup sugar, sifted
2 eggs
1 cup milk
⅓ cup walnuts, coarsely chopped

Preheat oven to 350° F.

Grease a loaf pan (9 by 5 by 3 inches).

Squeeze the orange, reserving the juice for the topping. Put the orange (rind and pulp) and the raisins through medium blade of a food chopper. Set these ingredients aside.

Resift the flour with the baking soda and salt. Beat the shortening (an electric mixer is recommended) until softened, gradually add the sugar, and continue to beat until the mixture is fluffy. Add the eggs, one at a time, beating well after each addition. At low mixer speed, or stirring by hand, add half the flour mixture and half the milk. Mix only enough to moisten ingredients. Add the reserved chopped orange and raisins; blend briefly. Add remainder of flour mixture and milk. Blend only enough to moisten. Add the walnuts. Pour the batter into the loaf pan and bake approximately 1 hour. Cake is done when a cake tester or a toothpick inserted in center of cake comes out clean. Leave in pan while preparing the topping.

THE TOPPING

Orange juice (reserved from cake recipe)
⅓ cup brown sugar, lightly packed

½ teaspoon cinnamon
⅓ cup walnuts, coarsely chopped

(continued)

Combine the reserved orange juice, the brown sugar mixed with the cinnamon and the remaining ⅓ cup of walnuts. Pour this mixture over the finished cake in pan while the cake is still hot. Let stand until cool. This cake should be sliced in its pan.

Note: The cake the author grew up on was made without the topping. The orange juice went into the cake. If you make your cake this way, reduce the milk content by ¼ cup.

SANTA CLAUS CAKES

Another old family recipe, this one was devised in England over a hundred years ago by the grandmother of a contemporary Vineyard cook, who has now passed it along to her son's bride. These chewy confections keep well when stored in an air-tight container, if you can hide them from the family until you are ready to put them out during the holidays. Traditionally, in their family of origin, two must be left on the hearth on Christmas Eve for Santa (he always manages to find them, assisted, perhaps, by one of the family poodles).

Makes 40 bars

2 cups dates, cut in small pieces (or buy precut ones)	½ teaspoon salt
3 egg yolks, beaten	1 cup coarsely chopped English walnuts (black walnuts are far better, if available)
1 scant cup sugar	
½ cup sifted flour	
1 tablespoon baking powder	3 egg whites, beaten stiff

½ cup sugar (more if needed)

Preheat oven to 375° F.

Grease a baking pan (about 10 by 14 by 2 inches).

Cut dates (kitchen shears work fairly well). If they are stuck together and hard to cut, sprinkle them with a bit of the flour, or dip scissors in hot water. Beat egg yolks until light yellow. Beat in the 1 scant cup sugar. Resift flour with baking powder and salt. Put dates and nuts into a fairly large bowl, sift flour mixture over them, mix well with a fork, coating them as well as possible. Add egg-yolk-and-sugar mixture; stir well. Beat egg whites until stiff; mix gently into fruit-nut mixture. Spoon out into the baking pan and spread evenly over bottom. Bake 5 minutes at 375° F.; lower heat to 325° F. and bake 20 minutes more. Cut with a silver knife into bars, 4 strips lengthwise and 10 strips crosswise. Cool in pan 15 minutes. Remove carefully with a pancake turner and roll each bar in the ½ cup granulated sugar while warm. Cool to room temperature before storing.

TWO-LAYER COOKIES
[*Brown-Sugar Nut Squares*]

These scrumptious cookies, favorites for years at an up-Island bakeshop, were one of the first things put down as essential when the plan for this cook book was conceived. But how to get the recipe? Even before then we had long tried to steal or cajole the secret from their maker. Then, to our joy, we found them in *Vineyard Fare,* the useful—and, fortunately for us, not copyrighted—collection of recipes published in 1963 by the Martha's Vineyard Hospital Auxiliary. So here they are.

Makes about 2 dozen 2-inch squares

COOKIE BASE

2 egg yolks
1 cup brown sugar, lightly
   packed
½ cup softened butter (or
   half butter, half
   margarine)

1½ cups sifted flour
1 teaspoon baking powder
½ teaspoon salt
1 teaspoon vanilla
¾ cup chopped pecans or
   walnuts

Preheat oven to 275° F.
Grease a 10 by 14 inch baking pan.
Beat egg yolks until light yellow, then combine with the brown sugar and butter. Beat well. Resift the flour with the baking powder and salt and gradually add to the egg-yolk mixture. Add the vanilla and blend well. Spread the mixture in the baking pan and sprinkle with the chopped nuts.

MERINGUE TOPPING

2 egg whites
¼ teaspoon cream of tartar

1 cup brown sugar, lightly
packed

Beat egg whites with cream of tartar until stiff peaks form. Lightly fold in brown sugar. Carefully spread this mixture over the cookie base and bake 1 hour. Let cool, then cut into squares.

BLACK-WALNUT MERINGUES

Makes about 3 dozen meringues

2 egg whites (at room
    temperature)
¼ teaspoon salt
1 cup sifted sugar

½ teaspoon vanilla
1 cup black-walnut meats,
    coarsely chopped

Preheat oven to 225° F.

Cover a cookie sheet with heavy brown paper.

Beat egg whites with salt until stiff peaks are formed. (An electric mixer does this efficiently.) Add the sugar in small amounts, no more than 2 tablespoons at a time. Beat well at high speed after each addition. The mixture should be thick and glossy. Fold in the vanilla and the nut meats.

Drop the meringues from a teaspoon onto the cookie sheet. A scant teaspoonful is sufficient for each meringue. Bake until dry, about 45 minutes. Turn off oven and allow the meringues to "cure" in the oven until cool.

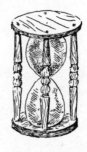

CONGO BARS

[*Brown-Sugar Brownies*]

Makes about 30 two-inch squares

1¾ cups butter (or half
butter, half margarine)
1 cup brown sugar, lightly
packed
3 eggs
2¾ cups sifted flour

2½ teaspoons baking powder
½ teaspoon salt
1 package chocolate bits
1 cup walnuts, coarsely
chopped

Preheat oven to 350° F.
Grease a baking pan (10 by 14 by 2 inches).

Butter and eggs should be used at room temperature. Cream butter, gradually add sugar, beating until light and fluffy. Add the eggs, one at a time, continuing to beat the mixture. Sift flour, baking powder, and salt together and add gradually, by hand, to creamed mixture, folding flour mixture in. Fold in chocolate bits and nut meats. Spread in the baking pan and bake about 30 minutes. Cool and cut into squares.

CHOCOLATE MERINGUES

Makes about 40 one-inch meringues

3 egg whites at room
temperature
½ teaspoon salt
½ teaspoon cream of tartar
1 cup sifted sugar

3 tablespoons cocoa
2 teaspoons water
½ teaspoon instant coffee
(optional)
Nut meats (optional)

Preheat oven to 225° F.
Cover a cookie sheet with heavy brown paper.

Beat egg whites with salt and cream of tartar until stiff peaks are formed (an electric mixer is fine for this). Using half the sugar, add it in small amounts, no more than 2 tablespoons at a

(continued)

time. Beat well after each addition. Combine the cocoa and remaining sugar. Add the water, a few drops at a time, alternately with the cocoa-sugar mixture. The coffee powder may be added also at this time. Beat the mixture until it is thick and glossy. Drop by scant teaspoonfuls on the cookie sheet, shaping into small cones. A nut meat may top each meringue, for decoration. Bake about 45 minutes, or until meringues are dry and will retain their shape. Turn off oven and allow them to "cure" in oven until cool.

FRUIT PASTRY SQUARES

Makes about 2 dozen squares

PASTRY

**Double recipe for 2-crust
pastry (or double recipe
Flaky Pie Crust, page 214),
chilled**

FRUIT FILLING

**3–4 cups applesauce seasoned
with cinnamon and
nutmeg (or 3–4 cups
mincemeat, or 3–4 cups
any favorite jam, with 1
or more tablespoons
lemon juice added to
reduce sweetness)**

**1 egg yolk mixed with 1
tablespoon water**

Preheat oven to 450° F.
A rimmed, 12- by 16-inch cookie sheet will be required.
Divide chilled pastry in half. Roll it on floured surface and fit one piece in bottom of cookie sheet. It should be about ¼ inch thick. Spread it with the applesauce, mincemeat, or jam. Roll the second piece of dough, fold it in half and place fold in middle of

pan. Unfold and adjust it to fit. Trim edges with a sharp knife and press together to seal. Make small slits in the pastry to allow steam to escape during baking.

Brush the crust with the egg-yolk mixture and bake 15 minutes or until crust is golden brown. Reduce heat to 350° F. and bake until pastry is done, a total cooking time of approximately 45 minutes to 1 hour.

Cool, then cut into squares or rectangles.

BLUE RIBBON GRAHAM BREAD

One of the pleasanter traditions on the Island is the festive three-day Agricultural Fair held each August at the fairgrounds in West Tisbury. Draft-horse pulling, dog show, and merry-go-round—there is something for everyone, including roast oysters, raw clams, and cotton candy. Competition among the exhibitors for the first-prize blue ribbons can hardly be called fierce, in most classes, but it is always a thrill to find one tucked under your five green tomatoes or the collage you assembled from beach litter picked up along the South Shore.

This bread, which has long delighted neighbors, guests, and family, won a blue ribbon when it was entered in the 1970 fair by the North Tisbury author of this book. Use of a somewhat gritty, rough-ground graham flour and a full-flavored dark molasses is important.

Makes 2 loaves

1 package granulated or
    compressed yeast
¼ cup lukewarm water
1 rounded teaspoon brown
    sugar
1 cup boiling water
1 cup evaporated milk,
    scalded
¼–⅓ cup dark molasses
2 tablespoons butter or
    margarine

2 scant teaspoons salt
4 cups graham flour (or 3 cups
    graham, 1 cup pumper-
    nickel)
1–2 cups white flour
3–5 tablespoons melted butter
    or margarine (for greasing
    loaves and loaf pans)

(continued)

Combine yeast, warm water, and sugar; mix well and set aside. (If using granulated yeast, water should be slightly hotter than lukewarm.) Pour boiling water and scalded milk into a large, heatproof bowl; add molasses, butter or margarine, and salt. Stir until thoroughly blended, then cool. When a few drops on your wrist feel just pleasingly warm, stir in yeast mixture. Then add graham flour, about ½ cup at a time, mixing it in well. A wooden spoon is good for this. Add white flour next, until dough stiffens (after the addition of about 5 cups of flour altogether). Turn dough onto a floured board, round it into a big lump, and knead it for about 8 minutes according to kneading directions given for Massa Sovada (see page 267). Greasing the hands from time to time with vegetable oil will make the kneading easier. Round kneaded dough mass and place in a large, greased bowl. Smooth a little vegetable oil or melted butter over top of dough, cover with a damp tea towel or waxed paper, put in a warm place and let rise until double its bulk. (If you are making this on a sunny morning on the Vineyard, the inside of your car or the attic of your old house might do. Otherwise, dough can be placed in closed, unlighted oven with a pan of hot water on a lower shelf under dough.)

When dough has doubled in bulk, empty it onto a floured board and knead it down gently for about 1 minute. Cut dough mass in half and shape 2 loaves, tucking the sides and ends under so that the top is smooth but not too tightly stretched. Place each loaf in a greased, standard-size loaf pan, put pans back into un-lighted oven (you can omit the hot water this time), and let loaves rise until double in size. Be sure to give the yeast time to work—whole-wheat bread dough rises more slowly than white.

Remove pans carefully from oven and keep them free from drafts while oven is heating to 400° F. Bake the bread 20 minutes, then reduce heat to 350° F. (this is a good time to see how your bread is faring), and bake another 35 to 40 minutes. Remove pans from oven. Brush melted butter lightly and evenly over top of each loaf. Remove loaves carefully from pans and place on wire rack to cool. Do not store bread away until it is completely cool—if you do it may mold.

TOGUS BREAD

We found this bread listed in an early book of Vineyard recipes and were intrigued by its name. Investigations made us suspect a typographical error in this earlier printing, for though "togus" was nowhere to be found, "togue" is, especially interesting to us, an Algonquian Indian word for the even more euphonious word (also of Indian origin), the namaycush, the name of a particular kind of large trout. Since the Vineyard Indians are a branch of the Algonquians, we think this should be called Togue Bread, and feel that the Gay Head Indians used to eat it with their togue, or namaycush. We made some and had it with baked fish, but recommend it also with such dishes as baked beans, since it strongly resembles—and may be a precursor of—Boston brown bread. Though the bread takes a long time to steam, it takes only a few minutes to mix up and is a comforting sort of thing to have bubbling on the stove on a winter morning.

Makes 1 round loaf

1½ cups sweet milk	1½ cups sifted Indian meal
½ cup sour milk or butter-	(yellow cornmeal)
milk	½ cup sifted white flour
¼ cup molasses	½ teaspoon soda
¾ teaspoon salt	

Grease a tall 1-pound coffee can.

Mix sweet and sour milk; warm molasses slightly in measuring utensil (so it will pour and mix more easily) and add to milk. Stir in well. Resift cornmeal and flour with soda and salt. Add milk-molasses mixture, a little at a time, to prevent lumping. Mix thoroughly; or put into a shaker and shake well to mix. Pour into the coffee can and seal top tightly with foil. (Be sure to leave a space of half an inch or so at the top of the can, since the bread will expand.) A heavy rubber band may be used to fasten the foil securely; also good is the paper-covered wire used for tying up

(*continued*)

garden plants. Place sealed, filled can on a rack in a kettle of boiling water deep enough to immerse about 90 percent of the can. Weight can with a plate to prevent floating, cover kettle, and steam in boiling water bath for 4 hours. Add hot water when needed to maintain original level. Let bread cool somewhat in can, then unmold and allow to cool to room temperature before slicing.

Note: This bread tends to mold, so keep it in a plastic bag in the refrigerator if it is to be kept more than a day or so. Allow to warm to room temperature before eating.

MARY ALLEY'S BANANA BREAD

The general store has been, as it should be, the social center of West Tisbury for many generations. "Dealers in Almost Everything" proclaims the sign that for many years has swung from the porch, and anyone in the neighborhood who ever has needed anything, from a piece of sandpaper to a pint of chocolate swirl ice cream, has taken the sign at Alley's Store quite literally.

One thing that Alley's doesn't deal in is this banana bread that is made in Mrs. Alley's kitchen in the big, old white house across the street and down a bit from the store. Its fame reached us from one of the Alleys' neighbors, who is given a loaf of it every Christmas. Its source, Mary Alley told us, was not a cook book but a long-ago friend in New Hampshire. She stressed that this is not cakelike, but breadlike, and thus very good for sandwiches. A filling of cream cheese and ground nuts should be especially good.

Makes 1 loaf

1¾ cups flour, sifted	1 scant cup sugar
½ teaspoon salt	2 eggs, lightly beaten
1 level teaspoon soda	3 large bananas, mashed
⅓ cup butter, softened	

Preheat oven to 350° F.

Oil a 9- by 5- by 3-inch loaf pan. (Mrs. Alley uses a piece of waxed paper on the bottom of her pan to facilitate removal of bread).

Resift flour with salt and baking soda. Cream the butter and sugar until light and fluffy; add eggs and mix well. Stir in bananas. Sift flour mixture into banana mixture about ½ cup at a time, mixing well but gently between each addition. Do not beat batter. Pour bread batter in pan. Bake 1 hour; cool slightly. Remove from pan and cool on rack. Let loaf cool completely before storing away.

CORNBREAD

"As a boy," says venerable Vineyard journalist Joseph Chase Allen, who grew up on a Chilmark farm, "I seldom ate cornbread or brown bread made from either white or bolted yellow meal. When we had those things, which was often, I would be sent to the barn and there I would get a bucket of the yellow meal ground for animal food. It had to be sifted more than the packaged meal, but we always thought that the food tasted better. I still do."

Such rustic procedures are no longer feasible for most of us, but this honest, simple food does deserve to be made and not just poured out of a cornbread-mix box.

8 to 10 portions

2 cups sifted all-purpose
    flour
4 teaspoons baking powder
¾ teaspoon salt
¾ cup sugar
1 cup yellow or stone-ground
    (white) cornmeal

2 eggs, beaten
⅓ cup melted butter, slightly
    cooled
1½ cups milk

Preheat oven to 425°.

Butter thoroughly a heavy glass or metal baking dish, 9 by 14 inches, or oil it.

Sift flour, baking powder, salt, and sugar into a large bowl. Mix in the cornmeal. Add eggs, melted butter, and milk and,

(continued)

working quickly, combine all ingredients thoroughly but only until well blended. Pour batter into the buttered baking dish and bake approximately 30 to 35 minutes. Cool slightly in pan, cut into squares, and serve warm.

BONA BREAD

When asked how she made these crunchy cheese-filled creations, the elderly North Tisbury lady responsible for inventing them replied: "Heavens, I don't know—I haven't used a cook book for fifty years!" She tried a few batches, then typed up instructions for us. These are especially good with a hot soup at lunch.

Makes about 40 bars (¾ *inch by 2 inches*)

1 cup sifted rye flour
1 cup sifted whole-wheat flour
1 cup sifted white flour
1 teaspoon salt
Freshly ground black pepper
    to taste
5 teaspoons baking powder

2 tablespoons caraway seeds
2 cups grated sharp Cheddar
    cheese
6 tablespoons vegetable oil
2 eggs, lightly beaten
Milk

Preheat oven to 450° F.
Lightly grease a cookie sheet.
Resift the three kinds of flour, salt, and pepper. Mix in the caraway seeds with the baking powder, and the grated cheese. Stir in oil, a little at a time, then stir in eggs. When well blended, add just enough milk to enable bread to be rolled out ½ to ¾ inch thick on a lightly floured board. Cut bread into finger-sized bars and place on the baking sheet. Bake 20 minutes.

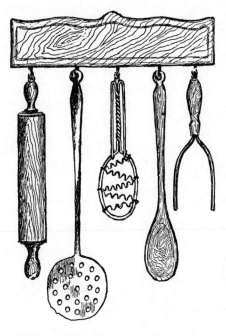

Pies, Puddings,
and Other Desserts

Chapter 9

PIES

In Colonial days New England housewives often baked as many as 100 pies at a time, stacked them in big jars, and stored them in a shed where they'd freeze. When a pie was wanted it was placed in the pie cupboard in the fireplace chimney and thawed out.

—FROM *The Yankee Cookbook,*
BY IMOGENE WOLCOTT*

Pies," says the *Columbia-Viking Desk Encyclopedia,* "were known to Romans, and were common in England by 14th cent.; mince pie early became a festive Christmas dish." Webster thinks perhaps the word derived from *magpie,* which brings to mind the "four and twenty blackbirds" that met such an inopportune end beneath a pastry crust. New Englanders—including Vineyarders—have never concerned themselves about how pies originated; they just originated their own with whatever was at hand or took their fancy—bits of cooked meat and vegetables, leftover fish or shellfish, any sort of fresh, dried, or preserved fruit, or almost any of these in seemingly ungastronomic combinations. Who first decided, for instance, that an apt mixture of roasting beef, molasses, lemon rind, beef fat, salt, raisins and a dozen or so other things, including a good dollop of brandy, would produce mincemeat? Some ingenious English kitchen lady of the Middle Ages, it seems, who might be pleased to know that her invention was brought to a new world centuries later and carried out with whatever of the standard ingredients were available in the snowbound kitchens of the New England settlements.

Pies have always been—and still are—traditional fare at Island gatherings. *Gazette* accounts of long-ago church suppers, Grange meetings, benevolent-society dinners, golden wedding celebrations, almost always include the word "pie," and they still do. Nowadays, far too many pies arrive in the kitchen via the grocery bag, done up and ready to defrost, brown and serve, or merely take out of the

* Coward, McCann, Inc., New York, 1963.

bakery box and slice. We don't disdain all ready-made pies, and certainly prepared pastry mixes and frozen ready-to-bake crusts are a blessing to those of us who simply can't roll a piecrust out of a wretched little heap of crumbly dough. But any cook who summers or lives year-round on the Vineyard should surely present her family with at least one summer-flavored delight—a fresh-baked rhubarb, blueberry, blackberry, or apple pie.

FLAKY PIE CRUST

Since standard cook books deal with various types of pie crusts, and many cooks also possess special favorites of their own, only one recipe for pie crust is given in this book (with the exception of the pastry formula for Beefsteak-and-Kidney Pie—see page 121). This crust is slightly sweet, flaky, and tender, but with a hint of cookie dough in its structure. The authors consider it interesting enough to wish to share it with their readers.

Butter is essential to the recipe, and so is lard, the latter having been used exclusively by New England cooks for generations, for it produces a crust of maximum flakiness. Hydrogenated shortenings, vegetable in origin, have almost replaced unfashionable lard, which is made from animal fat. A vegetable shortening may be used here, in combination with the butter, but it is not recommended.

Makes 2 nine-inch crusts

> 2¼ cups sifted all-purpose
> flour
> ½ teaspoon salt
> 1½ tablespoons sugar
> ⅓ cup butter, well chilled

> ⅓ cup lard or hydrogenated
> shortening, well chilled
> ½ cup commercially soured
> cream
> 1 egg yolk

In a chilled mixing bowl combine flour, salt, and sugar. Add butter and lard. Working quickly, blend flour-and-fat mixture with the fingertips until mixture resembles coarse meal. Add sour cream and egg yolk. Stir lightly with a fork until mixture is just blended.

Form into a ball, divide in two and refrigerate at least 1 hour. When it is thoroughly chilled, roll the dough on a lightly floured board and proceed with your pie recipe.

Note: When dividing the dough in two parts, one part should be slightly larger if to be used for two-crust pie. Use the larger one for the bottom crust.

BRANDIED APPLE PIE

This is the absolute favorite of one of the authors.

Pastry for 9-inch crust
(page 214)
6–8 tart apples, medium
size (or large windfall
apples)
1 cup brown sugar
½ teaspoon cinnamon

2 tablespoons butter, cut in
small pieces or melted
1 tablespoon lemon juice
2 tablespoons brandy
2 tablespoons cream or 1
tablespoon beaten egg
yolk

Prepare a single-crust pie dough and chill it. Peel, core, and slice apples; place in a large bowl with brown sugar, cinnamon, butter, lemon juice, and brandy. Mix well and let stand ½ hour.

Preheat oven to 450° F. while assembling pie.

Place apple mixture directly in a 9-inch pie pan. Roll out pie crust and place carefully over apple mixture. Flute edges of crust and prick in several places with a fork, or cut several slits. Brush crust with cream or with egg yolk combined with a little water. Bake at 450° F. for 15 minutes; reduce heat to 350° and bake another 20 to 30 minutes. (Apples may be tested for doneness by carefully inserting a paring knife into crust.)

LEMON-BLUEBERRY PIE

2 eggs, separated
1 cup sugar
4 teaspoons flour
⅛ teaspoon salt
Grated rind of 1 lemon

Juice of 1 lemon
1 teaspoon melted butter
¾ cup milk, scalded
9-inch unbaked pie shell
1½ cups fresh blueberries

(continued)

Preheat oven to 450° F.

Beat the egg yolks until light and thick. Combine sugar, flour, and salt; add the egg yolks, lemon rind, lemon juice, and butter. Beat well. Gradually beat in the scalded milk. Beat the egg whites stiff and fold them in. Pour the mixture into the unbaked pie shell and sprinkle the blueberries on top. Bake 10 minutes on middle shelf of oven. Reduce heat to 350° and bake an additional 30 minutes. Let pie cool; then chill it thoroughly and serve very cold. A little egg white brushed on the pie shell before filling it will help to prevent sogginess.

Note: Thinly sliced fresh peaches or rhubarb, or raspberries or strawberries could be used instead of blueberries. The mixture may also be baked as a fruit pudding, without the pastry.

BLACK-AND-BLUE PIE

Blackberries are often disdained because of their strong flavor and multiple seeds (not to mention the aggravations involved with picking them). True blackberry lovers, however, feel they are the finest of the wild fruits and, conversely, consider blueberries insipid-tasting and textureless. A pie pleasing to both extremes—and everyone in the middle as well—can be constructed by following a regular blueberry-pie recipe, but using half blueberries and half blackberries. A bit more thickening agent (1 tablespoon flour or 1 teaspoon cornstarch or arrowroot) should be added to the sugar to absorb the extra juice released by the blackberries.

DEEP-DISH BLACKBERRY PIE

For forty years or more, first in Kentucky, then in North Carolina, and now on Martha's Vineyard, the first blackberries picked every season have been preempted in one particular household by the cook of the family, who gave us this recipe. No complaints come from the berry pickers—only the insistence that she "make plenty of it."

Rather than reformulate what is basically a very simple dessert to prepare, we give you her instructions just as received.

Freshly picked blackberries. At least one cup per person with more if you can get them. Sprinkle with about one tablespoon flour per cup, tossing lightly with wide fork. Place in pretty, wide, shallow pottery dish. Cover with half as much sugar as berries.

Make a standard pie crust, only roll it a bit thicker than usual. Cover berries and prick top. Bake in moderate oven about three quarters of an hour or until fork finds berries well done and crust is nicely browned.

Serve with lots of rich cream or ice cream. Yummy.

An alternate method of preparation, which avoids any possibility of the flour lumping, would be to combine the flour with the sugar and sprinkle the mixture over the top of the berries after they are placed in the dish.

We suggest an oven temperature of 450° F. for 10 to 15 minutes, then 350° F. for the rest of the baking period. This particular cook likes things sweet; for some tastes, a ratio of one-third as much sugar as berries might be better.

MINCE PIE

The files of the *Vineyard Gazette* reveal some distinctive thoughts about mincemeat:

Mincemeat, in the eyes of the old school of Vineyard cooks, is a thing both sacred and seasonable . . . a survival of older customs, of course, when the native fruits ripened and could be obtained in profusion, when farmers killed and dressed their winter supply of meat and the supplies of spices from the south was greatest.

Some of the older cooks will declare that no meat is as suitable for mincemeat as beef cheekmeat and ox tongue. Others are equally certain that beef hearts produce the finest variety; others still use nothing but the better grades of corned brisket and the like. And nearly all will seriously assert that to produce the finest grade of mincemeat the common food grinder should not be em-

(*continued*)

ployed at all but that all ingredients should be laboriously chopped in an old-fashioned chopping bowl with the broad bladed chopping knife. Tedious labor this; nevertheless it is still performed by certain artists of the profession.

The apples must be sour; seeded raisins are not commonly adjudged as being quite as excellent as those with seeds, and the currants also vary in quality according to the best cooks.

When the mincemeat is gently spread in its bed of crust, covered with another ornamented with fans and scrolls produced by a scrimshaw jagging-wheel (produced by a whaling ancestor) and properly baked, this mince pie offers a temptation to a chronic dyspeptic and transports the ordinary diner to heights of ecstasy incapable of achievement by any baser variety of mince pie.

Suggested as a guide only, the following recipe may be adapted by the creative cook. It will produce five quarts of mincemeat. Whatever is not used at once for pies may be packed at once into hot, sterilized jars, sealed, and stored on the shelf that holds the other treasured home-canned foods.

Makes 5 quarts

2 pounds lean beef, chopped
1 pound beef suet, chopped
4 quarts (8 pounds) tart apples (greenings, Baldwin, windfall), peeled, cored, sliced
¼ pound candied orange peel, chopped
¾ pound candied citron, chopped
¼ pound candied lemon peel, chopped
1½ pounds sugar
1 quart cider, preferably aged

2 pounds seeded raisins
Juice and rind of 1 lemon
1 cup orange juice
2 teaspoons cinnamon
1 whole nutmeg, grated
1 teaspoon mace
1 teaspoon ground cloves
1 teaspoon salt
1 pound nut meats, coarsely chopped (optional)
Pastry for piecrust, as needed (for 2-crust pies)
1 or 2 tablespoons brandy per pie
1 beaten egg yolk per 2 pies

Combine all ingredients except pastry, brandy, and egg yolk and cook slowly for at least 2 hours, stirring frequently.

Preheat oven to 450° F.

Line 8- or 9-inch pie pans with unbaked pastry (see page 214). Fill each pie shell with at least 2 cups precooked mincemeat. Sprinkle brandy over mixture and cover with upper crust (rolling the top crust around the rolling pin and unrolling it over the pie simplifies this step). Flute edges; prick top of crust with fork or small knife in several places. Add a little water to beaten egg yolk and brush over tops of pies. Bake 15 minutes at 450° F., reduce heat to 350° F., and bake ½ hour longer.

Note: The prepared mincemeat will improve if allowed to mellow in a stone crock about a week before being used in pies.

ANOTHER MINCEMEAT

From the *Vineyard Gazette,* January 27, 1916.

3 pounds lean beef
1 pound beef suet
3 tart apples, peeled, cored, and coarsely chopped
2 pounds brown sugar
3 cups molasses
3 pints cider
½ cup cider vinegar
2 pounds seeded raisins
2 pounds currants
½ cup coarsely chopped citron

1 teaspoon nutmeg
1 teaspoon cinnamon
1 teaspoon ground cloves
1 teaspoon mace
1 teaspoon salt
⅛ teaspoon freshly ground pepper
Orange and lemon juice (optional)
1 cup quince preserves (optional)

In a heavy saucepan combine beef, suet, and water to cover. Cook until beef is tender. Strain beef and suet, reserving cooking liquid. Allow meat to cool. Continue to boil liquid until reduced to 1 cup. Chop the beef and the suet and combine it with the cooking liquid, then add apples, brown sugar, molasses, cider, vinegar, raisins, currants, and citron. Then slowly add spices, a little of each at a time, up to amount indicated. Add salt and pepper. Taste frequently. Be careful not to overseason. Cook over low heat about 1 hour, stirring frequently. For a richer mincemeat, include orange and lemon juice to taste and stir in the cup of quince preserves. The combination is delicious and as rich as one would want to eat.

TWO RHUBARB-AND-STRAWBERRY PIES

These two springtime fruits, both carefully cultured on the Vineyard, combine so delectably in a flaky-crusted pie that we are including two versions of this colorful dish. In one, the fruit is cooked briefly and eggs are added to create a sort of custard. This delicious filling has been used by Vineyard cooks for generations. The other method prescribes uncooked fruit, with mouth-watering results.

METHOD ONE (1-CRUST RECIPE)

8-inch pie shell, baked
    (page 214)
2 tablespoons butter
1½ cups sugar
2 cups 1-inch pieces of
    unpeeled young rhubarb

1 cup strawberries, hulled
    and washed, if necessary
2 tablespoons flour
2 egg yolks, lightly beaten
2 egg whites

Prepare and bake pie shell. Leave oven on at 300° F. Let pie shell cool while preparing filling. In a heavy saucepan melt butter over moderate heat; add 1 cup of the sugar, the rhubarb, and strawberries. Mix well and cook until sugar is dissolved. Mix ¼ cup sugar with the flour, add beaten egg yolks, combine thoroughly with fruit. Cook over low heat, stirring frequently, until mixture thickens and rhubarb takes on a slightly transparent look. Remove from heat, cool, then pour into pie shell. Beat egg whites until stiff peaks are formed, then gradually add the remaining ¼ cup sugar, beating constantly. Spread meringue over filled pie shell and brown in oven about 15 minutes.

METHOD TWO (2-CRUST RECIPE)

Pastry for 2-crust pie
    (page 214)
4 tablespoons flour
1½–2 cups sugar
3 cups 1-inch pieces young
    rhubarb, unpeeled

1 cup fresh strawberries
½ teaspoon grated orange
    rind (optional)
1 tablespoon butter

Preheat oven to 475° F.

Prepare pastry and line a 9-inch pie pan with about half the dough. In a large bowl combine flour and sugar, then add fruit, and orange rind if desired. Combine these ingredients gently but thoroughly. Fill the pie shell with fruit mixture and dot with butter cut into small bits. Cover with upper crust, crimp edges to seal, pierce with a fork or make several knife slits. Bake at 475° F. for 10 minutes; reduce heat to 350° F. and bake another 30 minutes, or until crust is golden brown.

A lattice crust makes an attractive topping for fruit pies: Cut long, narrow strips of pastry dough, place about ¾ inch apart on the filling, crossing at right angles. Moisten strips slightly where they meet the edge of the pie, then flute the pastry rim.

Note: Equal amounts of strawberries and rhubarb may be used for the filling, if preferred.

LEMON POT PIE

A fruit pot pie, like a meat pot pie, is a homely sort of dish with an old-fashioned sound, like chicken and dumplings—which is also a type of pot pie. Whatever the ingredients, a pot pie is made by simply cooking dumplings on top of whatever slightly thickened mixture you choose to use. Old recipe books and files contain numerous instructions for fruit pot pies, made with berries, peaches, or almost any serviceable fruit. Since lemons are a fairly universal favorite in dessert making, we choose this recipe to represent fruit pot pies.

4 portions

LEMON SAUCE

2 lemons, sliced very thin
1 pint water (or 1½ cups water, ½ cup lemon juice)

1 cup sugar
2 tablespoons butter

(continued)

Combine all ingredients in a saucepan, bring to a boil over moderate heat, reduce heat, and simmer 10 minutes. Remove from heat.

DUMPLINGS

1 cup sifted all-purpose flour	1 teaspoon sugar (optional)
2 teaspoons baking powder	½–¾ cup milk
¼ teaspoon salt	

Resift the flour with the baking powder, salt, and sugar (if used). Add sufficient milk so that the dumpling dough will drop readily from a spoon. Return lemon mixture to stove and bring to a simmer over low heat. Drop the dumpling dough from a tablespoon onto the lemon sauce—the dumplings should measure 1½ to 2 inches across. Cover pan tightly and cook 15 to 20 minutes. Spoon the dumplings into shallow soup plates and cover with the lemon sauce.

GREEN-TOMATO-AND-APPLE PIE

After the first "white" frosts of the autumn (which kill the tenderer crops such as green peppers and eggplant) and before the first "black" frost, dreaded by every vegetable gardener who has gone out one still, chill fall morning to find his beloved garden blackened and devastated by the first true touch of winter—somewhere between these yearly harbingers, the provident gardener will pick all the unripened tomatoes from his vines and store them in a cool place until he finds time to convert them into pickles, a tart relish, a tasty marmalade, or this unusual pie. (The finest of the green tomatoes can be wrapped in newspapers, stored in a cool dark place and opened and used as they ripen—a process that can sometimes be sustained into early December.)

Pastry for 2-crust pie
(page 214)
3 medium-sized tart apples
2 cups sliced green tomatoes
1 cup sugar (half white and
half brown is suggested)
1 teaspoon cinnamon
¼ teaspoon nutmeg

¼ teaspoon allspice (optional)
2 scant tablespoons flour
1 tablespoon lemon juice
2 tablespoons butter
1 tablespoon cream or melted
butter (or 1 tablespoon
beaten egg yolk)

Preheat oven to 450° F. Prepare pastry and use half to line a 9-inch pie pan. Peel and core apples and cut into ½-inch slices. Slice tomatoes to match. In a large bowl combine sugar, spices, and flour. Mix lightly, then gently mix in tomatoes, apples, and lemon juice. Fill pie shell with this mixture; dot with bits of butter. Add top crust. Crimp edges. Brush with melted butter, cream, or egg yolk mixed with a little water. Cut several slits in top crust, or prick with fork. Bake about 15 minutes, or until crust is golden brown. Reduce heat to 350° and bake for a total of about 1 hour.

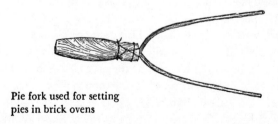

Scrimshaw Jagging Wheel

Pie fork used for setting
pies in brick ovens

PUDDINGS AND OTHER DESSERTS

> . . . the puddings which accompanied them . . . were of
> many varieties ranging from the aristocratic plum-pudding of
> English vintage to the lowly "Gap and Swallow" with its sauce
> of thick maple syrup.
>
> Among the jewels of the pudding family were the floating
> islands, sweetened with rosewater, the flummeries made by
> turning rich custard over cake and topping it all with the
> beaten whites of eggs, and the syllabubs with their foundations
> of *good sweet cream*. . . .
>
> —FROM *The Yankee Cookbook,*
> BY IMOGENE WOLCOTT

The mere word "pudding" sounds fattening and delicious; and
most puddings are both. Almost anything cooked up with flour,
tapioca, eggs, rice, milk, fruits, spices, and—always—some sort of
sweetening can be termed a pudding. Through the years, needless to
say, puddings and variations of puddings have been developed in
numbers that boggle the mind and would certainly incapacitate the
stomach, were it suddenly confronted by all of them. Since there are
instant puddings and canned puddings and frozen puddings in every
food store to tempt the time-conscious cook, we have not included
many puddings in this book. For most puddings demand leisure—
they need to be sifted, whipped, rolled, patted, steamed, baked. Yet
in the end, a good homemade pudding is a comforting object to set
before your family as the last course of a pleasant evening meal.

Simpler desserts usually involve fruit or fruits, and aside from
omitting a last course altogether, nothing is more appropriate after
a rich, heavy meal. Many fruits can simply be served raw—washed,
sometimes peeled, but often left just as they are. Many respond well
to poaching in wine or fruit juice, a bit of lemon juice or peel, a dash
of spice. Really good fruit, like really good vegetables, should not
be tampered with or its innate flavor is altered. Experiment, but
with discretion.

STEAMED OR BAKED BLACKBERRY ROLL

6 generous portions

2 cups sifted flour
4 teaspoons baking powder
1 tablespoon sugar
2 teaspoons salt
2 tablespoons butter (or more, as desired)
1 egg, beaten
⅔ cup milk (approximately)
2 cups fresh blackberries or huckleberries

¾ cup sugar
1 tablespoon lemon juice
2 tablespoons melted butter (optional)
Heavy cream, Berry Sauce (page 249), or Foamy Sauce I or II (pages 248–49)

Sift flour, baking powder, 1 tablespoon sugar, and salt into a large bowl. Work in butter with pastry blender or fingertips. Combine egg and milk; stir gradually into flour mixture. The dough should be firm enough to roll. Add more milk if necessary. Roll out on a floured board to form a rectangle about ⅓ inch thick.

Combine berries, ¾ cup sugar and lemon juice; sprinkle over dough. Roll up like a jelly roll. Tuck ends in. Place roll on a lightly floured clean dish towel and tie or sew the cloth loosely in place. Place on a trivet or rack in a large saucepan, cover with boiling water, and steam for 1 hour over low heat.

To bake this pudding, place it on a buttered shallow baking dish without the dish-towel wrapping. Brush the roll with 2 tablespoons melted butter and bake in a preheated 450° oven for about 30 minutes.

Serve hot with heavy cream, Berry Sauce, or Foamy Sauce I or II.

BLACKBERRY, HUCKLEBERRY, OR BLUEBERRY FLUMMERY

Flummeries were made in medieval times, as various conglomerations of oatmeal, sugar, flour, eggs, and eventually fruit, something between a gruel and a pudding, it seems. The British were fond of them, and it is very likely that some English lady brought along her favored recipes for flummery when she settled her household on Martha's Vineyard several hundred years ago. Somewhere along the line, the name dropped out of usage, for though we found numerous residents who remembered eating this dish in their childhood—and some housewives who make it still—none of them knew of it as flummery, but simply as a berry pudding. And, as in earlier days, there are still different sorts of flummeries. These two distinctly different preparations are the ones used on the Vineyard. However you make them, and whatever you call them, flummeries are lovely inventions.

FLUMMERY I

4 portions

1 quart blackberries, huckleberries, or blueberries (frozen may be substituted)	¼ teaspoon ground cinnamon
	8 slices (or more) home-style white bread, crusts removed
1 cup sugar	Softened butter
1 tablespoon lemon juice	Whipped cream (optional)

Preheat oven to 350° F.

Remove stems and leaves from fruit. Wash it and let it drain in a colander for a while. Combine berries, sugar, lemon juice, and cinnamon in a 2-quart saucepan and cook over moderate heat only long enough for the mixture to come to a simmer. Remove from heat. Butter the bread slices generously. Cut several slices of bread to fit bottom and sides of a 2-quart bowl or charlotte mold; place in bowl and spoon half the berry mixture over bread slices. Lay additional bread slices over berries; cover with remainder of fruit, and lay bread slices over top. Bake 20 to 25 minutes. Allow to cool, chill thoroughly, and serve with whipped cream if desired.

Note: This dessert may also be served unbaked. Simply prepare the mixture as above, then place a plate and heavy skillet or kitchen weight on the top of bread slices. Allow weighted dessert to remain in the refrigerator overnight before serving.

FLUMMERY II

4 portions

2 cups blackberries, huckle-berries, or blueberries	½ cup sugar
	3 tablespoons cornstarch or arrowroot powder
2 cups water	¼ cup cold water
1 tablespoon lemon juice	

Whipped cream (optional)

Remove stems and leaves from berries, rinse carefully with cold water, and drain. Combine berries with water and lemon juice and cook over low heat, simmering gently, for 10 minutes. Mix sugar and cornstarch or arrowroot, blend in ¼ cup water, and carefully stir into fruit. Simmer another 5 minutes. Cool slightly and pour into glass bowl or individual glass serving dishes. Chill thoroughly and serve very cold. Garnish with whipped cream if desired.

Note: Freshly picked red raspberries—or the rare but delectable black ones—are admirably suited to this recipe in place of the berries specified.

QUEEN OF PUDDINGS

Small wonder that old-timers were fond of this wonderful dessert—it is handsome to look at and a delight to the palate.

(continued)

6 to 8 portions

1 cup soft bread crumbs (use French or Italian, or home-style bread, if possible)

2 cups milk

1 tablespoon butter

¾ cup sugar

Grated rind of ½ lemon

¼ teaspoon salt

3 egg yolks, lightly beaten

½ cup raspberry jam (or ¾ cup fresh raspberries)

3 egg whites

Preheat oven to 350° F.

Combine, in a saucepan, crumbs, milk, butter, ½ cup of the sugar, lemon rind, and salt. Place over low heat and cook only until milk comes to a simmer. Remove from heat, beat in the egg yolks thoroughly, pour into a buttered 8-inch round baking dish, about 2 inches deep. (A deepish pie plate will do.) Set baking dish in a pan of hot water that comes halfway up the sides of the pudding dish and bake about ¾ hour, until it is firm. It is done when a knife inserted in center of pudding comes out clean. Remove dish from oven. Melt jam over low heat; pour over pudding. If using fresh berries, sprinkle on top of pudding.

Beat the egg whites until soft peaks are formed; add the remaining ¼ cup sugar gradually, beating constantly until a firm meringue develops. Spread the meringue over the pudding (or use a pastry bag to pipe the meringue decoratively over the top). Return pudding to oven to brown the meringue delicately, for 10 to 15 minutes.

QUINCE PUDDING

The library of the Dukes County Historical Society in Edgartown is an enchanting place to while away a rainy afternoon looking at stereopticon slides of places and people long gone, or reading whaling journals or accounts of the early settlers.

In an 1829 householding book from the library's collection, we came across this receipt for a quince pudding. With an added meringue, and baked in a fluted ironstone bowl, it came out of the oven looking so pretty that it seemed a shame to eat it.

A somewhat tart flavor and an unusual texture distinguish this creation from most custard-type baked puddings.

6 to 8 portions

3 medium-sized quinces, quartered, peeled, and cored	3 egg yolks
	¾ cup sugar
	½ teaspoon ginger
1 cup milk	¼ teaspoon cinnamon
1 cup medium cream or evaporated milk	¼ teaspoon salt
	3 egg whites

½ teaspoon cream of tartar

Preheat oven to 350° F.

Put quince pieces in a saucepan and barely cover with water. Bring to a boil and cook gently about 10 minutes, or until fruit is soft enough to purée. Remove from heat and put through a food mill. In same saucepan, combine milk and cream or evaporated milk. Heat to scalding; remove from heat. Beat egg yolks lightly and combine quince purée, ½ cup of the sugar, spices, and salt, mix well, then add scalded milk. Pour mixture into a 1½- to 2-quart ovenproof bowl (about 3 inches deep), set bowl in a pan of hot water (water should come up sides 1 or 2 inches), place in oven, and bake 30 minutes.

Beat egg whites with cream of tartar until they form stiff peaks, then beat in the remaining 4 tablespoons sugar a little at a time. Remove pudding from oven and spread meringue over its top with back of a wooden spoon, spreading to edge of bowl so meringue will not shrink when baked. Replace pudding in oven, raise oven temperature to 400° F. and bake another 10 minutes. Serve pudding either warm or cooled (not cold).

GOOSEBERRY FOOL
[*Or Raspberry or Blackberry*]

Although the dictionary defines this use of fool as relating to the word "trifle" (also a dessert term) or "surprise," describing it as a "dish of crushed fruit with whipped cream and sugar," we were unable to find the origin of this entertaining name. Perhaps early cooks considered the dish to be a foolishness. We suggest that it is a delicious foolishness, good enough to be prepared two ways. One variation uses whipped cream, the other has a custard base.

VARIATION I

6–8 portions

1 quart fresh, ripe gooseberries (or raspberries or black-berries)	1 cup sugar 3 cups heavy cream, whipped

Remove stems from berries; discard bruised or damaged fruit. In a heavy saucepan combine berries with the sugar and cook over moderate heat until the fruit is tender, about 20 minutes. Stir frequently, pressing down on the berries to extract their juices. Press the cooked fruit through a colander or purée in a blender. Refrigerate until thoroughly chilled. Just before serving, whip the cream and fold it into the chilled fruit.

VARIATION II

1 quart fresh, ripe goose-berries (or raspberries or blackberries)	4 egg yolks, beaten until light 4 egg whites, beaten stiff
2 cups water	3 tablespoons confectioners' sugar
1 cup sugar	½ teaspoon grated lemon rind (optional)
¼ teaspoon salt	
1 tablespoon butter	

Prepare berries as in Variation I. Put berries and water in a heavy saucepan and cook over moderate heat until tender, about 20 minutes. Press mixture through a colander or purée in a blender. Return mixture to saucepan and add sugar, salt, and butter. Cook over low heat until butter is melted, then fold beaten egg yolks lightly into fruit mixture. Immediately remove from heat. Pour into a serving bowl and refrigerate until thoroughly chilled. Just before serving, beat egg whites until very stiff; beat in confectioners' sugar, beating constantly. Heap the meringue on the fruit mixture and serve immediately.

Optional and attractive: sprinkle ½ teaspoon grated lemon rind on the meringue.

RHUBARB FOOL

6 to 8 portions

1½ cups sugar	Peel of ½ lemon, cut in strips
1 quart rhubarb cut in 1-inch lengths	4 whole coriander seeds
	4 whole cloves
1 cup water	2 tablespoons flour
1 pint light cream	4 egg yolks, well beaten
1½-inch piece stick cinnamon	Nutmeg

Combine 1 cup of the sugar with rhubarb in a saucepan, add water, bring to a low boil, and simmer gently for 5 minutes. Let cool while preparing cream mixture.

Place cream in a medium saucepan. Tie cinnamon stick, lemon peel, coriander, and cloves in a small piece of cheesecloth and simmer in cream for 10 minutes. Remove pan from heat. Discard cheesecloth and contents. Combine remaining ½ cup sugar with flour and stir in beaten egg yolks. Return cream mixture to low heat and stir in egg mixture. Cook slowly on low heat until mixture thickens somewhat, stirring constantly. Do not boil. Pour thickened mixture into large bowl. Cool. Put rhubarb through a food mill or colander. Stir into cooled cream mixture. Mix well. Chill thoroughly. Serve with dash of nutmeg atop each serving.

PEARS IN GRAPE JUICE

An old, wind-bent Bartlett pear tree brushes the living-room windows of one hillside North Tisbury house, and every September its owner gathers from it a bushel or more of fine big pears, leaving at least that many more on the ground for the yellowjackets, bumblebees, ants, rabbits, and deer that always manage to have made prior claims. A long row of canned pear products appears on the kitchen shelf—plain, gingered, spiced, pear butter, pear-tomato chutney—and still there are more pears to be used up. Since this is also wild-grape season, this becomes a highly favored dessert at that time of year, made from the tangy juice of the wild fruit.

4 portions

8 raw pears, peeled, cut into halves, and cored
1 pint grape juice
½ teaspoon ginger or ½-inch piece cinnamon stick

½ cup sugar
1 teaspoon grated lemon or orange rind (or ½ cup sour cream)

Put pears into an appropriate saucepan, add grape juice, ginger or cinnamon, and sugar. Bring to a boil, lower heat, and poach gently for about 25 minutes, or until pears are tender. Turn fruit several times so it will color evenly. Cool to room temperature, and serve with a sprinkle of grated lemon or orange rind or with a dollop of sour cream on each portion. Or the cooking liquid may be boiled down to one-half volume, allowed to cool, and poured over the pears.

Do not serve this dish cold, as this impairs the delicate flavor.

MIXED BERRIES WITH HONEY CREAM

4 to 6 portions

1 quart ripe berries (any mixture of strawberries, black or red raspberries, blueberries or blackberries)
Pinch of salt

1 cup whipping cream, chilled
½ cup honey
½ teaspoon spices (ginger, cinnamon, nutmeg—optional)

Use berries at room temperature. Pick over fruit, removing any stems or bits of leaves. Do not wash unless absolutely necessary. Add salt to whipping cream and whip until quite thick. Warm honey slightly by placing measuring utensil in hot water, then whip it into the cream. Spices, if used, may be added at this time also, or they may be sprinkled over the cream when dish is served. Place fruit and whipped cream in separate bowls and serve.

THREE-FRUIT ICE

Makes 2 quarts

2 scant cups sugar
3 cups water
3 lemons
3 oranges

3 bananas
½ teaspoon grated orange and lemon rind

Combine sugar and water in a saucepan, stir to mix, and bring to a boil. Cook long enough to allow sugar to be thoroughly dissolved. Cool.

Extract juice from lemons and oranges. Cut up the bananas, combine with fruit juices, and blend in a blender briefly. (Do this in several batches or you will have banana spattered about.) In a large bowl, combine the sugar syrup and blended fruit mixture. Add grated rinds. Beat well to mix. Pour mixture into a 2-quart freezing pan (a large loaf pan may be used), place in freezer and freeze until mushy, about 1 hour. Turn mixture into

(continued)

large bowl again, beat well until smooth, pour back into freezing pan, and freeze again until mushy, about $\frac{1}{2}$ hour. Return to bowl once more and beat, then replace in freezing pan and freeze until firm. A piece of foil placed over top of pan helps to prevent ice crystals.

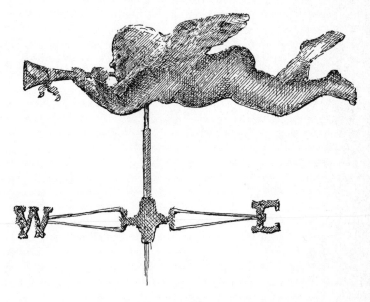

Sundries

Chapter 10

Mrs. Mayhew Look, grape sauce, 1st prem., 1.00 . . . Mrs.
A. S. Tilton, b'lkberry preserve and chili sauce . . . Mrs. Sarah
B. Russell, pickled onions and cucumbers . . . Mrs. Z. A.
Athearn, preserves, pickles, chow chow, piccalili, 1.40 . . .
Mrs. Edgar West, spiced pears . . .

—FROM THE LIST OF AWARDS,
COUNTY AGRICULTURAL FAIR,
WEST TISBURY, SEPTEMBER 26,
1895

An adaptable word, sundries may be used to refer to various types
of miscellaneous collections. It seemed an apt heading for this chapter, which contains recipes for marmalades, herb sandwiches, pickles,
sauces, and other good things that don't quite fit into the other
sections of this book.

The Vineyard is a delightful place to make many of these sundries—
using end-of-summer garden leftovers, a handful of herbs, a basket
of gnarled fruit from a deserted farmstead. Some of them can be
bottled and sealed in a canner or steam bath, then packed up and
carried home at summer's end, along with the beach stones, bits of
driftwood, gull feathers, and other flotsam you can't bear to throw
away—pleasant ways of taking a little of the Vineyard home with you.
A pot of rose-hip jam on Sunday morning, or artichoke relish,
zucchini pickles, and cranberry chutney with your Thanksgiving
turkey or Christmas ham can evoke memories of the bright days of
your Island vacation and sustain your nostalgia until you return.

MILLION-DOLLAR PICKLES

An elderly gentleman in West Tisbury who still loves to gather
and preserve the fruits of his garden gave us this wonderful
pickle recipe, which he learned many years ago from a Negro
neighbor of his in the South. The directions came to us well an-
notated with such remarks as "4 or two qts. sliced cukes (original

recipe not clear, depends on how much you want)," and, at the bottom of the typewritten page: "(Unfortunately mice (?) had chewed original recipe sheet and amounts are only approx. Determine how much needed by testing by taste)." We appreciate, in principle, this fairly casual approach to cookery; and after both testing and tasting found the proportions given below produce flavorsome and memorable pickles. You may prefer them made with less spices and a bit less sugar.

These pickles, by the way, were sold one summer during pickling season at a small roadside vegetable stand in North Tisbury, and each time they appeared, Theresa Morse, a celebrated cook and cook-book author in her own right, appropriated every quart to serve at her delightful Menemsha guest house, Beach Plum Inn.

Makes about 4 quarts

4 quarts sliced cucumbers	2 green peppers, chopped
8–10 small onions, sliced	½ cup salt

Put cucumbers, onions, and green peppers into a crock or other large receptacle (do not use metal). Mix well with a long wooden spoon; add salt and mix in thoroughly. Add cold water barely to cover cut vegetables. Lay a towel or piece of cheesecloth over top of crock and place in a cool spot overnight. In the morning, remove vegetables a quart or so at a time into a colander, press as much water as possible from them, and transfer them all to a large saucepan (at least 6-quart size). Taste vegetables as you work—if they seem too salty spray some cold water over one batch or more to remove some of the salt. Prepare syrup.

SYRUP

4 scant cups sugar	2 teaspoons mustard seed
1 quart vinegar	1–3 teaspoons mixed pickling
1 teaspoon celery seed	spices
1 teaspoon turmeric	

In a smaller saucepan, combine sugar, vinegar, and spices. Let mixture come to a boil, stir to dissolve sugar thoroughly, then pour syrup over cucumber mixture.

Bring pickles to a boil; cook over moderate heat about 15 to 20 minutes, until vegetables are fairly tender but not soggy. Mix and stir several times during cooking period. A wooden spoon is best for this. If pickles are to be canned, have four hot, sterilized quart jars ready for use, pack well with pickles, and seal. If desired, cook pickles only ten minutes, pack and seal, and process 5 minutes in boiling-water bath. Pickles may also be put into clean quart jars, allowed to cool, and stored for some months, tightly capped, in the refrigerator or in a very cool part of the basement.

BABY ZUCCHINI PICKLES

Makes 1 quart

Enough tiny (3–4-inch) zucchini squash to fill quart jar	2 cloves garlic, peeled and sliced
1 teaspoon salt	1 teaspoon olive oil
¼ teaspoon cayenne pepper (optional)	Sprig of fresh tarragon, dill, or basil
	1 cup vinegar

1 cup water (approximately)

Allow 2 or 3 extra squash, as they should be well forced into the jar when packed. Wash squash well, remove stems and blossom ends, let soak in a bowl of hot water while you assemble other ingredients, then pack carefully and neatly into clean hot quart jar. Add salt, cayenne (if used), garlic, and olive oil. Heat vinegar and water almost to boiling and pour over zucchini. Use a knife if necessary to remove any air at bottom of jar. Place sprig of tarragon, dill, or basil on top of squash, seal, and process 10 minutes in hot water bath.

If pickles are to be eaten soon rather than canned for later use, place squash in saucepan, add seasonings, oil, and herb sprig,

(continued)

and pour on enough of the vinegar-water mixture barely to cover
the squash. Bring to a boil, lower heat, and simmer 5 minutes.
Squash should be crisp, not tender. Let cool, pour off excess
liquid and store pickles in closed containers in the refrigerator.

RAW ARTICHOKE RELISH

A refreshing raw relish can be made very simply from grated raw
unpeeled Jerusalem artichokes and Vinaigrette Dressing (see
page 247). During the fall and winter, when interesting lettuces
and other spring and summer delectables are prohibitively expensive or infrequently available, serve this as salad with your
evening meal, if you have been farsighted enough to raise this
unique vegetable (for details on storage, see Steamed Jerusalem
Artichokes, page 158).

Scrub half a dozen or so raw artichokes, grate on medium
grater blade, and add 2 tablespoons Vinaigrette Dressing to each
cupful of raw artichokes. Mix well and allow to marinate for
several hours in the refrigerator. Serve chilled but not too cold,
with a dusting of freshly ground black pepper or cayenne pepper,
and a sprinkling of chopped fresh parsley.

Note: A tablespoon of grated raw onion may be stirred into
this relish to give added tang.

CAROLINA ARTICHOKE RELISH

Like most of the best recipes, this one has been handed down
through generations of cooks. It originated many years ago on a
South Carolina plantation and came into the family of one of this
cook book's authors from a Southern friend, a descendant of the
plantation owners. Guests have been known to eat a pint of this
relish at one sitting, so try to make a large batch at one time. It is
easy to can—merely follow any standard pickling directions, processing the jars 10 minutes in a boiling water bath.

Makes about 4 quarts

2 quarts ground unpeeled Jerusalem artichokes (cut up biggest ones before measuring)	1½ gallons cold water
	1½ cups salt
	2 tablespoons turmeric
	4 tablespoons white mustard seed
1 quart cut-up green peppers (or mixed red and green bell peppers)	4 cups brown sugar, lightly packed
1 quart cut-up onions	2 quarts cider vinegar

Scrub artichokes well (soak in cold water if necessary to remove dirt), put through food chopper, using medium blade, until you have about 2 quarts ground vegetable. Grind cut-up peppers and onions. Soak ground vegetables in water and salt overnight—use large nonmetallic container for this purpose. In the morning, drain well, taste to be sure vegetables are not too salty (if they are, rinse part of them in a colander under cold water). Mix turmeric and mustard seed into ground vegetables. In a large kettle (at least 6-quart size), mix brown sugar and vinegar. Place kettle over heat; stir until sugar dissolves. Add ground vegetables. Bring mixture to a boil and simmer 3 minutes, stirring constantly.

If relish is to be canned, place in sterilized jars and process 10 minutes. If preferred, simmer relish another 8 to 10 minutes, stirring occasionally, cool, and store in glass jars or plastic containers in the refrigerator.

PICKLED NASTURTIUM SEED PODS

Pickled nasturtium seed pods, though quaint sounding, can be prepared as easily and satisfactorily from a summer garden today as they could when an early eighteenth-century herbalist advised housewives to put their "Nerstusan Seeds . . . into an Earthen pott and Power the pickle upon them. . . ." For centuries, the pickled flower buds (prepared in the same manner as the seed pods) have been used as we use capers, but they have a bite and a tang that are distinctively their own.

(continued)

1 pint white-wine vinegar
2 teaspoons salt
10 black peppercorns

4 cloves
½ teaspoon mace
1 garlic clove

Nasturtium seed pods

Combine all ingredients except nasturtium pods in a kettle and bring to a boil. Allow mixture to cool, then pour into a quart bottle (one with a tight top). Add the nasturtium pods as they ripen. (Pick the knobs that form after the flowers have wilted, when they are firm but not dry.) Keep bottle tightly sealed and in a cool, dark place. Allow pods to pickle several months (or until you return to the Island the following summer) before eating them.

Note: If white-wine vinegar is not available, use white vinegar diluted in the proportion of 3 parts vinegar and 1 part water.

GREEN-TOMATO MARMALADE

Barbara Nevin, wife of Edgartown's Dr. Bob Nevin, not only manages an enormous house and household but busies herself in such other areas as politicking for town offices, novel writing, and cooking all manner of delights. All sorts of helpful ideas and suggestions began to arrive from her as soon as she heard this book was being compiled; one recipe she sent us was this version of tomato marmalade, which offers a practical disposal of those green tomatoes you pick off just before the first frost threat and never know what to do with.

Makes about 3 quarts

6 pounds green tomatoes
   (about 20, preferably
   small ones)
2 pounds sugar
6 lemons
1½ teaspoons salt
1 cup water

½ teaspoon whole cloves
   (optional)
1-inch piece stick cinnamon
   (optional)
½ teaspoon whole allspice
   (optional)

Cut tomatoes into 1-inch chunks and place in a large bowl. Add sugar and stir. Cut lemons into paper-thin slices, sprinkling them with salt as you go. Cook the lemons in the water for 5 minutes, then combine with sugared tomatoes in a large sauce-pan and cook over very low heat until mixture reaches the boiling point. Continue cooking on low heat, stirring constantly, until mixture thickens, about 50 minutes. Pack marmalade into sterilized jars and seal with paraffin.

If a spiced marmalade is preferred, tie spices in a cheesecloth bag and drop into pot after fruit comes to a boil. Remove spice bag before pouring marmalade into jars.

QUINCE HONEY

Anyone fortunate enough to have a quince tree on the premises usually guards it carefully as quince season approaches, then parcels out some of the hard, knobby yellow-green quinces to special friends and relatives, saving the rest for home use—to be baked whole (sweetened and spiced) and served with cream (plain or whipped), or to be converted into preserves or some other delicious sweetener. A few Vineyarders have quinces, and in mid-October comes the call: "The quinces are ready." Our quinces came from a tree in the yard of a very old farmhouse nestled back in the valley off Lambert's Cove Road, and were picked on a bright October morning from an old tree entwined with a scarlet-hued Virginia-creeper vine.

We used them to make up this "honey" from a recipe in an old book of Vineyard recipes. "Honey" seems to have been an old-fashioned New England term for what newer cooking guides call preserves, which is actually what this is since the cooked fruit is not strained out but left in. We just like calling it quince honey.

Makes 4 jelly glasses

8 medium-sized quinces		Juice from 1 lemon
	Sugar	

(continued)

Wash the quinces, quarter them, then core and peel them,
saving cores (unless too wormy) and parings. Quinces darken
even more rapidly than apples, so if you want a light-colored
honey, drop your peeled quinces into a bowl of water to which
the juice of a lemon has been added. Put parings and cores into
a saucepan, barely cover with water, bring to a boil, lower heat,
and simmer 20 minutes. While they cook, grate or finely chop
the peeled quince quarters. Cover with waxed paper to retard
darkening, if desired; or grate just before parings are through
cooking. Strain liquid from parings, measure, and add enough
water to make 3 cups liquid. Combine this liquid and the grated
or chopped quinces in a saucepan, bring to a boil, lower heat, and
simmer 15 minutes. Measure cooked quince and add an equal
amount of sugar; replace in saucepan, stir well, return to a boil,
lower heat, and simmer about 15 minutes, stirring frequently so
mixture will not stick. Skim if needed, then pour into hot, clean
jelly glasses and seal.

TEA LANE CHUTNEY

Every Christmas for many years, certain favored up-Island households have been the recipients of a jar of this prized apple chutney. A foil-wrapped and beribboned jelly glass always appears in
the mailboxes of this cook-book's authors; but though they have
tried for years to extract the recipe from its eighty-six-year-old
owner, it was only given to them the day before this manuscript
was sent off to the publisher. With the recipe came the story of
its origin on Martha's Vineyard, which we now pass along.

Almost thirty years ago, a charming Englishwoman appeared
at the door of one of the two year-round farmhouses on Tea Lane
and asked if she and a friend might pick blueberries on that
property. Since the lady of the house was also English, a friend-
ship developed that lasted for many years, and each summer the
lady came back to pick blueberries and have a pleasant afternoon
tea. Over the tea things, this recipe was divulged, copied out, and
placed in the recipe box of the house on Tea Lane. That Christ-

mas, the apple chutney was sent around to dear friends, as it has been each subsequent Christmas. But the recipe, invariably sought, was never divulged.

When asked how much the recipe makes, the chutney maker got out a 1942 diary, which is used each year to record brief notes on planting times, first frosts, bird visitors, egg production, and canning records. "Nine containers" was the amount given, but "I always put up big jars for certain people and small ones for the others," the cook said, so the figure given below may not be quite accurate.

One caution: This chutney is extremely hot when made with the full amount of red pepper. Use about half the amount stated; if you want more after testing your chutney, stir in a little more at a time, tasting after each addition.

Makes about 8 standard jelly glasses

2 pounds apples
1½ pints vinegar
2 pounds moist (dark brown) sugar
1 pound raisins or chopped dates
2 heads (cloves) garlic, minced (or 1 large onion, chopped fine)

4 ounces crystallized ginger, chopped fine
1 dessertspoon (about 1½ teaspoons) dry mustard
1 teaspoon salt
1 tablespoon dried red pepper flakes (see caution in text above)

Peel, quarter, and core apples. Cook them in the vinegar until they are soft and mushy. Add the other ingredients, using only half the red pepper. Mix well. Bring to a boil and cook over moderate heat about 10 minutes. Taste chutney. Then add remainder of red pepper if a very hot chutney is desired. Cook about 15 minutes more, stirring occasionally. Pour into hot, clean containers and seal. The chutney will keep indefinitely, the recipe card notes, if "tied down" in jars.

HERB SANDWICHES

2 to 3 tablespoons chopped herbs
  per sandwich

English traditions linger in many Vineyard homes, as they do in much of New England. The social life of several elderly Island residents centers on occasional visits from friends who live in another part of the Island. As the tea things are passed around, topics range from the oriole at the feeding station to the defeat of the zoning law at the last town meeting.

Fresh herbs, good white bread, and sweet butter combine exquisitely with tea's delicate flavor, and in summer and fall herb sandwiches at teatime make a nice change from oversweet cakes and other sugary goodies. Collect a handful or two of herb sprigs and cut or chop them as fine as possible. Experiment with combinations and proportions, but don't cut too much of the more overpowering herbs like sage, tarragon, thyme, mint, fennel, and marjoram. Parsley, basil, chives, rosemary, chervil, dill, lovage, and savory are all flavorsome. Two pleasing combinations are equal parts of parsley, basil, chives and dill; or about one-third each of lovage, parsley and dill and a small bit of tarragon. Whimsical gardeners could snip in some nasturtium leaves and flowers, scented geranium leaves, or maybe a marigold or two.

Butter one side of both slices of bread, or use a good mayonnaise on one side of the sandwich. This helps keep the herbs in place. White bread is recommended, but oatmeal, pumpernickel, and rye are also quite good. Spread 2 or 3 tablespoons chopped herbs on one buttered slice and top with another. Press slices together lightly to imbed the herbs in the butter. Cut into desired shapes and serve. Don't prepare these sandwiches ahead and refrigerate them—they should be freshly made.

PARSLEY STUFFING

[*For fish or chicken*]

This stuffing will be sufficient for a small chicken, if one is roasting a broiler or fryer. It is delicious with fish to be baked, or for stuffing fillets such as flounder or small haddock.

Makes about 2 cups

1½ cups soft bread crumbs, preferably made from day-old French or Italian bread

1 cup coarsely chopped fresh parsley (Italian type is best)

1 medium onion, grated

1 teaspoon ground sage (a little more if fresh is used)

½ teaspoon salt

Freshly ground black pepper to taste

Juice of ½ lemon

1 teaspoon soy sauce

2 tablespoons melted butter or vegetable oil

Combine all ingredients in a mixing bowl and mix well with a fork.

VINAIGRETTE DRESSING

1 generous cup

1 clove garlic, finely minced or put through garlic press

½ teaspoon salt

⅛ teaspoon freshly ground black pepper

½ teaspoon any sharp mustard, preferably Dijon type

⅛ teaspoon dried basil or tarragon, or both

1 cup olive oil, or any good vegetable oil

¼ cup red-wine vinegar

Combine all ingredients thoroughly in a quart bowl, stirring with a wooden spoon and pressing down the garlic. Or place all ingredients in an electric blender and whirl for 15 to 20 seconds.

MAÎTRE D'HÔTEL BUTTER

[*Lemon Butter*]

Makes about ¾ cup

½ cup butter, slightly
softened

1 tablespoon chopped fresh
parsley

1 tablespoon chopped fresh
chives

1½–2 tablespoons lemon juice

Beat butter, using electric mixer if available, until it is very soft, light, and fluffy. Beat in the herbs. Gradually beat in the lemon juice, a little at a time, until it is well blended. Finished butter may be shaped into teaspoon-sized balls or formed into a roll. If the latter is wished, turn the mixture onto waxed paper, wrap it up, and store it in refrigerator until needed.

About 1 teaspoon per serving is sufficient.

FOAMY SAUCE I

Makes about 2 cups

1 cup confectioners' sugar
½ cup softened butter
1 egg yolk

1 teaspoon vanilla extract
1 egg white
⅛ teaspoon salt

Sift the sugar. Beat the butter until it is creamy. Add the sugar gradually. Beat in the egg yolk. Add the vanilla. Cook over very low heat in a heavy saucepan, stirring constantly. Do not overheat or the sauce will curdle. Cook until the mixture coats the spoon

Beat the egg white until it holds stiff peaks, then beat in the salt. Fold the egg white lightly and carefully into the sauce. The sauce may be served hot or cold.

FOAMY SAUCE II

Makes about 1 cup

½ cup butter
½ cup sugar

1 tablespoon water
1 egg

½ teaspoon vanilla

In a heavy saucepan combine butter, sugar, and water. Cook over extremely low heat until butter and sugar are well blended. Beat the egg until light and foamy. Add to the sauce with the vanilla. Serve immediately.

Note: This sauce may be made ahead by keeping the butter-sugar-water mixture warm in the top of a double boiler and adding the beaten egg and vanilla just before sauce is to be served.

BERRY SAUCE

Makes about 2 cups

⅓ cup soft butter
1 cup sifted confectioners'
sugar

1 egg white, beaten lightly
⅔ cup blackberries or
huckleberries

Beat the butter until very soft, add the sugar gradually, beating until well blended and fluffy. Add the egg white and continue beating until completely blended. Crush the berries slightly; fold into the sugar mixture. Chill thoroughly and serve very very cold.

SOFT CHOCOLATE FROSTING

Enough for 1 cake

1½ cups sugar, sifted
4 tablespoons cornstarch
½ teaspoon salt
1½ cups milk

4 squares baking chocolate
(unsweetened)
3 tablespoons butter
1 teaspoon vanilla

Combine sugar, cornstarch, and salt in a heavy saucepan, then stir in milk and add chocolate squares. Cook over moderate heat,

(continued)

stirring frequently, until chocolate melts and mixture begins to
bubble. Cook a few minutes more, stirring constantly (a wire
whisk is useful for this). Remove saucepan from heat and stir in
butter and vanilla. Cool mixture slightly before spreading on
cake.

RUM TEA

Beach picnics, cookouts, clambakes, or just a sandwich from a
fisherman's back pocket—any food enjoyed at the seaside seems
enhanced by one's surroundings. The pleasantest beach outing
remembered by one Edgartownian took place some years ago at
Katama. On the long-anticipated day, it rained; but being
primed and prepared, the family voted to go anyhow. It was
really only a typical midsummer mizzle, the husband observed.
Cold chicken, good garlicky salami, marinated artichoke hearts
with capers, cherry tomatoes, homemade dill pickles, Camembert, Italian bread, stuffed eggs, homemade oatmeal cookies, a
quart of rich-red strawberries, and two Milkbones for the poodles
were laid out along a flat board that had been washed up by the
sea, and the rum tea was poured. An Elysian period ensued.

Rum tea came to us from late-fall luncheons at Max Eastman's
house, where it was served with the meal in large white cups. It
is fine for chilly days at home, but even better on the beach.
Prepare large vacuum bottles of good, strong, boiling-hot tea.
Use a regular blend, not something fancy, and allow at least a
pint of tea per person. Sweeten the tea slightly, and take along
extra sugar in case someone wants it. Put the rum (a light Puerto
Rican type is good, but you may prefer something else) in an
appropriate bottle, allowing for about a tablespoon per cup of
tea, and take a small jar of milk. The rum and the milk, if desired, are added to each cup as it is poured.

The concoction is especially recommended for sunless, windy
days when you have to eat your lunch wrapped in a blanket or
crouched behind a rock or dune. Also fortifying after a chilling
swim in the surf.

MAX EASTMAN'S DAIQUIRIS

Sitting outside the hilltop house in East Pasture with Max and Yvette Eastman on an idyllic summer afternoon and sharing their panoramic view of Menemsha Pond, Vineyard Sound, and the Elizabeth Islands is a memory treasured by many of their friends. The daiquiris Max often served us to enhance our pleasure were as inimitably delightful as everything else about this great man. When we began to compile this book, we asked him to tell us how he made them. He credited their invention to his first wife, Eliena, saying that "like all her creations, they were speedy, spontaneous and very simple."

> One ounce of light rum,
> One ounce of dark rum,
> The juice from half a succulent lime.
> My mother's sugar-spoon level full of sugar,
> A leaf or two of mint,
> Mixed in a blender with oodles of ice.

Herring Gull

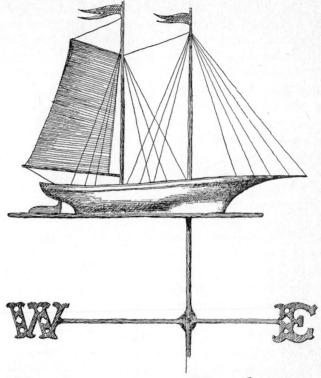

Portuguese Cookery

Chapter 11

Albion Alley & Co., General Store; Amaral Brothers Plumbing and Heating, Inc.; Ben David Motors, Inc.; De Bettencourt's Taxi; De Sorcy Contracting Co., Inc.; Manuel M. Maciel, Inc., Plumbing; Raul B. Mederios, Jr., Contractor; Arthur T. Sylva Oil Company, Inc.

—FROM THE MARTHA'S VINEYARD
TELEPHONE DIRECTORY

On Vineyard storefronts and mailboxes Portuguese names are almost as common as long-familiar New England ones like Daggett, Luce, Manter, and Mayhew. When whaling ships set sail from the Edgartown wharves two centuries or more ago, they often left without a full crew and stopped by the Azores and the Cape Verde Islands to sign on a complement of Portuguese sailors, renowned for their seafaring skills. Some of these vigorous, industrious men brought their families to the new land of America when their seagoing days were over, and it is fortunate for Martha's Vineyard that they did, as most of the Island's services are owned and run today by the descendants of these sea specialists—men who are as hard-working and as rugged as their forefathers were. The Island's Portuguese are noted also for their friendliness; anyone caught in a snowbank or with a flat tire or an injured animal never has to wait long for aid—and the odds are high that his savior will be a Portuguese.

Mingling easily and cordially with their New England neighbors, the Portuguese people of the Island have nonetheless maintained many aspects of their heritage with pride and care. Not the least appealing of these is the Mediterranean-oriented cooking that is the backbone of their cuisine. All the local grocers stock tasty linguica and chorizo sausages, and the Portuguese bakery in Oak Bluffs turns out a delicious massa sovada, the traditional sweet bread. One local Portuguese housewife attributes her family's good health—and that of her people in general—to the ingestion of huge amounts of parsley, both raw and cooked, citing it as one essential to Portuguese cookery, along with mint and, when possible, fresh coriander leaves. The cuisine in the Island's Portuguese households is still traditionally Azorean cooking, and differs from the cuisine of mainland Portugal in somewhat the way the Vineyard's food differs from that of the rest of New England. Azorean recipes specify white cornmeal, for instance, whereas most Portuguese ones use yellow meal. (One of the world's most ubiquitous foods, cornmeal figures importantly in the diet of the Vineyard's three principal cultural families—the British colonists, the Indians and the Portuguese.)

In general, Portuguese food might be said to be hearty, interesting, and delightful—words that could also describe the people whose cuisine these dishes are drawn from.

PORTUGUESE CHOWDER

The Mediterranean influence is evident in the fish chowder prepared by some of the Vineyard's Portuguese cooks. The basics are constant—fish, salt pork, onions, potatoes—but the addition of spices and vinegar results in a somewhat piquant dish instead of the more traditional bland one.

6 portions

¼ pound salt pork, cut in
  ½-inch dice
2 large onions, chopped
  medium fine
3 medium potatoes, cut in
  ½-inch dice (about 3 cups)
6 cups water
About ½ teaspoon salt
1 tablespoon vinegar

1 teaspoon dried orégano
¼ teaspoon saffron
Freshly ground black pepper
  to taste
About 2 pounds cleaned
  boned fish (haddock,
  halibut, cod, flounder, in
  any proportion), cut in
  chunks

Cook salt pork in a heavy aluminum kettle or Dutch oven over moderate heat until golden brown. Remove and drain on a paper towel. Reserve. Add chopped onions to fat and cook slowly until transparent and tender. Add potatoes, water, and seasonings. Bring to a slow boil and cook gently until potatoes are tender. Do not overcook. Add chunks of fish and cook gently about 5 minutes, until fish flakes easily when poked with a fork. Test for seasoning—more salt may be needed. Add browned salt pork bits just before serving.

CALDO VERDE

[*Kale Soup*]

A celebrated creation, popular in the Island's Portuguese households and familiar to almost every Vineyard housewife, kale soup provides a hearty and satisfying meal when served with a platter of fresh, hot cornbread, a simple fruit dessert, and a bottle of dry red wine. Mainland Portuguese cooks prepare Caldo Verde without beef and beans. This recipe, a Vineyard one by way of the Azores, calls for both; but other variations are allowable. The sausage and onions may be sautéed together briefly before being tossed into the soup pot. A few chopped fresh tomatoes, a handful of thinly sliced cabbage, a cup or so of fresh or frozen green peas—any or all of these may be added. A non-Portuguese but otherwise valid substitution is the use of fresh spinach, or mustard or beet greens, instead of the traditional kale. Good soups, good stews characteristically develop according to the taste of the individual cook and her household. Kale soup exemplifies this principle admirably.

8 generous portions

1 large beef shinbone
1 cup coarsely chopped
  onions
1½ teaspoons salt
1 clove garlic (optional)
6–8 cups water
1½ pounds (approximately)
  linguica, cut in ½-inch
  slices (chorizo or a garlic-
  flavored smoked pork
  sausage may be substi-
  tuted if linguica is
  unavailable)

1 pound fresh kale, shredded
2 cups raw potatoes, peeled
  and cut into 1-inch cubes
1 can (2 if preferred) red
  kidney or shell beans
3 or 4 sprigs fresh mint

(continued)

Simmer shinbone, onions, salt, and optional garlic in water for about 2 hours. Skim off any surface scum as needed. Add linguica and simmer another half hour. Add kale, potatoes, and beans. Continue to simmer until potatoes are almost tender, about 20 minutes. Add mint; cook another few minutes until potatoes are soft. Remove from stove and take out shinbone. Cut meat into small pieces; trim off fat and gristle. Return meat pieces to pot. Taste soup for seasoning. The soup may be cooled and the fat removed before soup is reheated.

The flavor is improved if the soup is allowed to mellow a day or so in the refrigerator before being served.

Indian mortar and pestle

HOLY GHOST SOUP

[*Kale Soup*]

A variation of the traditional method of preparing kale soup is offered as a memento of a Vineyard summer festival sponsored by the Portuguese-American community: the Feast of the Holy Ghost. A Vineyard prelate claims no one really knows the origin of Holy Ghost Soup except that it all began back in the old country, some say in honor of a queen who was extremely generous to the poor. In Oak Bluffs the affair is sponsored by St. John's Holy Ghost Society. Most of the people concerned, or their forebears, came from the Azores during old whaling days. "Not shanghaied," the good priest says, "but as honorable crew members and paid."

Hundreds are fed this soup. All they want. And free. The proportions below won't feed hundreds, but should satisfy 6 to 8 hungry people.

2 pounds marrow bones, cut into 3-inch pieces
Vegetable oil, if needed
3 pounds beef chuck, cut in 1-inch cubes
4 medium onions, coarsely chopped
Salt
Freshly ground black pepper
1 bay leaf
4 allspice seeds
3 whole cloves garlic
8–10 cups water
3 or 4 hot Italian sausages (linguica may be substituted), sliced ½ inch thick
3 or 4 medium potatoes, peeled and cut into 1-inch cubes
1 pound kale, coarsely shredded
Loaf of French or Italian bread
Sprigs of fresh mint

Brown the marrow bones in a heavy 8-quart kettle over moderately high heat until the marrow can be extracted. Reserve the bones. Using the marrow (and a little oil if needed), brown the meat and then the onions. Add salt and pepper to taste, the bay leaf, allspice, and garlic. Return the marrow bones to the kettle and add the water, enough to cover all ingredients by at least 2 or 3 inches. Simmer over low heat, covered, until beef is tender, about 2 hours. Add sausages, potatoes, and kale and simmer another ½ hour.

Slice the bread in 2-inch chunks; crisp them in a preheated 400° F. oven about 10 minutes. Place one or two pieces in each bowl, lay several sprigs fresh mint over the bread and ladle the soup over bread and mint. Serve immediately before bread softens.

MARINATED PORK CHOPS

4 portions

MARINADE

3 cloves garlic, chopped fine
½ cup vinegar (preferably white-wine vinegar)
½ cup dry white wine
1 large onion, cut in ½-inch slices
Pinch of cinnamon
1 tablespoon salt
1 hot red pepper, coarsely chopped (pickled may be substituted)

(continued)

Combine marinade ingredients in a large glass, ceramic, or stainless-steel bowl. Place pork in marinade and refrigerate 24 hours; or marinate 12 hours at room temperature. Turn the meat occasionally.

8 lean pork chops (or 8 slices pork loin, cut 1 inch thick)	1 teaspoon flour
	2 tablespoons water
3 tablespoons lard or vegetable oil	Lemon wedges
	Pimiento slices

Remove pork from marinade. Drain it well and dry it with paper towels. Reserve the marinade. Add lard or oil to a heavy skillet; melt over moderately high heat. Brown the pork evenly on both sides. Remove from skillet. Pour off fat from skillet. Strain 1 cup of the marinade and add it to skillet. Bring to a boil over high heat, scraping the brown particles from the bottom and sides of the skillet to incorporate them in the marinade. Return pork to skillet, reduce heat to low, cover tightly, and simmer 30 minutes, or until meat is tender. Sauce may be thickened slightly by slowly stirring in 1 teaspoon flour mixed to a smooth paste with 2 tablespoons water.

Serve with a garnish of lemon wedges and strips of canned pimientos.

LIMA BEANS AND LINGUICA

4 generous portions

1 cup dried lima beans	1 pound linguica, cut in 1-inch slices
1 large onion, coarsely chopped	Salt
2–3 tablespoons butter (or half butter, half vegetable oil)	Freshly ground black pepper

Soak lima beans overnight in water to cover. Drain, cover with 3 cups fresh cold water and bring to a boil over high heat. Reduce heat to low and let simmer. In a small, heavy skillet cook onion in butter or butter-oil mixture until golden and transparent. Add linguica slices and brown lightly on both sides, then add onions and linguica to lima beans. Cover tightly and barely simmer until beans are tender (see note below regarding cooking time). Season to taste with salt and pepper. Linguica has a high salt content and it may not be necessary to add salt to this dish.

Note: Soaking period for dried beans may be hastened as follows: Drop beans into 3 cups rapidly boiling water, bring back to the boil and cook over moderately high heat for 2 minutes. Remove saucepan from heat and let beans soak for 1 hour, then proceed with recipe.

It is nearly impossible to give even an approximate cooking time for dried beans. Too many factors are involved—the length of time the beans have sat on the grocery-store shelf, for instance. Beans soaked overnight will cook up more quickly than those soaked in the method given in the preceding paragraph. Sometimes specially treated beans may be purchased which presumably do not require soaking.

CODFISH CAKES

Makes 6 large fish cakes

1 pound salt cod (the Canadian fillets are recommended)

2 cups day-old French or Italian bread, coarsely crumbled

¾ cup olive oil (or part olive, part other vegetable oil)

2 tablespoons chopped parsley

2 tablespoons chopped fresh coriander, if available

1 teaspoon chopped fresh mint

Freshly ground black pepper

3 cloves garlic, peeled and cut in half

Parsley sprigs

6 poached eggs (optional)

Freshen the cod by soaking at least 12 hours in cold water to cover. Change water several times during this period. Drain fish, rinse it, place in a saucepan, and add sufficient cold water to cover it by 1 inch. Bring to a simmer over moderate heat and cook over low heat about 20 minutes, or until fish flakes easily when pierced

(continued)

with a fork. Do not let it boil at any time. Drain the fish and let it cool, then shred it fine with the fingers, discarding any bones or skin.

In a large bowl combine bread crumbs, ½ cup of the oil, chopped parsley, coriander, mint, and pepper. Stir vigorously. Add flaked codfish and beat well. Shape mixture into flat, round cakes, about ¾ inch thick. The hands may be lightly moistened with water before shaping fish cakes. Heat the remaining ¼ cup oil in a heavy skillet with the garlic until almost at the smoking point. Add the fish cakes to the pan and cook over moderate heat until golden brown on each side. Drain briefly on a paper towel, then serve on a heated platter with a garnish of parsley sprigs. A poached egg may top each fish cake.

SALT COD WITH POTATOES

4 to 6 portions

1½ pounds salt codfish fillets (the Canadian fillets are excellent)

¾ cup olive oil (or half olive oil, half other vegetable oil)

4 medium onions, peeled and cut into ¼-inch slices

½ teaspoon finely minced garlic

6 medium potatoes, boiled without salt, peeled, and cut into ½-inch slices

Salt

Freshly ground black pepper

2 tablespoons finely chopped fresh parsley

4 hard-boiled eggs, cut into 16 wedges

18–20 pitted black olives

Lemon wedges

Freshen the cod by soaking at least 12 hours in cold water to cover. Change the water several times during this period. Drain the fish, rinse it, place in a saucepan, and add enough cold water to cover it by 1 inch. Bring to a simmer over moderate heat, then cook over low heat about 20 minutes, or until fish flakes easily when pierced with a fork. Do not let it boil at any time. Drain the fish; let it cool. Shred fine with the fingers, discarding any bones or skin.

Heat half the oil in a heavy skillet over moderate heat and cook the onions in it until golden and transparent. Stir often. Stir in the garlic, immediately remove the skillet from the heat. With a slotted spoon, remove onion-garlic mixture and set aside.

Preheat oven to 375° F.

Place half of the sliced potatoes in a heavy 8- to 9-inch casserole, 4 inches deep. Salt them very lightly. Cover with half of the onion-garlic mixture, then with half of the codfish. Season with a little black pepper. Repeat layering process with remainder of potatoes, onions, cod, and black pepper. Now pour remainder of the oil over the contents of the casserole. Bake about 20 minutes, or until top is lightly browned. Sprinkle with parsley and garnish with egg wedges and olives. Serve immediately.

Offer, as an accompaniment, lemon wedges—and, for those who wish it, coarsely ground black pepper.

STEAMED CLAMS IN WHITE WINE AND SEASONINGS

This variation of a classic dish is prepared by a Spanish friend who cooks sublimely in Portuguese as well.

2 portions (as main course)
4 portions (as first course)

2 tablespoons olive oil
1 tablespoon butter
½ cup finely chopped onions
1 tablespoon finely chopped
  garlic
½ cup coarsely crumbled day-
  old French or Italian
  bread, crusts removed
¼ cup chopped parsley
¼ cup pine nuts (*pignoli*), if
  available (or ¼ cup sliv-
  ered almonds)

24 small hard-shelled clams
  (little necks), scrubbed
  clean
1 cup dry white wine
Freshly ground black pepper
Salt, if needed
Lemon wedges
Parsley sprigs

(*continued*)

Heat oil and butter in a heavy casserole or skillet over moderate heat until foam subsides. Reduce heat to low, add onions and garlic and cook until onions are golden and transparent. Add bread crumbs, parsley, and nuts; cook about 5 minutes, adding a little additional oil or butter if needed. Add clams and wine. Cover pan tightly and cook over low heat 8 to 10 minutes, or until clam shells open. Remove clams to a heated platter, add pepper and salt (if needed) to sauce and pour it over clams.

Garnish with lemon wedges and sprigs of parsley.

PORTUGUESE EGGS WITH VEGETABLES

4 portions

2–3 tablespoons butter (or half butter, half vegetable oil)

½ pound linguica sliced in ½-inch circles (chorizo or any garlic sausage may be substituted)

½ cup finely chopped onions

1½ cups cooked fresh or frozen peas (or cooked small zucchini, cut in ½-inch slices)

½ cup fresh chicken stock (or canned chicken broth)

2 tablespoons finely chopped parsley

2 tablespoons finely chopped fresh coriander (cilantro, or Chinese parsley)

1 teaspoon tomato paste

Salt

Freshly ground black pepper

6 eggs, beaten

1 tablespoon grated Parmesan cheese (optional)

Preheat oven to 375° F.

Melt butter in a heavy flameproof 10-inch shallow casserole over moderate heat. When foam subsides, brown the sausage slices on one side only, then remove from pan. Add the onions and cook until golden and transparent. Remove casserole from heat. Add the peas (or zucchini), chicken stock, parsley, and coriander, and stir in tomato paste. Season with salt and pepper to taste.

Arrange the sausage slices in a circle around edge of casserole, leaving vegetable mixture in center. Pour beaten eggs over vegetable mixture. If using the grated cheese, sprinkle lightly over the eggs. Bake until eggs are set, 10 to 15 minutes. Serve from casserole.

As a variation, eggs may be used whole. Slip them, one at a time, from a saucer onto the vegetable mixture, keeping each one apart from its neighbor.

Note: Fresh coriander, if one is fortunate enough to have a source of supply, imparts a distinctive flavor to many Portuguese dishes. It can often be found in Chinese markets or in Spanish neighborhoods.

PORTUGUESE CORNBREAD

Traditionally served in Portugal as an accompaniment to Caldo Verde, or Kale soup (page 257), this coarse-textured cornbread may be prepared with either white or yellow cornmeal. In the Azores, where a large group of the Portuguese people on Martha's Vineyard originated, the white meal is preferred. Serve it also with any hearty soup, or with a good salad. Or serve it at breakfast, cut into wedges and generously buttered.

4 to 6 portions

1½ cups white cornmeal (or yellow)
1½ cups boiling water
1½ teaspoons salt
2 tablespoons sugar
2 tablespoons butter
1 package compressed or granulated yeast dissolved in ¼ cup warm water (water for granulated yeast should be slightly more than lukewarm)

½ cup milk
3–4 cups (approximately) sifted all-purpose flour (a mixture of 2 parts pastry flour and 1 part all-purpose flour may be used and will make a softer dough)

(continued)

Grease a 9-inch round pan, 2 to 3 inches deep.

In a large bowl combine cornmeal, boiling water, salt, sugar, and butter. Stir vigorously until smooth. Cool slightly. Add the yeast mixture and blend well. Add milk and flour, using enough flour to produce a moderately firm dough. Place dough on a lightly floured board and knead by pressing down on it with the heel of the hand, lifting the mass off the board and then throwing it back onto the board. Continue this process until dough becomes smooth and elastic, about 5 minutes. Avoid overflouring the pastry board. Place dough in a buttered bowl, cover with a clean, dampened towel, and let it rise in a warm, draft-free place. The oven, unheated, is a good spot. Set the bowl over a pan of hot water to hasten rising. When the dough has doubled in bulk, after about 1½ to 2 hours, punch it down in its bowl, then take it out and knead it again two or three times. Shape dough into a ball, place in baking pan and allow it to rise again until doubled in bulk, about 1 to 1½ hours. Bake in a preheated 350° F. oven until the top is golden brown, 45 to 50 minutes.

Note: The cornbread will be lighter in texture if dough is allowed to rise twice in the bowl before final rising in the pan.

PORTUGUESE SWEET BREAD

[*Massa Sovada*]

This is the sweet bread for the Sabbath—perfect with hot, freshly brewed coffee. Toasted and accompanied by a firm white cream cheese and jelly—beach plum, especially—it is the purest of pleasures.

Another name for these light and airy loaves is Easter bread. When the bread is made during that season, one hard-cooked egg in the shell for each child in the family is placed in the dough before the second rising.

Makes 2 medium loaves

2 packages granulated or
    compressed yeast
½ cup warm water
¼ teaspoon sugar
1 cup milk
¼ pound softened butter
1 teaspoon vanilla extract
½ teaspoon powdered mace
    (optional)
Pinch of powdered saffron
    (optional)

About 6 cups sifted flour,
    preferably unbleached (2
    parts pastry flour and 1
    part all-purpose flour may
    be used)
1¼ cups sugar
1 teaspoon salt
5 or 6 eggs, well beaten
1 beaten egg yolk, mixed with
    2 tablespoons water (or
    granulated sugar)

Grease two 9-inch round pans, preferably 2 inches deep.

Combine yeast, warm water, and ¼ teaspoon sugar and set aside. (If using granulated yeast, water should be slightly hotter than lukewarm.) In a small saucepan heat milk and butter. Add vanilla and the mace and saffron, if used. Remove from heat when butter has melted. Cool slightly. In a large mixing bowl combine 4 cups of the flour, 1¼ cups sugar, and the salt. Make a well in the center, add cooled milk and yeast mixture. Beat vigorously. The electric mixer works well up to this point. (If your mixer has a dough hook attachment, you can use it to do the rest of the mixing if you wish.) Add beaten eggs, mix well. Add remaining flour, ½ cup at a time, until a firm dough is achieved (additional flour may be needed). Place dough on a lightly floured board or marble slab; knead by pressing down on bread mass with heel of hand, lifting mass off board, then throwing it back. Knead about 5 minutes, or until dough becomes smooth and elastic. Place dough in a buttered bowl and let rise in a warm, draft-free place such as an unheated oven (set bowl over a pan of hot water to hasten rising). When dough has doubled in bulk, turn out on a floured board and knead again for a few moments. Cut dough into two equal pieces, shape lightly into round balls, and place one ball in each cake pan. Brush loaf tops lightly with beaten egg mixture, or sprinkle a little granu-

(continued)

lated sugar over the loaves. Let bread rise until doubled in bulk, about 1½ hours. Bake in preheated 350° F. oven approximately 1 hour.

Note: Instead of the 5 or 6 eggs specified, up to 12 eggs are sometimes used to make this bread, in which case additional flour is required to stiffen the dough.

PORTUGUESE BREAD PUDDING

A deliciously different bread pudding that typifies the Portuguese fondness for sweets prepared with many eggs. It is a departure from standard bread puddings using bread slices (this one contains bread crumbs); and the caramel mixture coating the baking dish melts during the cooking process, adding another dimension of flavor.

6 to 8 portions

½ cup sugar, sifted
2 tablespoons water
2 cups milk
6 tablespoons sugar
½ teaspoon grated orange rind
2 tablespoons butter

2 cups fine bread crumbs, made from day-old French or Italian bread, crusts removed
5 or 6 beaten eggs (4 whole eggs and 2 egg yolks may be used)

Preheat oven to 350° F.

Combine ½ cup sugar and water in a small, heavy saucepan. Cook over moderate heat, stirring with a wooden spoon, until sugar melts. Continue to cook, swirling the pan now and then, until the liquid turns caramel-brown. Immediately remove saucepan from heat and pour the caramel into a 6- to 8-cup baking dish, at least 4 inches deep, or a 1½- to 2-quart charlotte mold. Tilt the baking dish so that the bottom and sides are coated with caramel, which will harden as it cools. In a saucepan combine milk, 6 tablespoons sugar, and orange rind and heat to scalding (the scalding point is reached when tiny beads or bubbles appear around the edges of the pan) . Remove from heat.

Add the butter and crumbs to the milk mixture. Stir the beaten eggs into this mixture, then pour into the caramel-lined baking dish. Set it in a container holding about 2 inches of boiling water and bake in middle of oven 45 to 50 minutes. Custard is done when a knife inserted in its center comes out clean. Cool thoroughly in mold, then chill in refrigerator for several hours. Unmold by running a knife around the sides of the baking dish, then placing serving plate over pudding and inverting. Spoon some of the caramel over each serving

The Old-Timers

Chapter 12

Flour, per barrel	$ .59	Veal, per pound	.03
Wood, per load	1.00	Pork, per pound	.05
Potatoes, per bushel	.25	Butter, per pound	.10
Beef, per pound	.04	Cheese, per pound	.05

—FROM AN 1829 GROCER'S ADVERTISEMENT
IN THE *Vineyard Gazette*

. . . the Vineyard was not only self-supporting but self-sustaining for nigh onto two centuries. Only spices, sugar, tea, coffee, breadstuffs and the rum, which was considered quite essential, were imported. . . . Meat, beef, pork, and mutton; fish, both fresh and cured; vegetables and fodder; the clothes people wore, their shoes . . . all were raised, caught, grown or made on the Island.

—FROM *A Short History of Martha's
Vineyard*, ELEANOR R. MAYHEW, ED.

Nostalgia for times past lingers in many sections of the Vineyard. The hazy, halcyon days of summer and fall often evoke the shade of some former Islander, and though you will no longer pass one of the Reverend Mayhews riding his mare along a cowpath on his way to minister to an ailing farmer, you may very well buy your lobsters from a contemporary member of this distinguished family, or chat with another one of them at the airport as he waits for a plane to Boston to attend meetings of the legislature as a state representative. Mayhew, Norton, Athearn, Manter, Luce, Pease, Allen—the old names survive; the families still live here.

Like other New Englanders, Vineyarders settled in for the winter prepared for almost anything. "In those days," says John Daggett, "we had no warning that a storm was coming until it practically reached us. However, we never worried but took it in stride because we usually had pork, bacon, chickens, eggs and also vegetables in the cellar. We always had a barrel of flour, another of sugar, and usually one or two of apples, as well as 100 pounds of prunes."* Travel was precarious during much of the year—and tediously slow, because of

* *It Began With a Whale,* by John Daggett, privately printed (1963).

innumerable sheep and cattle bars across the roads. As a result, an Edgartown lady might see her brother in Chilmark only once or twice a year. On arriving from the mainland by boat, the traveler lodged for the night at a Holmes Hole (now Vineyard Haven) tavern before he "sett forward" on the road to Gay Head.

Food was a vital concern. Remarkable ingenuity was displayed by industrious housewives in both preserving and preparing what foodstuffs they had. A few pecks of oysters, bedded down in sawdust and partially frozen, could be feasted on for weeks. Deer, rabbits, and other small game were easy targets on snow-covered fields and could be drawn and hung in outsheds until needed for food. On good days there was ice fishing in some of the Great Ponds. Pickles and jellies put up on hot summer days added tang to late-winter meals; and when beans and cornmeal, and salt pork, potatoes, and onions were about all there was left, Yankee inventiveness remained as active as ever. Thus a simple combination of three basic ingredients—salt pork, potatoes, and onions—became many things: Potato Bargain, Necessity Mess, Tilton's Glory, or Scootin'-'Long-the-Shore (the latter being the shipboard name because the dish was often prepared in ships' galleys as the fishermen were scooting along the shore). And if you became *very* hungry about the middle of March, there was always Field Mouse Pie, which, however, was not made out of the Vineyard's white-footed mice that crept in from the fields to winter in the basement, but involved sausages and other prosaic ingredients.

JOSEPH CHASE ALLEN'S
DRY BEEF STEW*

Joseph Chase Allen probably knows more and has written more about Martha's Vineyard than anyone else around—with the exception of his long-time associate at the *Vineyard Gazette,* Henry Beetle Hough. An old-style talespinner and humorist, a fisherman and historian and Yankee to the core, Joe Allen was raised in a beautiful old weatherbeaten farmhouse that still sits

---

* Old-timers' stews presumably were prepared like soups; their "dry" stews contained only enough water to braise the meat.

tight-built on the earth in a windswept Chilmark meadow, with
the rambler roses and grapevines and lilacs of his childhood now
gone wild among the grasses.

We reprint this recipe just as he sent it to us, feeling it should
not be tampered with.

I don't know whether people ever made a "dry" beef stew anywhere save on the Vineyard, but to me it is one of the best ways
of serving beef normally too tough for steaks or roasts. My wife
turns out a splendid kettle of it, always sufficient for at least two
meals for us, because "it's better every time it's warmed over."

Here's how you do it, regulating your quantities according to
the mouths to be fed:

Select beef that has some fat on it and leave it there. Cut it, or
have it cut, into pieces that will weigh a quarter of a pound or
even more. (Incidentally, it doesn't matter a whoop what part of
the animal it comes from; neck to tail it can be used.)

Boil this meat with some salt and onions until you can almost
separate it with a fork. Then drop your vegetables into the same
kettle, potatoes, white and sweet, if you like them; turnip, more
onions, carrots, that's it.

It's a good idea to cut these vegetables into relatively small
pieces, say, halve the potatoes, cut the slices of turnip in two. While
they are cooking, mix up some flour dumplings, quite stiff, and
about the size of a human fist. Drop those into the kettle on top of
everything and steam the whole until everything is done.

Then, the dumplings have to come out first, then skim out meat
and vegetables and put 'em on a platter. Heat up the liquid in the
kettle and thicken it with flour to whatever consistency you like
gravy. Your dry stew is ready to serve.

The diner fills his plate with meat, vegetables and a dumpling
broken into several pieces and then ladles a cupful of the gravy
over the whole.

After that a deep silence falls upon the scene and lasts until the
plates are empty.

We should add that Mr. Allen's comments about Vineyard cooking included the following: "The oldest and best cooks always
swore that no cooking utensil could impart flavor to food like

(continued)

cast iron. Be it boiled, baked or fried, they insisted that this is true. My grandmother even made her baking powder biscuits in an iron frying pan on top of the stove." For this stew and other such "receipts" we suggest using a cast-iron Dutch oven with a tight-fitting lid.

RED FLANNEL HASH

The meat and vegetables left over from the New England boiled dinner create this savory dish. It is a delicious dividend and attests to the inventiveness of the old-timers. Its name is derived from the brilliant color given to it by the beets.

6 generous portions

¼ pound salt pork, cut into
    ½-inch dice
¾ cup finely chopped onions
3 cups finely chopped cooked
    corned beef
3 cups coarsely chopped
    cooked potatoes
1½ cups cooked beets, cut into
    ½-inch dice

1 small clove garlic, finely
    chopped (optional)
1 tablespoon finely chopped
    celery leaves (optional)
½ cup cream
Salt
Freshly ground black pepper
6 poached eggs (optional)
1 tablespoon chopped parsley

Brown the salt pork in a 10- or 12-inch heavy skillet over moderate heat. Remove dice from pan and drain on a paper towel. Reserve. Pour off all but 2 or 3 tablespoons of the fat. Reserve extra fat. Add the chopped onions and cook slowly until transparent, transfer to a mixing bowl. Add to mixing bowl the diced salt pork, corned beef, potatoes, beets, and, if desired, garlic and celery leaves. Then add the cream and stir thoroughly to blend. Taste for seasoning, adding salt if required, and freshly ground black pepper.

Return the reserved fat to preheated skillet, add the hash ingredients, press down with a spatula to cover the skillet evenly and cook uncovered over moderate heat until the bottom is crusty brown, about 25 to 30 minutes. Or place skillet in preheated

425° F. oven for 20 to 25 minutes, or until browned crust forms.

To remove from skillet, slide a spatula or narrow pancake turner along the sides and carefully work under the hash without crumbling it. Then fold hash in half as you would an omelet. Transfer to a heated platter.

Serve topped with poached eggs, if desired, and sprinkle with the chopped parsley.

CHICKEN AND OYSTER STIFLE

Certain quaint, early-English culinary names occur frequently in old cook books, in old newspapers, and in talks with the elderly on Martha's Vineyard. "Flummery" fascinates. So does "fool." The dictionary defines the former as a "custard of *blanc mange*"; the latter is a "sweet made with heavy cream and stewed fruit." The kitchen-oriented use of "stifle" is not listed under that word as either verb or noun, but "smother"—a good term familiar in southern kitchens—is one synonym. Smothered chicken and chicken stifle are prepared in much the same way: the meat is well browned, then braised in a seasoned, slightly thickened liquid until tender.

Here is an ancient recipe, several hundred years old, using two ingredients with great empathy toward each other—chicken and oysters.

6 portions

2 tablespoons butter	Freshly ground black pepper
2 tablespoons cooking oil	1 tablespoon flour
2 fresh broiler chickens, quartered	1 cup milk
	1½ cups medium cream
1 teaspoon salt	1 quart drained fresh oysters

Preheat oven to 350° F.

In a skillet, heat the butter and oil until foam subsides. Add the chicken pieces, first seasoning them with salt and pepper, and

(*continued*)

cook over moderate heat until golden on each side. Don't over-crowd the skillet. Remove chicken pieces from skillet and place in a large casserole. Add the flour to the fats in the pan and cook, stirring, until smooth. Add the milk and stir until a smooth sauce is obtained and the mixture comes to a simmer. Strain the sauce over the chicken pieces in the casserole, and bake, covered, for about 1 hour, or until the chicken pieces are tender. Pour in the cream, top with the oysters and return casserole to the oven for 15 minutes, or until the edges of the oysters curl, then remove casserole immediately.

Place chicken and oysters on a heated platter, pour the sauce over all and serve.

FISH STIFLE

4 to 6 portions

½ pound salt pork, cut into
    ½-inch slices
2 medium onions, thinly sliced
2 tablespoons cider vinegar
8 whole cloves
2 pounds any fresh fish: cod,
    haddock, scup (porgy),
    halibut, cleaned and cut
    in 2-inch pieces

2 tablespoons catsup
1 clove garlic, minced fine
    (optional)
Sprinkle of cayenne pepper or
    a dash of Tabasco
¼ teaspoon salt
¼ teaspoon freshly ground
    black pepper

In a heavy 4- to 6-quart kettle cook salt pork over moderate heat until crisp and golden. Remove it, drain on a paper towel, and reserve it.

Cook the sliced onions in the fat in pan until golden and transparent. Add remaining ingredients, including the reserved salt-pork slices, cover the kettle tightly and simmer gently over low heat until the fish is tender, about 20 to 25 minutes, depending on the thickness of the fish.

Note: It is unnecessary to remove skin and bones from the fish pieces.

CLAM STIFLE

From a 1921 issue of the *Vineyard Gazette* come the following instructions:

> One quart clams is of course the essential part of the dish. Separate the stomach from the ribs and chop the ribs thoroughly before combining with the stomachs. Strain the juice carefully before using.
>
> Take a baking dish, and put in a layer of potatoes, a layer of scallions, and a layer of clams, and repeat until all the clams are used.
>
> Add at least a half a pint of milk and all the butter, applied in generous dabs, that your conscience will let you use. Put several slices of salt pork over all. This is important. Salt and pepper to taste. Bake for two hours.

These directions, quoted in full, were obviously written by a cook—and we suspect a male one—who feels that anyone who is messing around in the kitchen in the first place should know intuitively about proportions and other mundane technicalities, such as how to distinguish a clam's ribs from its stomach. Agreeing in principle, we give you the recipe just as it appeared.

BOILED SALT COD DINNER

[*Sometimes called "Picked Fish"*]

4 generous portions

1 pound salt cod (the Canadian fillets are good)	6 medium potatoes, peeled
Freshly ground black pepper to taste	½ pound salt pork, cut into thin strips

Soak salt cod at least 12 hours in sufficient cold water to cover it by 1 inch. Change the water several times during this period. Drain fish; rinse it in cold water. Place in a kettle or saucepan of appropriate size, and add sufficient cold water to cover the fish

(continued)

by 1 or 2 inches. Bring to a simmer over low heat and cook about 20 minutes. Do not let the fish boil. Drain it, remove skin and bones, if any, and keep warm. Dust lightly with a little freshly ground black pepper.

Boil the potatoes in unsalted water until tender.

Cook the salt pork in a heavy skillet over moderate heat until crisp and golden. Remove and drain on a paper towel. Reserve the pork and the liquid fat.

To serve: Vineyard people place the salt cod in one serving dish, the potatoes in another, the salt pork in still another. The liquid fat is poured into a pitcher. The diner breaks a potato open on his plate, heaps salt cod on top, crumbles the salt pork over both, then pours some of the pork fat over all, and happily sets to.

A variation is to make a cream gravy with some of the liquid fat and serve that instead of the liquid pork fat.

Cooked, diced beets are a good accompaniment, as is Egg Sauce (see page 39).

Note: Some New England cooks set the salt cod flesh side down on clothespins in a large kettle, allowing the salt to sink to the bottom of the container.

POTATO BARGAIN

[*Also known as Poverty Hash or Necessity Mess*]

Quaintly, even forthrightly named, this recipe has persisted for generations, perhaps because today it is as appetizing in taste as it was in other, less affluent times. Its appearance on the menu in those earlier days was dictated by what was left in the food or root cellar along about February or March. There was always the salt-pork barrel to be dipped into; and usually still a few rations of potatoes and onions were left. Mrs. Welcome Tilton's great-great granddaughter supplies this recipe. She says her father, when sailing as a young man on the *Alice B. Wentworth,* claimed it was "better after two or three days but tiresome after a week of being served up daily."

4 portions

4 slices of lean salt pork, cut
    in ½-inch dice
4 medium onions, sliced thin
4 medium potatoes, pared and
    sliced thin

Boiling water
Pepper to taste
Salt if needed

In a heavy aluminum pot with a tight-fitting lid, or a black iron skillet with a good lid, fry the salt-pork dice until a crisp, golden brown. Remove them from pan and drain on a paper towel. Add the sliced onions to the fat in pan and cook until golden and transparent. Return pork dice to pan, add the sliced potatoes and enough boiling water barely to cover ingredients. Add freshly ground pepper, and salt, if needed. Cover the pan tightly and cook slowly, turning the food from time to time. The potatoes, when tender, should have absorbed most of the water.

The Tilton recipe, handed down through the years, suggests that "the secret of a good Bargain is not too much water but cook slow and let the steam cook them."

OLD VINEYARD–STYLE BAKED BEANS

Early Vineyarders made baked beans much the same way as other New Englanders. A slight variation, according to one native Chilmarker whose memories go back seventy-five years to his mother's cooking, is boiling the salt pork before putting it in the bean pot with the beans. He comments that "the pork should be boiled until nearly done before it is put in the beans, which should also be boiled. Then score the rind on the pork and leave it exposed. It will bake until it crackles when chewed and the heft of people enjoy it."

(continued)

8 portions

1 quart dried pea beans	1 teaspoon dry mustard mixed
3 small onions, or 1 large	with a little water
onion	⅓ cup molasses
3 or 4 cloves, inserted in one	2 tablespoons brown sugar
of the onions (optional)	½ pound salt pork, cut in 2 or
2 teaspoons salt	3 chunks
½ teaspoon freshly ground	Additional brown sugar
black pepper	(optional)

Soak beans overnight in cold water to cover. In the morning, simmer them in a large pot until the skins break. (Test for this by placing several beans in a spoon and blowing on them.) Or without soaking the beans, put them in a large saucepan; pour in enough cold water to cover them by several inches. Bring to a boil, cook over moderate heat for 2 or 3 minutes. Allow the beans to stand in their water for about an hour, then turn into a 4-quart bean pot or heavy casserole. Bury the onions in the pot. The bean water should just cover the beans. Reserve any left-over liquid. Add the salt, pepper, mustard, molasses, and brown sugar. Place the salt pork (preferably boiled first), after scoring it with a sharp knife, on top of the beans; it should protrude about ½ inch above the beans.

Cover the beans and bake in a 200° to 250° F. oven for about 8 hours. Do not stir them. Check the liquid level from time to time, keeping the beans barely covered. Use the reserved bean liquid, if any; otherwise add water. Uncover the beans the last half hour of cooking. A little additional brown sugar may be sprinkled over their surface at this time.

BAKED BEAN SOUP

Economical in its use of leftover beans, this is a hearty, different, but delicious soup—perfect for luncheon on a crisp autumn day or during a driving summer northeaster.

6 to 8 portions

2 tablespoons butter

4 tablespoons finely chopped
onion

2 tablespoons flour

2 cups baked beans

4 cups beef stock (or 4 cups
boiling water with 3
bouillon cubes dissolved in
it)

2 cups canned tomatoes (or
4 or 5 large, fresh un-
peeled tomatoes, coarsely
chopped)

Freshly ground black pepper
to taste

½ teaspoon salt

Croutons (optional)

Melt the butter over moderate heat in a heavy 3- to 4-quart
saucepan. When the foam subsides, add the onions and cook, stirring occasionally, until transparent but not brown. Add the flour,
mixing thoroughly to blend it with the onions. Add the baked
beans, the beef stock or bouillon, and the tomatoes. Grind some
black pepper over the pot and stir in the salt. Bring ingredients
to a simmer and cook 20 to 30 minutes.

Purée the soup in a food mill or force it through a strainer.
Return the soup to the saucepan, taste for seasoning, and reheat.

Garnish with croutons, if desired.

PUMPKIN SOUP

New Englanders—and Vineyarders—seem to have used "pumpkin" and "squash" interchangeably when they spoke of making
fall and winter dishes from this or these vegetables. What would
be a pumpkin pie in the South would be made with a squash
filling in Massachusetts; and many northern cooks disdain
pumpkins altogether except as something to set out on the porch
as a traditional symbol that fall has arrived and jack-o'-lantern
season is approaching.

In a way, everyone is right in this particular culinary issue: the
Cucurbitas include both pumpkins and squashes (as well as
gourds), and *C. maxima,* according to Norman Taylor's *Encyclopedia of Gardening,* "includes very large squash that pass for
pumpkins."

(continued)

So here is an old-fashioned recipe for a pumpkin—or squash—soup. Actually, sherry and cream, two of its ingredients, bring it close to the category of *haute cuisine,* and it is doubtful that early New Englanders would have condoned their use. The other ingredients, however, were available in their larders at all times, despite the long, cold winters and dwindling food supplies.

In any case, the soup is a delight served hot or thoroughly chilled, and is recommended as an unusual prelude to a Thanksgiving dinner.

4 to 6 portions

2 tablespoons butter
3 tablespoons chopped onion
2 cups chicken stock (or canned chicken broth)
2 cups cooked pumpkin, fresh or canned (or cooked hubbard squash)

2 cups milk
Small pinch each of ground cloves, ground ginger, ground allspice
½ teaspoon salt
½ cup heavy cream
¼ cup dry sherry

Whipped cream for garnish

Melt the butter over moderate heat in a heavy 4-quart saucepan. When the foam subsides, add the onion and cook until transparent and golden. Add chicken stock, pumpkin or squash, milk, spices, and salt. If fresh pumpkin or squash pulp is used, it should be well drained and put through a food mill or strainer before use. Mix ingredients well and bring to a boil, stirring thoroughly. Reduce heat and simmer, stirring from time to time, for 15 or 20 minutes.

Purée the soup in a food mill or force it through a fine strainer. Return purée to saucepan. Add the cream and sherry and heat the soup carefully without allowing it to boil. Taste for seasonings. Garnish each serving with a spoonful of stiffly beaten heavy cream, lightly salted. May be served chilled, using the same garnish.

APPLE MUFFINS

This recipe comes from Annie Lord's 1912 cooking class, which met in the First Baptist Church in Vineyard Haven.

Makes 1 dozen

2½ cups sifted flour	½ cup sugar
3½ teaspoons baking powder	1 egg, beaten
½ teaspoon salt	1 cup milk
¾ teaspoon cinnamon	1 cup chopped or coarsely
¾ teaspoon nutmeg	grated apples (peel them
4 tablespoons butter	first)

2 tablespoons brown sugar

Preheat oven to 400° F.

Sift the flour, baking powder, salt, and ½ teaspoon each of the cinnamon and nutmeg together into a bowl. In another bowl, cream butter and sugar until well blended. Stir in egg. Add flour mixture alternately with milk. Add apples. Stir only enough to moisten. (See instructions for Blueberry Muffins, page 182.) Pour into greased muffin tins. Combine brown sugar and remaining cinnamon and nutmeg; sprinkle over top of muffins. Bake 25 minutes.

SEA VOYAGE GINGERBREAD

Mentioned by Henry Beetle Hough in his introduction to this cook book, here, for the curious, is the recipe for Sea Voyage Gingerbread exactly as it appeared in the *Vineyard Gazette* in an issue dated August 28, 1857.

Sift two pounds of flour into a pan, and cut up in it a pound and a quarter of fresh butter; rub the butter well into the flour and then mix in a pint of West Indian molasses and a pound of the best brown sugar.

Beat eight eggs until very light. Stir into the eggs two glasses or

(continued)

a gill of brandy; add also to the egg a teacup full of ground ginger and a tablespoon of powdered cinnamon, with a teaspoon of soda melted in a little warm water. Wet the flour, etc. with this mixture till it becomes a soft dough.

Sprinkle a little flour on your paste board, and with a broad knife spread portions of the mixture thickly and smoothly upon it. The thickness must be equal all through; therefore spread it carefully and evenly, as the dough will be too soft to roll out. Then with the edge of a tumbler dipped in flour, cut it out into round cakes.

Have ready square pans, slightly buttered; lay the cakes in them sufficiently far apart to prevent their running into each other when baked. Set the pans into a brisk oven and bake the cakes well, seeing that they do not burn.

These cakes will keep during a long voyage and are frequently carried to sea. Many persons find highly spiced gingerbread a preventive to seasickness.

HASTY PUDDING

[*Cornmeal Mush*]

That this homely preparation has long been eaten on Martha's Vineyard is evident from this quotation from an early journal: "April 10, 1714. The wind being excessive high we did not goe to Holmes' Hole, but . . . sat awhile in the Wigwam where Elizabeth, Stephen Spokes' Widow dwells: eat roste Alewive and very good Hasty Pudding."*

One of the humblest of foods, and one of the simplest to pre-pare, cornmeal mush, plain or elaborated on, has warmed the innards of generations of New Englanders on wintry days or evenings. Like most old-time dishes, it acquired a variety of folk names—"Stir-about Pudding," because it must be con-stantly stirred about; "Hasty Pudding," because it can be put together hastily. It has its southern counterpart in the traditional breakfast grits (though this uses a coarser stone-ground meal from white corn rather than yellow meal); and fried mush with

---

* *History of Martha's Vineyard,* Vol. I, Dukes County Historical Society, Edgartown, Massachusetts (1966).

molasses has sustained whole families as breakfast, dinner, and supper in a sharecropper's cottage during hard days.

A heaped, steaming plateful of Hasty Pudding, with a pool of butter in the middle and crisp bacon bits sprinkled over the top, makes a nourishing, satisfying supper if the cook is too tired to cook; or a bowl of it at breakfast, served with cream and some type of sweetening—maple sugar, honey, molasses, or brown sugar—will get most people through a frigid morning in fine style.

A depressing sign of the instant-food age is that the Quaker Oats cornmeal box no longer gives instructions for making cornmeal mush.

4 portions

½ cup yellow cornmeal   Few dashes of cinnamon and
3 cups water   mace (optional)
½ teaspoon salt

Mix cornmeal with 1 cup of the water. Bring 2 cups water to a boil; add salt. Stir in cornmeal mixture, lower heat, and cook 10 to 15 minutes, stirring frequently. Add spices if desired. Mixture may be started in the top half of a double boiler, then covered and placed over boiling water and steamed for half an hour or longer. This eliminates the need for frequent stirring, and some feel it also improves the flavor of the finished mush.

If the mush is to be fried, mix 2 tablespoons flour with the cornmeal before adding the cold water. Cook in same fashion, then pour into an ungreased loaf pan (rinsed first with cold water) and chill several hours or overnight.

Slice cold mush, dust with flour and fry in butter or bacon fat until slices are nicely browned.

CRACKER PUDDING

Annie Lord's 1912 cooking class in the First Baptist Church of Vineyard Haven prepared this old-fashioned pudding. The directions from *Vineyard Recipes* state: "Bake slow. After set add a cup of milk." One suspects the milk is not stirred in, like that used in Baked Indian Pudding I (see page 289). No portions are given for the finished dish; presumably it will feed 6 people.

1 quart milk
1 cup sugar
1 cup cracker crumbs (preferably prepared from common crackers, crushed)
1 cup raisins (less may be used)
2 tablespoons melted butter

¼ teaspoon ground cinnamon
¼ teaspoon ground cloves (or ¼ teaspoon ground nutmeg)
¼ teaspoon salt
½ teaspoon vanilla
2 eggs, lightly beaten
1 cup milk (optional)

Preheat oven to 325° F.

Combine milk, sugar, crumbs, raisins, butter, spices, salt, and vanilla in a saucepan; cook over low heat until the mixture almost simmers. Immediately remove from heat and stir the beaten eggs thoroughly into the mixture. Pour into a baking dish; bake approximately 1 hour, or until pudding is set. If desired, pour the optional cup of milk over the pudding (do not stir it in) and bake another ½ hour.

BAKED INDIAN PUDDING I

The "Indian" part of this pudding is the cornmeal, a foodstuff long used by various Indian tribes that was quickly adopted into the diet of the first white settlers. Cornmeal is still referred to as Indian meal in many old recipes, including several found in old Vineyard records.

This is generally agreed on as the basic recipe. Most cooks, however, have added—and still add—personal touches: suet instead of butter, a different blend of spices, a handful of raisins. If you're cooking your pudding on the Island, why not slice some windfall apples from a roadside tree into the baking dish?

If a soft-centered pudding seems more traditional, reserve some of the milk, pour it over the combined ingredients without stirring it in, then bake.

8 portions

3 tablespoons butter	½ cup yellow cornmeal
⅔ cup dark molasses	½ teaspoon salt
5 cups milk	6 tablespoons sugar
¾ teaspoon cinnamon	Heavy cream, whipped cream,
¾ teaspoon nutmeg	or vanilla ice cream
½ teaspoon ginger (optional)	

Preheat oven to 300° F.

Grease a baking dish, about 8 by 10 inches and at least 3 inches deep.

In a saucepan heat the butter, molasses, and 4 cups of the milk. In another saucepan, thoroughly combine the spices, cornmeal, salt, and sugar. Then stir in the heated milk mixture. Cook over moderate heat, stirring frequently, until it thickens. Pour into the baking dish. Add the remaining cup of milk but do not stir it in. Bake at least 3 hours without stirring.

Serve warm with heavy cream, whipped cream, or a scoop of rich vanilla ice cream.

BAKED INDIAN PUDDING II
[*A Durgin-Park recipe*]

The proprietors of Boston's famed Durgin-Park Restaurant, an ancient establishment known to many Vineyarders, supply this recipe in an amusing brochure they offer to their diners. They claim this pudding recipe was taken to sea by clipper-ship captains, who were among their early patrons, and made in ships' galleys from Valparaiso to Hong Kong. In the course of a current year, Durgin-Park claims, they make enough Indian pudding "to float the *Queen Mary,* the *Queen Elizabeth* and one small rowboat."

12 portions

1½ quarts hot milk	½ teaspoon salt
1 cup yellow cornmeal	¼ teaspoon baking powder
½ cup black (dark) molasses	2 eggs, slightly beaten
¼ cup sugar	Heavy cream, whipped cream,
¼ cup butter	or vanilla ice cream

Preheat oven to 500° F.

Grease a stone crock (preferably) or a baking dish.

Using half of the hot milk (3 cups), combine and thoroughly mix all ingredients. Pour into the stone crock or baking dish. Bake until the pudding comes to a boil. Then stir in the remaining milk. Reduce oven heat to 200° F. and bake the pudding for 5 to 7 hours.

Serve warm with thick, heavy cream, whipped cream, or a scoop of vanilla ice cream.

FRIED CHEESECAKES

These pan, griddle, or whatever cakes, adapted from a very old New England recipe, are unexpectedly good. Try them for Sunday brunch with crisp bacon slices and broiled garden-fresh tomatoes.

2 portions (8 pancakes, 3 to 4 inches in diameter)

1 cup grated store (Cheddar)
cheese (Alley's Store in
West Tisbury has a fine
one)
3 tablespoons flour
½ tablespoon grated lemon
rind

½ teaspoon salt
⅔ cup sour cream
3 egg yolks, lightly beaten
3 stiffly beaten egg whites
(optional)

Combine cheese, flour, lemon rind, and salt in a mixing bowl. Stir in sour cream and beaten egg yolks.

Heat a griddle or large heavy skillet over moderate heat. Grease it lightly. When the griddle is hot enough (test with a drop of water; it should sputter on the griddle's surface), spoon the mixture into cakes averaging 3 to 4 inches in diameter. Brown lightly and turn. Two to 3 minutes a side should cook them properly. Do not overcrowd the griddle. Remove first batch to a heated platter and keep warm. Grease the griddle lightly again if necessary and finish baking the cakes.

Note: If used, the egg whites may be beaten to stiff peaks and folded into the griddle cakes. Or use them in Chocolate Meringues (see page 203) or Black Walnut Meringues (see page 202).

PRISCILLA HANCOCK'S
CHOCOLATE NUT FUDGE

As an only child on her father's chicken farm at Quenames, near South Beach, Priscilla Hancock spent many happy hours in her "kitchen" out under the trees, making splendid concoctions from flour, water, mud, and whatever else was appropriate and at hand. When she grew up, she moved indoors, and for forty years—until she retired in 1956—Miss Hancock turned out in that Quenames kitchen the tastiest confections ever produced on the Vineyard or, some thought, anywhere else. Her success, according to an article on her published in a February, 1970, issue of the *Vineyard Gazette,* she attributes largely to "never using anything but the finest ingredients, always taking plenty of time, and thinking up interesting taste combinations. 'I'd always use sweet chocolate for anything with fruits and nuts in it, but then I'd dip butter creams and peppermints in bittersweet. But there wasn't really anything so remarkable about it all. There's no great secrecy to candy-making except never changing the quality of your ingredients.' "

Gone now are the long quiet walks down the woodsy road to the candy lady's house; and gone is the West Tisbury general store where Miss Hancock used to "gam" with her friends James Cagney and Clarence Budington Kelland and a former policeman named McNamara, who'd been in the movies and studied voice with Caruso. Miss Hancock and her friend Lucy Wiig now live in a pleasant old West Tisbury house, with a big ginger cat and rooms filled with Victorian antiques. But there are still quiet woodsy roads to stroll down, and comfortable country kitchens where a Vineyard dweller can mix up her own batch of one of Miss Hancock's specialties—this luscious fudge.

Makes 4 pounds

4 cups sugar	5 or 6 tablespoons butter
1½ teaspoons salt	2 teaspoons vanilla
1½ cups light cream	1½ or 2 cups coarsely chopped
2 tablespoons corn syrup	walnuts or pecans
6 squares Baker's unsweet-	
ened chocolate	

Bring sugar, salt, cream, and corn syrup to boiling point in a large saucepan and cook slowly for several minutes, then add chocolate. Reduce heat and cook without stirring to the soft-ball stage, or 234° on a candy thermometer. Put butter and vanilla in mixture but do not stir. Cool to lukewarm; beat until creamy, then add nuts. Pour onto a buttered platter and allow to harden before cutting into squares.

Note: In a recent conversation, Miss Hancock stressed the importance of allowing the fudge to cool sufficiently before beginning to beat it. This prevents graininess in the finished confection.

Gingerbread cottage in Oak Bluffs

End Page

Summer is over. The signs on the shops have been taken down and the NO TRESPASSING signs nailed up. Shutters are closed on the summer houses; chains hang across roadways; gates are closed. Out at Squibnocket, the rocks roll in on the rising tides and begin covering the summer sand; and the only sounds heard there besides the wash of the water and the crying of the gulls is the occasional plop of a few handfuls of sand as little by little the precious, coveted sea cliffs of Martha's Vineyard erode in the wet wind and the slashing fall rains, drop to the beach, and wash away forever into the sea. The Island is disappearing; through the millenniums to come it will be washed away.

But for the moment—and, hopefully, for the rest of our time—the Vineyard is safe, unless we who live on it destroy it in other ways. Rum cherries, wild grapes, beach plums, rose hips, late blackberries hang richly ripe on the moors and in the thickets. Schools of tinker mackerel and pollock swarm in and out of the Great Ponds with the tides. The fat black-faced Canada geese settle in Farmer Greene's empty cornfield beside the tattered scarecrows and glean the last hard kernels of grain; restless, they take off again and circle aimlessly over West Tisbury in a loose V, then head for Chilmark and the Keith pond, debating noisily en route whether to migrate or count on being fed all winter on the Island.

The opulence of fall pervades the Vineyard, as all the people and creatures who live on it and plants and trees that grow on it prepare for the short, cold days of winter. For Martha's Vineyard is not only a summer place but a place to be born and grow up, a place to live and work and thrive year-through, nourished by the bounty that its soil and shore offer to all who are provident enough to seek and use it.

Index

ABOUT THE AUTHORS

LOUISE TATE KING has been cooking professionally for over twenty years. She is one of the co-founders of Blueberry Hill Farm in Chilmark. She now owns and operates her highly successful French provincial-style restaurant in Edgartown during the summer season. She has studied at the Cordon Bleu in Paris, spent considerable time visiting the great vineyards of France, and supervised various restaurants in the West Indies during the winter months.

JEAN STEWART WEXLER spends most of her time on Martha's Vineyard where she operates a small horticultural business, grows flowers and special vegetables for the seasonal farmers' market, and tends to the house and three acres of land she and her husband own in North Tisbury. Winter months are spent in New York City with her editor husband, writing gardening articles and working on a mystery novel set on the Vineyard.

GRAMBS MILLER was born and raised in Peking, China. She came to America on a scholarship to the Art Students League in New York. In a varied career since then she has illustrated children's books, nature books, and cook books, and has drawn for many of America's leading magazines. She spends as much time as she can in her house on Chowder Kettle Lane in Menemsha.

3⁵⁰　　　Gen 12/14 TO